WITHDRAWN

❧ REQUIEM ❧

Requiem

MUSIC
OF
MOURNING
AND
CONSOLATION

by

Alec Robertson

CASSELL · LONDON

CASSELL & COMPANY LTD
35 Red Lion Square, London WC1
Melbourne, Sydney, Toronto
Johannesburg, Auckland

© Alec Robertson 1967
First published 1967

Printed in Great Britain by
The Camelot Press Ltd, London and Southampton
F.667

In loving memory of my brother,
MAC ROBERTSON,
*killed in action in France
on 22 May 1915,
and for H.C., D.D., and M.T.*

CONTENTS

Foreword   ix

PART ONE
THE LATIN REQUIEM MASS

1 The Funeral Rites and Prayers of the Early Christians   3

2 The Origins of the *Missa pro defunctis*   8

3 The Plainsong Mass of the Dead   11

4 The Requiem Mass to the End of the Sixteenth Century

    1. DUFAY, OCKEGHEM, BRUMEL, DE LA RUE   25

5   *2.* MORALES, PALESTRINA, ANERIO, ASOLA,
       VICTORIA   42

6 The Requiem Mass in the Seventeenth Century   55

7 The Requiem Mass from the Eighteenth to the Twentieth
Century

    1. MICHAEL HAYDN AND MOZART   60

8   *2.* CHERUBINI AND BERLIOZ   75

9   *3.* VERDI AND DVOŘÁK   96

10   *4.* FAURÉ, DURUFLÉ, AND PIZZETTI   117

PART TWO
HOLY WEEK MUSIC

11 *Stabat Mater*   133

12 Liszt's *Via Crucis*   154

13 The Holy Week Office of *Tenebrae*   159

PART THREE
LUTHERAN FUNERAL MUSIC

14 German Requiems: Schütz and Brahms   171
15 Six Bach Church Cantatas   183

PART FOUR
ANGLICAN FUNERAL MUSIC

16 Anglican Funeral Music: Purcell, Croft, Davies   205

PART FIVE
MEMORIAL MUSIC AND LAMENTS

17 Memorial Music and Laments   213

PART SIX
MODERN ELEGIAC WORKS

18 Elgar's *The Dream of Gerontius*   239
19 Hindemith's *When Lilacs Last in the Door-yard Bloomed*   252
20 Requiems of the First World War: Foulds, Elgar, Bliss,
   Delius   260
21 Britten's War Requiem   265

   Index   287

FOREWORD

An extensive literature has been devoted to the history of the Mass of the Roman rite but very few books to a study of the vast amount of music associated with it. A comprehensive study would, of course, prove to be a daunting task, even if not taken beyond the sixteenth century. It is strange, however, that no one, so far as I know, has undertaken a separate study of the music of the *Missa pro defunctis* or, to use the commonly accepted term, the Requiem Mass, a much more manageable proposition and one that will, I hope, attract a musicologist at some future time.[1]

My aim has been to enlarge the general reader's knowledge of Requiem Mass settings, which may well begin with Mozart and end with Fauré. I have, therefore, tried to fill out the picture by giving a brief account of the funeral customs of the early Christians, which in the course of some nine centuries were to lead through the normal Mass offered on behalf of the souls of the departed to a specific Mass for the Dead. I have included the Latin texts, with English translations, of the parts of the Requiem Mass available for setting to music, together with a commentary on their structure and the music accompanying them. This will provide the proper background for the Requiem Mass settings of the polyphonic era, from the fourteenth to the sixteenth centuries, and those for solo voices, chorus, and orchestra which followed in the succeeding centuries, and up to the present day. The book could well have been limited to this material but I have taken the opportunity to extend the subject matter to include settings of *Stabat Mater*, Lutheran and Anglican funeral music, motets (or anthems), part-songs and solo songs relevant to the main themes of death, mourning, and remembrance, and works such as Brahms's German Requiem and Britten's War Requiem, that are *sui generis*.

My choice of material in the space available is, I need hardly say, highly selective and personal but, as far as can be, it is also practical in that a considerable amount of the music is obtainable in print, and has been recorded,[2] and that much of it is certain to be heard

---

[1] *Charles Warren Fox compiled a catalogue of Requiem settings from the fifteenth century to the present time. Of the 1,000 works he listed only forty-five appeared before 1615. From a paper on 'The Polyphonic Requiem before about 1615'.* Bulletin of the American Musicological Society, *11 January 1941.*

[2] *Works of which recordings are available at time of going to press are indicated by means of an asterisk in the Index.*

from time to time, on the B.B.C's extensive Music Programme, in the concert hall, or, more rarely, in church. With regard to the repertoire works, I have a standing quarrel with those who glibly say 'but everyone knows *that*'. Half a century's experience of the public has taught me that everyone does *not* 'know that', and that even if they do there is, as I myself constantly discover, always something more to know. I lay claim to no special revelations or insights, but hope that what is said, even about the familiar Requiem Masses and other works, may add to the knowledge of the kind of reader whom I have had continually in mind and make his listening more fruitful.

It may seem strange to admit that I have enjoyed writing a book of this character but a part of the answer lies in the experience of those who habitually fill our concert halls to hear a performance, let us say, of Verdi's *Requiem*. Whatever their beliefs may be, their response is not, I believe, merely emotional, it is also spiritual. The music that rises to the height, or nearly so, of 'the great argument' is among the most beautiful that has ever been composed, and, whatever the failings and shortcomings of this book, I greatly hope that what is said may deepen appreciation of the way in which the most sublime of all themes has inspired composers of all ages.

I owe a large debt of gratitude to Miss Annette Carter, my literary editor at Cassell's, for constant advice and for her hard labour in putting my untidy manuscript in order for the printers. I am also most grateful to Mrs. Barbara Tucker, who coped so successfully with my illegible handwriting in typing the manuscript, to Mrs. Cicely Moulding who drew out the musical examples with such admirable clarity, to Donald Beswick for special help over the earlier chapters of the book, and to Mrs. B. Horton for going over the galley proofs with me and making many valuable suggestions.

ACKNOWLEDGMENTS

The author is grateful to the following for allowing him to reproduce extracts from the material specified.

TEXT

Mr Harold Owen and Chatto & Windus for extracts from *The Collected Poems of Wilfred Owen*; Mr Harold Owen, Sir Osbert Sitwell, Oxford University Press and Chatto & Windus for quotations from Wilfred Owen's letters; J. M. Dent & Sons Ltd for Dylan Thomas's 'Do not go gentle into that good night'; David Higham Associates for 'Still falls the rain' from *The Collected Poems of Edith Sitwell*; the Trustees of the Hardy estate, Macmillan & Co. Ltd and the Macmillan Co. of Canada Ltd for 'The Oxen' from *The Collected Poems of Thomas Hardy*; Sheed & Ward Ltd for Father Philip Hughes's *A History of the Church*; and Penguin Books Ltd for the translation of Strauss's 'Im Abendroth' from *The Penguin Book of Lieder*.

MUSIC

Snr Higino Anglès, President of the Pontificio Istituto di Musica Sacra for Morales' *Missarum Liber Secundus*; Bärenreiter Verlag for Dufay's *Credo* and *Ave Maria*, and Schütz's *Absalom*; Boosey & Hawkes Music Publishers Ltd for Britten's War Requiem and 'Still falls the rain', Stravinsky's 'In Memoriam Dylan Thomas', and Richard Strauss's 'Im Abendroth'; British & Continental Music Agencies Ltd for Michael Haydn, Palestrina, Casciolini, Cherubini (D minor) and Berlioz Requiems, Palestrina's Lamentations, and Bach's 'Todessehnsucht' and six Cantatas; Broude Bros Ltd for Caldara's *Stabat Mater* (© 1954 by Broude Brothers); G. Schirmer Inc, New York (Chappell & Co. Ltd, London) for Schütz's Requiem; J. & W. Chester Ltd for Lennox Berkeley's *Stabat Mater* and Josquin Des Prés's *Déploration*; Hamelle & Cie for Fauré's Requiem; Mercury Music Corporation for Arcadelt's *Deh come trista*; Novello & Co. Ltd for Brahms, Mozart, Dvořák and Cherubini (C minor) Requiems, Elgar's *The Dream of Gerontius*, Palestrina, Rossini and Dvořák *Stabat Mater*, Croft Burial Service and Handel's *Saul*, and for de la Rue and Brumel Requiems as agents for Möseler Verlag; Verlag Friedrich Pustet for Victoria's *Tenebrae*; G. Ricordi & Co. Ltd for Verdi and Pizzetti Requiems, and Verdi, Pergolesi and Scarlatti *Stabat Mater*; Editions Salabert S.A., France for Poulenc's

Stabat Mater; Schott & Co. Ltd for Hindemith Requiem and Jeremiah Clarke Music on Purcell's Death; Stainer & Bell for two Weelkes extracts, Morley's 'Hark Alleluia', four Byrd extracts and Tomkins 'When David heard that Absalom was slain'; Universal Edition (Alfred A. Kalmus Ltd) for Szymanowski's *Stabat Mater*; United Music Publishers Ltd for Duruflé Requiem.

I

The Latin Requiem Mass

CHAPTER ONE

THE FUNERAL RITES AND PRAYERS
OF THE EARLY CHRISTIANS

The origins of prayers to and for the dead that were to lead, over nine centuries, to the *Missa pro defunctis* are to be found in the catacombs, the underground cemeteries of the early Christians. It is at first a chilling and, for the claustrophobic, even a frightening experience to descend from the bright Roman sunshine into this city of the dead whose galleries and chambers, faintly illuminated by the taper given one by the custodian of this or that catacomb, have been estimated to stretch for about ninety-six miles under the living city above. But as one gazes at the paintings on the walls and ceilings, and reads the inscriptions scratched on the tombs, imagination overcomes the chill, or the fear, and one begins to people the place with the life that once thronged here. It is well described by Father Philip Hughes in the first volume of his *A History of the Church* (Sheed & Ward, 1958):

> The Roman practice by which great families opened their private cemeteries to their dependants: the sacredness in the eyes of the Roman law of the tomb and the cult of the dead: the ancient Roman custom of family re-unions at the tombs of its deceased members: all these favoured the development of the system of catacombs.
>
> The Christians, once gathered in their cemeteries were secure, not only from mob hostility, but even from the attention of the police during persecutions. These Roman catacombs go back to the days of the Apostles themselves. Still, today, the pilgrim can wander through the miles of their underground galleries and the chambers hewn out of the *tufa* where, nearly two thousand years ago now, the Mass was said and the homilies delivered and the neophytes baptized. He can look upon the sites of the tombs of the earlier martyr-popes, and upon the hundreds of funeral inscriptions that tell the names and qualities of these long dead Christians and that attest to many of the doctrines they professed: and he can look upon the earliest Christian paintings, and study, there again, not merely the quality and development of the artistic inspiration, but the beliefs to which the paintings witness and the religious practices of which they are the mute unchanging testimony.

The looting of the tombs by the Goths in 537 and the Lombards in 755 caused the relics of the martyrs to be moved to the churches. Veneration of the martyrs and saints was now, therefore, transferred to the churches, and during the Middle Ages the very existence of the catacombs—except for those of St Sebastian, the only ones so called by the early Christians—was forgotten. The St Sebastian catacombs, alone, were probably remembered because the bodies of St Peter and St Paul were temporarily transferred there from St Peter's and St Paul's 'Without the Walls' in 258, during the persecution of Valerian.

> On May 31, 1578, a man digging for *pozzolana* [volcanic sand] in a vineyard near the Via Salaria broke into a tunnel and found himself in a world of the dead. He saw a narrow, rock-hewn passage lined on each side with tomb niches, and as he ventured inside he found the gallery to be interesected by others leading on into a labyrinth. His discovery amazed Rome. The men of that time were more excited by the thought that a city of the dead existed unsuspected beneath their feet than by the fresh and beautiful world of early Christianity which had emerged after its long entombment: the funeral lamps, the glass chalices with portraits of St Peter and St Paul, the pictures of the Good Shepherd, the touching epitaphs. [H. V. Morton: *A Traveller in Rome* (Methuen, 1957).]

Just over fifty years later the importance of the discovery began to be estimated and in 1864 G. B. de Rossi published the first of three volumes of his classic work, *La Roma Sotterranea Cristiana.*

The first thing that strikes one about the paintings in the catacombs is their lightness and gaiety. The artists copied the Graeco-Roman art they knew in their world and so we find the most serious subjects, the rite of Baptism, the Eucharist, the raising of Lazarus, the sacrifice of Isaac, depicted in a style of smiling grace. There is no hint here of damnation and hell and it is not, indeed, until much later that these concepts appear in art. These artists were not concerned with doctrine, the figures and symbols they employed were tantamount to prayers for the deceased. These early Christians lived unafraid near to death, for to die for Christ's sake was a privilege. Most interesting of all are their representations of Christ, who is depicted as a young man with the radiant beauty of Apollo (a concept far removed from the stern and bearded oriental type that was later to prevail), as Hermes, the Good Shepherd, Helios, the Sun-God or as Orpheus. These were symbols, not realistic portraiture, a spiritualization of pagan cults. By the mid-fourth century, however, God himself is depicted, on a ceiling of the Catacomb of Commodilla, as a specific personage with distinctive features.

4

The *graffiti*, the scratchings on the walls of the tombs, are most touching. The word has been applied, in our time, to the defacing of ancient buildings, including churches, abbeys and cathedrals (and much lower forms of architecture!) by those who seek to perpetuate their ignoble names, but this exhibitionism was far from the minds of those who wrote 'Peter and Paul, remember us' or 'Paul and Peter, pray for Victor'.

The pagans, whose ornate tombs rise on the Via Appia not far from the catacombs, could only write 'Ave atque vale' as Catullus did in a poignant threnody to his dead brother.

> Yet take these gifts, brought as our father bade
> For sorrow's tribute to the passing shade.
> A brother's tears have wet them o'er and o'er,
> And so, my brother, hail, and farewell evermore.

It was not with these dismissive words that the Christians addressed their dead, but with such affirmative phrases as 'Vivas in Deo' (Live in God); 'In pace Christi' (In the peace of Christ)—by which was meant 'In the friendship of Christ'.

There are many prayers *for* the dead person but even more *to* the dead person. Here is a prayer for the dead person.

> Begging forgiveness for his many sins.
> For salvation and forgiveness of sins.
> In your mercy, overlook his shortcomings—
> the sins he knew he had done
> and the faults he was not aware of.
> Grant him forgiveness for his sins.

And here a prayer to the dead person.

> Pray for your parents.
> Pray for your children.
> May he pray for us.
> Pray for us. Pray that we may be saved.
> Pray for the one child you have left behind you.
> Live in Christ and pray for us.

I add this deeply moving prayer to a young child.

> Anatolius, our first-born, ours for a little while,
> pray for us.[1]

---

[1] *Early Christian Prayers, ed. Adalbert Hamman, O.F.M. Translated by Walter Mitchell (Longmans, 1961).*

Death had no finality for these Christians, it led to the true life.

> Alexander is not dead, but lives above the stars, and his body rests in this tomb, a rest that will end with a resurrection.

Requiem, rest, the word that was to become the leading theme of the Mass for the Dead, is everywhere to be found—rest, and sleep, and peace. A perceptive mediaeval pilgrim to the catacombs wrote on the walls, 'There is light in this darkness, there is music in these tombs.'

The catacombs were sited outside the city as, by Roman law, no one could be buried within it, and so when the authorities delivered the bodies of the martyrs for burial—as Pilate had delivered the body of Jesus to Joseph of Arimathea—the mourners set out quietly and at night along the great highways leading out of the city. The presence of a priest was indispensable at the burial rite, at which psalms and prayers were recited and sung. St Jerome (c. 342–420) mentions that the kind of psalms in use were those with an 'Alleluia' refrain. He was, of course, writing at the time when the persecution had been ended by the Edict of Milan, signed by the Emperors Constantine and Licinius in 310, which led to great activity in the building of churches and made burial in the catacombs unnecessary. It is interesting that in *The Liturgy Constitution* promulgated by Pope Paul VI at the second session of the Vatican Council, a section, devoted to burial rites, deprecates 'the natural gloom of mourning that has tended to stifle at times the joyful hope of resurrection which belonged originally to the funeral rites of the Church', and expresses the hope that the paschal colour of white should replace the sombre black, and the *Alleluia* (still found in the Eastern rites) sung instead of *Dies irae*.

The Pope's words are mild when one thinks of the appalling vulgarity of the funeral pomp, the black-caparisoned horses with nodding plumes drawing the hearse, of later years, and of the money wasted on such extravagant displays.

There was a belief, brought into the Church by pagan converts to Christianity, that the spirits of the dead hovered round their tombs for a space, particularly at the beginning of November, and needed refreshment—a concept most familiar to us in the tombs of the Pharaohs. An inscription in the Catacomb of St Sebastian reads, 'I, Tomius Coelius, partook of a refreshment-meal for Peter and Paul'. It is easy to see how this touching custom led to drunkenness and debauchery, especially during the all-night vigils, and why St Augustine, having seen so-called Christians revelling round a martyr's tomb, cried, 'The martyrs hear your bottles, the martyrs hear your frying pans, the martyrs hear your drunken revels.' The ecclesiastical authorities acted sternly against these practices, echoes of which were sounded—and perhaps still are—in the 'wakes' (a watch by the corpse before burial) held in various parts of the world.

But the memory of such abuses cannot disturb the faith, hope and love that so move one in contemplating the inscriptions and paintings that illuminate the darkness of the catacombs. These one can see: one can hear Mass—and it is a wonderful experience—in the funeral halls where these early Christians may sometimes have heard it, albeit the much simpler form of the celebration of the Eucharist that is given in a second-century account by St Justin Martyr (*c.* 100–*c.* 165).

But one thing that has to be imagined is the music sung at the burial or the memorial rites. The converts from Jewry, who must have included 'elders' who had led the chanting in the synagogues, would have wished to use the ancient melodic formulas they had known in their psalm-singing, but the Greeks—and Greek was the liturgical language of the Church up to the second half of the fourth century—would have contributed their own folk-songs. Of the melodies of these we have no knowledge, though the so-called Oxyrhynchus hymn to the Holy Trinity, written *c.* 300, may provide a faint clue.

CHAPTER TWO

THE ORIGINS OF THE *MISSA PRO DEFUNCTIS*

The first reference to the dead in the Roman Mass, as we have it today, comes in the Canon, its central and most solemn part. The Canon—a Greek word meaning something fixed and unchanging—begins after the Preface and Sanctus and ends with a doxology just before the Lord's Prayer, which stands at the beginning of the preparation for Communion. The Canon contains a prayer for the living before the Consecration of the Bread and Wine, and the following prayer for the dead follows soon after:

> Remember also, O Lord, Thy servants, N and N, who have gone before us with the sign of faith and who rest in the sleep of peace. To them, O Lord, and to all who rest in Christ, we beseech Thee to grant a place of cool refreshment (*refigerium*), light, and peace. Through Christ Our Lord. Amen.

This interpolation, signified by the word 'also', was made, in the earliest extant texts of the Roman Mass books, about the seventh century. The Memento of the Dead was made, in general terms, from the fifth century, in the *Kyrie* Litany, an introductory act to the Mass 'filled out with song and prayer.'[1]

It is not until the close of the tenth century that one can speak of a specific 'Requiem' Mass. Before that as far as we know Masses for the Dead were not distinguished from others, but the Memento of the Dead, now said silently by the celebrant, was omitted on Sundays and Feastdays in the Roman rite. In Gaul, however, the opposite was the case.

> Throughout the land it was, too, a prominent feature on those days precisely when the churches were full, Sundays and feast days. The names were read aloud so that all might hear, distinct and apart from the text of any prayer. The prayers themselves 'continually dwell on

---

[1] *Joseph A. Jungmann, S.J.,* The Mass of the Roman Rite *(Burns, Oates, 1959).*

the names of the dead, friends or relatives known to all: "our dear ones" as the Gallican formulae are never weary of calling them, with that strong affection and deep sense of family relationship that, inherited from a remote past, characterises the French people still.' [*The Mass of the Roman Rite.*]

It is not surprising, in view of this, that Amalar of Metz (*c.* 780–850) speaks of a special day in commemoration of the dead and that in 998 St Odo, Abbot, from 994 to 1048, of the great Benedictine Abbey of Cluny, founded by William, Duke of Aquitaine, about 927, fixed 2 November for the commemoration of all the Faithful Departed (All Souls' Day). This is, by a happy inspiration, the day following All Saints' Day. Odo ordered that the Office of the Dead be said in Choir, and public and private Masses celebrated. There is a legend that Odo was sent a message from a hermit who lived on a small island near Sicily, near which great fires belched forth (the volcano of Etna, perhaps), to the effect that through the prayers and almsgivings of Odo and the monks of Cluny, the Devil was cheated of many souls he was intending to thrust into the fires, whereat the angels rejoiced. All religious houses subject to Cluny observed All Souls' Day and, after it had been approved by a succession of Popes, the commemoration was everywhere observed by the thirteenth century. By this time the doctrine of Purgatory, amplified by St Thomas of Aquinas (*c.* 1225–74) and other theologians, and foreshadowed since the third century, was universally accepted, and Masses for the Dead became a general feature of parish life.

The Mass for the Dead, substantially as we have it today, is of Franco-Gallican origin. In 772 Charles the Great, who became the first Emperor of the Holy Roman Empire in 800, asked Pope Hadrian I to send him the Missal that bears Pope St Gregory's name. Now Charles was never more pleased with himself than when presiding in his own Chapel and setting everybody to rights. He had an orderly mind and was determined to put a stop to the liturgical anarchy in his kingdom. To this end he imposed the Gregorian *Antiphonale* on the Franks; but, considering it too austere for his people, he enriched it with a supplement selected from the liturgical books already in use in France, with the result that as Jungmann says, 'about the middle of the tenth century the Roman Liturgy began to return in force from Franco-Germanic lands to Italy and to Rome, but it was a Liturgy that had undergone radical changes and a great development'. This importation entailed supplanting the local form of the Roman Liturgy by its Gallicized version, even at the centre of Christendom. Rome, as far as is known, made no protest at all. She had never shown, as Cardinal Newman said, any marked gift for origination (except in the case of some great popes) and all the parts of the Proper and Ordinary of the Mass were adopted by her, mainly from the East, and not invented. And so the Mass and the Office of the Dead, as we have them today, and the source of all the settings to be described, are clearly of Franco-Gallican origin.

Rome's sobriety and Christian sensibility are shown in the fact that while France and Spain had a dozen or more different formulae for the Mass for different classes of dead persons, Rome had one for all, king or pope, peasant or pauper. To point the moral, when Joseph II died his body was taken in state to the austere building of the Capuchin Monastery in Vienna, founded by the Empress Anna, on the west side of the Neuer Markt, below the church of which lie the imperial vaults. When the cortège arrived there an official knocked loudly on the door and answered the cry of 'Who is there?' with a recital of the dead Emperor's styles and titles. To this imposing catalogue the porter replied from within, 'We do not know him.' Again the official knocked and in reply to the same question said, 'A poor man.' The door was then opened and the body received for burial. A formality, no doubt, but one to which Joseph II had perforce to conform!

CHAPTER THREE

THE PLAINSONG MASS OF THE DEAD

At the twenty-fifth and final session of the Council of Trent, held on 3–4 December 1563, the revision of the liturgical books, the Missal and Breviary, was discussed and handed over for consideration by Pius IV, but there is no clear account of the proceedings. The lines of reform were evidently the basis of a Bull issued by Pius V on 14 July 1570, making the proposed reforms binding—with certain reservations—on the whole Western Church. The intention was to restore the Missal 'to conform' with the original norms and rites laid down by the Holy Fathers—of which the Pope's advisers can only have had a very limited know-ledge—but churches able to demonstrate a two hundred years' custom for their own usage were permitted to retain that usage. This fortunately allowed the diocese of Milan to keep its ancient rite and I shall allude later to one way in which the Milanese Mass for the Dead differs from the Roman rite, the main subject of this chapter. Many variations of text appear in the polyphonic settings of the Mass composed before Pius V's Bull was promulgated and these, indeed, continue right up to the eighteenth century. Com-posers had a choice of at least four texts for the Introit, Tract, and Offertory, and six for the Communion. In general, settings of the Proper of the Mass—that is, the texts that vary with the changing events of the Church's calendar—have never attracted composers for the obvious reason that their music would only be heard on the specified day in the calendar; whereas the Mass for the Dead was not limited to All Souls' Day, 2 November, but could be celebrated at almost any time as, for example, when some important person had died, and when his death was subsequently commemorated. (Less important persons have usually to be content, if only for economic reasons, with a Low Mass of Requiem, that is, one said and not sung.)

It is true, also, that the Church wished the Proper of any Mass to be sung in her own plainsong and for long considered polyphony, even of the Ordinary, out of place in the Requiem Mass. Polyphonic settings can unduly lengthen the ceremony; and even in plainsong the Sequence, *Dies Irae*, immediately following the Gradual and

Tract, holds up the singing of the Gospel. In practice, many composers of both polyphonic and orchestrally accompanied Requiem
Masses, intended for church use, often omit the Gradual and Tract,
and some others omit the Sequence, but in all such cases the omitted
portions have to be sung in plainsong.

The polyphonic Requiem Mass differs from the normal Mass—in
which, usually, only the Ordinary is set—not only in including all,
or more often some, of the items of the Proper, but in generally
preceding various sections with the relevant plainsong intonations
and introducing them in the course of these.[1]

THE PLAINSONG REQUIEM MASS

INTROIT

This, as the word implies, is properly a processional chant and
antiphon with psalm verses, sung as the celebrant, his ministers, and
attendants move from the sacristy to the altar. In large churches,
cathedrals, and abbeys, where the distance might be considerable, a
sufficient number of verses of the psalms would be sung up to the
moment when the procession reached the Sanctuary. The signal was
then given for the Introit to be repeated.[2] (The modern Roman
Gradual preserves two verses in the Requiem Mass, only one in the
normal Mass.)

Requiem aeternam dona eis, Domine, et lux perpetua luceat eis. *V.* Te decet hymnus, Deus, in Sion, et tibi reddetur votum in Jerusalem. *V.* Exaudi orationem meam, ad te omnis caro veniet. Requiem aeternam, etc.	*Eternal rest grant them, O Lord, and let perpetual light shine upon them.* V. *Thou shalt have praise, O God, in Sion, and to Thee let the vow be paid in Jerusalem.* V. *Heed my prayer! All flesh must come before thy Judgement seat.*

The text of the opening lines before the verses is based on a passage
from the Fourth Book of Esdras (2: 34–35) 'And therefore I say unto
you, O ye people that hear and understand, look for your Shepherd,
he shall give you everlasting rest . . . be ready for the reward of the
Kingdom, for the everlasting light shall shine on you for evermore.'
'Rest' and 'light' are at once proclaimed as the leading themes of the
Mass. 'Rest' in the sense of St Augustine's words 'Our souls are
restless till they rest in Thee', a rest that is now eternal, a light that is
all enlightening.

---

[1] *Composers vary their treatment so much that one can only indicate general lines of approach.*

[2] *This practice, long in disuse, is now allowed to be resumed by the Sacred Congregation of Rites where conditions are suitable.*

The simple melody breathes peace; its basic motif is made up of the notes F, G, A, in the opening phrase at 'aeternam', repeated at 'dona', 'Domine' and finally at 'eis'. Such repetitions are of the very essence of plainsong 'composition' (a word the monk-craftsmen would not have recognized); the building-in of melodic formulae out of a common stockpot, but shaped by artistic instinct.

Re — quiem ae — ter — nam do — na e-is ——— Do-mi ——— ne —

Ex. 1

The words of the psalm verse (64: 1–2) are sung as befits the occasion to a solemn psalm tone.

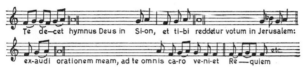

Te de—cet hymnus Deus in Si-on, et ti-bi reddetur votum in Jerusalem:

ex-audi orationem meam, ad te omnis ca-ro ve-ni-et Re—quiem   etc.

Ex. 2

KYRIE

Kyrie, eleison.	*Lord, have mercy on us.*
Christe, eleison.	*Christ, have mercy on us.*
Kyrie, eleison.	*Lord, have mercy on us.*

The *Kyrie* continues in the same peaceful and confident vein. There is none of the dramatic fervour here, or in the polyphonic settings, that was to become associated with the orchestral settings. The opening phrase is repeated for each of the nine petitions except the last. Here, as in some measure in nearly all the plainsong *Kyries*, the final petition is varied. In this instance there is a new phrase for 'Kyrie' but the same one as before for 'eleison', a nice point of unification.

Ky——ri-e ✴e ——— le-i-son, Ky-ri-e ——— ✴e —— le—i-son

Ex. 3

GRADUAL

This word is derived from the Latin *gradus* (step) and has been in use since the ninth century to specify the psalm (now only a portion of it) sung after the reading of the Epistle. In earlier days the psalm was probably sung between readings from the Old and New Testaments, the congregation responding between the verses, with some refrain such as 'For his mercy endureth for ever', or 'Alleluia', etc. In the modern Missal there remains only a short extract from the psalm, or other source, divided into Responsory and Verse. But 'responsory' is merely a technical term, for the cantors intone the opening words —in this case 'Requiem', etc.—the choir continues with them and the cantors sing the verse. Musically speaking the form requires a *da capo*, as in the Alleluia with verse, but as plainsong Graduals tend to be drawn out, this is not now generally observed. The 'step' mentioned above was the one, or more, that led up to the pulpit from which the deacon chanted the Gradual. No ritual action takes place at this point in the Mass, all attention is fixed on the singer, and the florid nature of the Graduals, sometimes excessive, shows that a virtuoso technique was required at least for the more elaborate examples, such as the celebrated and magnificent *Haec dies*, *quam fecit Dominus* ('This is the day which the Lord hath made') sung on Easter Day.

St Gregory, disgusted at the vanity of the deacons who, delighted with the sound of their voices, and forgetting they were supposed to be singing 'to the greater glory of God', forbade them to undertake this task, considering that thereby they were endangering their souls. He therefore allotted it to clerics of a lower order, whose souls, apparently, were of less importance.

The text of the Gradual in the Requiem Mass repeats that of the Introit but adds, in the verse, from Psalm 111, the words, 'In memoria aeterna erit justus: ab auditione mala non timebit' ('Men will remember the just man for ever: no fear shall he have of evil tidings').

Among the alternative chants found in manuscripts of the tenth and eleventh centuries the best of the two preserved in the Milanese rite is to my mind preferable to the Roman. It derives its text from the second responsory in the first Nocturn of the Office for the Dead (about which I shall have something to say later) and speaks of the raising of Lazarus from the grave after four days. The verse has the same words as in the Roman Introit. The plainsong melody is much simpler and has no extended vocalizations. The Roman Gradual is modelled on melodic formulas shared by eight or nine other Graduals in the second Mode. The words of these express very different sentiments, and this underlines the fact that it is the word that determines the expression; the melodic formulae by themselves are incapable of expressing anything other than a neutral succession of notes. The word 'luceat' illuminates the whole phrase below.

Ex. 4

TRACT

The Tract, originally sung after the second of the three lessons (the Epistle), is so called because, unlike the Gradual, it generally consists of a psalm, or more usually a portion of a psalm, chanted straight through, and so is not of a responsorial kind. Its place is taken, in the normal Mass, by the Alleluia, but it is still sung there instead of the Alleluia in seasons of penance such as Lent. In the Mass for the Dead the text is not taken from the Bible.

Absolve, Domine, animas omnium fidelium defunctorum ab omni vinculo delictorum. *V.* Et gratia tua illis succurente, mereantur evadere judicium ultionis. *V.* Et lucis aeternae beatitudine perfrui.

Lord, release the souls of all the faithful departed from every bond of sin. V. *By the help of thy Grace enable them to escape avenging judgement.* V. *And to enjoy bliss in everlasting light.*

'The Tracts', Professor Wagner says in his Introduction to *The Gregorian Melodies*, 'are extremely old and venerable monuments of the chants of the Latin Church, and they preserve the forms of solo psalmody of the Mass in the shape they were used up to the fourth and fifth centuries in Italy, when the solo singers began to deck them out with richer melismata than before, and by this innovation brought about the abbreviation of the psalm.'

The phrase below at 'defunctorum' recurs twice in the verse, at 'succurente' and at 'aeternae', a beautiful underlining of the prayer-ful words: and a vocalize on 'perfrui' depicts the bliss the holy souls may hope to enjoy.

Ex. 5

SEQUENCE

We come now to the famous Sequence *Dies irae, dies illa*, which was not introduced into the Mass until the fourteenth century and then not universally.

The authorship of *Dies irae, dies illa* is disputed; Thomas of Celano, a Franciscan, the friend and biographer of St Francis, appears to be the most likely candidate. However that may be, the author drew his inspiration from the responsory *Libera me, Domine, de morte aeterna* sung in the Absolution at the end of the Mass, in which the second verse begins with the words 'Dies illa, dies irae, calamitatis et miseriae, dies magna et amara valde'. These words are a gloss on the magnificent passage in the Vulgate from the prophet Sophonias (called Zephaniah in the Authorized Version) who was of royal descent and lived in the days of Josias, King of Judah, 640–609 B.C. Sophonias makes a stern call to repentance and for the abolition of idolatory. The technique is that of the hell-fire sermon, but he ends with a 'Song of Consolation', an assurance of God's love for His people. I give the noble text, music in itself, and its English translation in the Moulton version:[1]

Juxta est dies Domini magnus: juxta est, et velox nimis; vox diei Domini amara, tribulationibus ibi fortis. Dies irae, dies illa, dies tribulationis et angustiae, dies calamitatis et miseriae, dies tenebrarum et caliginis, dies nebulae et turbinis, dies tubae et clangoris super civitates munitas et super angulos excelsos (i. 14–16).	*The great Day of the Lord is near: It is near and hasteth greatly! Even the voice of the Day of the Lord: The mighty man crieth there bitterly. That Day is a day of wrath A day of trouble and distress, A day of wasteness and desolation, A day of darkness and gloominess, A day of clouds and thick darkness, A day of the trumpet and alarm Against the fenced cities, And against the high battlements!*

Our author also draws on a seventh century Advent hymn *Apparebit repentina dies magna Domini* ('The great day of the lord will suddenly appear'), an acrostic with the first verse beginning with A, the third with B, the fifth with C, and so on, and it is probable that the first liturgical use of *Dies irae* was for the first Sunday in Advent. Other sources are Our Lord's stern words in Matthew 25: 41, about those who lack charity and at the judgement stand on His left hand. 'Go far from me, you that are accursed, into that eternal fire which has been prepared for the devil and all his angels. For I was hungry, and you never gave me food, I was thirsty, and you never gave me drink,' etc. The third line of the opening stanza 'Teste David cum Sibylla' ('As David and the Sibyl say'), gave offence to later theologians, and some versions of *Dies irae* replace it with 'Crucis expandens vexilla' ('The banners of the Cross streaming forth'), but, as Archbishop Chevenix Trench states in his book *Sacred Latin Poetry* (1874), the line is quite in the spirit of early and mediaeval theology. In those uncritical ages the Sibylline verses were not seen to be the transparent forgery which indeed they are: but were continually appealed to as only second to the sacred Scriptures in prophetic authority.

The Archbishop does not mention the mysterious Sibylline women whom Michelangelo included in his painting in the Sistine

---

[1] The Modern Reader's Bible, *ed. Richard G. Moulton (Collier-Macmillan, 1943).*

Chapel and who, in the more liberal era of the High Renaissance, seem to have been accepted without demur.

According to John Julian's *Dictionary of Hymnology* (1892) there were at that time over 150 English translations of the Sequence, and several have been added since. The enormous popularity of the *Dies irae* does not, however, justify its presence in the Requiem Mass. It is a personal meditation based on the Gospel for the first Sunday in Advent (Luke 21: 25–33), and the sources before stated. The Sibyl (as also such psalms as XCVII, 1–6: and more definitely Peter II. 3: 7–12) was supposed to have prophesied the destruction of the world by fire and water, a fact St Augustine alludes to in his *De Civitate Dei*. The poem is written in an unusual form, each line of each three line verse having eight syllables in trochaic metre 'Dies irae, dies illa', etc., the second and third lines rhyming with the first. This led a German commentator to call every word, 'weighty, yea, even a thunderclap', and a French one, more accurately, to describe the effect of the triple rhythm as 'blow following blow of the hammer on the anvil'. (This is vividly borne out in the orchestral part of Verdi's setting of the first two stanzas.) The following translation is from a *Manual* of 1673, and is perhaps by J. Austin (d. 1669).

Dies irae, dies illa,
Solvet saeclum in favilla:
Teste David cum Sibylla.

Ah, come it will, that direful day
Which shall the world in ashes lay
As Daniel and the Sibyl say.

Quantus tremor est futurus,
Quando judex est venturus,
Cuncta stricte discussurus!

How men will tremble and grow pale
When Justice comes with sword and
*   scale*
To weigh the faults and sort the fates
*   of all!*

Tuba mirum spargens sonum
Per sepulcra regionum,
Coget omnes ante thronum.

A trumpet first shall rend the skies
And all, wherever laid, must rise
And come unto the Bar in prisoner's
*   guise.*

Mors stupebit, et natura,
Cum resurget creatura,
Judicanti responsura.

Nature and Death amazed will stand
To see each one rebodied, and
Brought to reply, himself, to each
*   demand.*

Liber scriptus proferetur,
In quo totum continetur,
Unde mundus judicetur.

A written book lie open shall
Containing each one's charge; and all
By those grand evidences stand or fall.

Judex ergo cum sedebit,
Quidquid latet, apparebit;
Nil inultum remanebit.

Then the Judge seats himself and tries;
No shifting from all-seeing eyes
Nor 'scaping, then. Who e'er deserves
*   it dies.*

Quid sum miser tunc dicturus? Quem patronum rogaturus, Cum vix justus sit securus?	*O then, poor I! What shall I do?* *Which friend or patron take me to,* *When saints themselves are scarce* *secure from woe?*
Rex tremendae majestatis, Qui salvandos salvas gratis, Salva me, fons pietatis.	*Dread King, to thee thyself run I,* *Who savest the saved, without a why,* *And so mayst me, thou source of* *clemency.*
Recordare, Jesu pie, Quod sum causa tuae, viae: Ne me perdas illa die.	*Think! Who did once thy pity move* *And drew thee from thy throne above?* *Cast me not off, at last, thy former* *love!*
Quaerens me sedisti lassus, Redemisti Crucem passus: Tantus labor non sit cassus.	*Thou tired'st thyself in seeking me,* *For my sake didst die on a tree:* *Let not in vain such pains and labour* *be.*
Juste judex ultionis, Donum fac remissionis Ante diem rationis.	*True: thou art just and repayest love!* *Yet acts of grace mayst deign to save* *At least, before that day of reckoning* *come.*
Ingemisco, tamquam reus: Culpa rubet vultus meus: Supplicanti parce, Deus.	*And I am guilty, ere thou try me:* *My very looks, and blush, descry me:* *But mercy, Lord, do not deny me.*
Qui Mariam absolvisti Et latronem exaudisti, Mihi quoque spem dedisti.	*Thou, who didst once a Magdalen* *spare* *And of a thief condemned took'st care,* *Bid'st me by these examples not* *despair.*
Preces meae non sunt dignae; Sed tu bonus fac benigne, Ne perenni cremer igne.	*Nay, not that my prayers aught can* *claim* *But thou art good! Be still the same,* *That wretched I burn not in th'endless* *flame!*
Inter oves locum praesta, Et ab haedis me sequestra, Statuens in parte dextra.	*When from the goats thou shalt divide* *Thy sheep, let me with thee abide,* *Placed in eternal bliss on thy right* *side.*
Confutatis maledictis, Flammis acribus addictis; Voca me cum benedictis.	*And then, those great Assizes done,* *And all the cursed i' the fire thrown,* *Say: 'Come ye blessed', meaning me* *for one.*

Oro supplex et acclinis,	*Lord, this I beg on bended knee,*
Cor contritum quasi cinis:	*With heart contrite as ashes be:—*
Gere curam mei finis.	*That thou take care both of my end*
	and me.
Lacrimosa dies illa,	*Alas, that day fulfilled of tears*
Qua resurget ex favilla,	*When man before his throne appears*
Judicandus homo reus.	*Who makes and only can appease*
	our fears!
Huic ergo, parce, Deus.	*Gentle Lord Jesus*
Pie Jesu Domine, dona eis	*Give rest to them. Amen.*
requiem. Amen.	

A Sequence or trope is something that follows after and the early history of the form shows it as 'following after' the verse of the *Alleluia* of the Mass and added to its repeat. Music always seeks to be autonomous and the *Alleluia* had long given opportunity for a vocalization on the last vowel, the wordless song of joy of which St Augustine so eloquently speaks in the *Confessions*. No doubt it was improvised in his day but by the end of the ninth century there was a unity of melodic tradition that made what we inaccurately call Gregorian chant a closed art. The creative instinct could therefore only find an outlet in the trope and sequence. A trope (from a Greek word *tropus*, which originally meant a melody) came to signify the addition of words or music, or both, to an existing chant. The chants of the Ordinary of the Mass, as they stand in the modern service books, have sub-titles such as 'Orbis factor' (No. XI), the first words that were added to the melismatic phrases of the *Kyrie eleison*. This practice, extended to nearly all parts of the Proper and Ordinary of the Mass, was tolerated but never officially recognized, and was banished entirely by the Council of Trent, with the exception of the kind of trope called the Sequence. Four examples are left in the liturgy: *Dies irae, dies illa, Lauda Sion Salvatorem, Veni sancte Spiritus,* and *Victimae Paschali laudes. Stabat Mater* was not admitted until 1727. Sequences grew out of the addition of words and music to the repetition of the Alleluia after the verse, with the final result that they became independent compositions. Each one of those listed above differs in musical construction, but we are concerned here only with the *Dies irae*. There are three melodic phrases (each divisible into three sub-phrases) each immediately repeated and so covering verses 1–2, 3–4, 5–6, after which the same pattern is repeated. It can be expressed as A, a, B, b, C, c. It is interesting that the range extends by one note in verses 3–4, 5–6. A has a compass of a 7th, B and C of an octave. But whereas A and C are low pitched, B goes at once to the top of the stave and only touches one note below the lowest of the four lines. This means that treble voices are only comfortably situated in B and basses only in C. This wide difference in compass is found in all the Sequences left in the Roman *Graduale* (the book of Mass chants). The three phrases are given below. The last five lines were

Exs. 6, 7, 8

supplied by an unknown person. Horrified by the use of the first person singular in the Sequence, he added the prayer 'Pie Jesu Domine, dona eis requiem' so as to include all the souls of the departed.

Ex. 9

This personal meditation on death and judgement disturbs the solemn serenity of the Requiem Mass and from the liturgical point of view there is no doubt that an Alleluia with a suitable verse, following on the Tract, would be preferable as expressing peace and light and hope, the leading motives of the Mass. It may be that, in accordance with Pope Paul's words in the *Liturgy Constitution*, this reform will soon be carried out. It would leave the great settings of Berlioz and Verdi undisturbed, for these are essentially concert, not liturgical, masses; but one would certainly regret, on musical grounds, the loss of the best of the polyphonic settings, for they can only be in their right place within the liturgy.

OFFERTORY

The Offertory, the next piece to be sung, retains, in having a verse, the semblance of the processional chant it once was—an antiphon with a number of psalm verses, separated by the repeat of the antiphon—or part of it—as a refrain, while the people brought their gifts of bread and wine and wax, etc., to the altar steps. It is, in the

Requiem Mass, textually a strange piece of unknown, but certainly not Roman origin, and it is suspect by orthodox theologians in regard to the doctrine it presents of the particular judgement of the soul. It came to Rome from the ancient Gallic rite and as Anton Baumstark says in his book *Comparative Liturgy* (Mowbray, 1958): 'If we examine the substance of the text we are at once transported to Egypt, for only there do we meet with analogies to the "signifer sanctus Michael" ("the standard-bearer St Michael"). Here in Egypt we find the iconographical type, widespread in all Coptic art, of the Archangel weighing the merits of the dead.' Professor Baumstark quotes a Greek funerary inscription of 409 which bids God receive the soul of the departed woman 'through Thy holy and illuminating Archangel Michael'. The Offertory was inserted in the Requiem Mass some time between the ninth and eleventh centuries.

Domine Jesu Christe, Rex gloriae, libera animas omnium fidelium defunctorum de poenis inferni, et de profundo lacu: libera eas de ore leonis, ne absorbeat eas tartarus, ne cadant in obscurum: sed signifer sanctus Michael repraesentet eas in lucem sanctam: quam olim Abrahae promisisti et semini ejus.

V. Hostias et preces tibi, Domine, laudis offerimus: tu suscipe pro animabus illis, quarum hodie memoriam facimus: fac eas, Domine, de morte transire ad vitam. Quam olim Abrahae promisisti et semini ejus.

O Lord Jesus Christ, King of glory, deliver the souls of all the faithful departed from the pains of hell and from the deep pit: deliver them from the jaws of the lion, lest they fall into darkness and the black gulf swallows them up. But let thy standard-bearer, blessed Michael, bring them into that holy light, which of old thou didst promise to Abraham and his seed.

V. We offer unto thee, O Lord, this sacrifice of prayer and praise: do thou receive it on behalf of the souls of those whose memory we this day recall: make them, O Lord, to pass from death unto life. That life of which of old thou didst promise to Abraham and his seed.

The plainsong to these words is really an ornamented version of the second of the eight psalm tone formulas, and the music continually centres round its basic notes.

The most decorated words are 'Rex gloriae' and 'quam olim Abrahae promisisti et semini ejus', but the 'lucem sanctam' into which Michael the Standard-bearer brings the souls of the faithful departed shines out already at 'repraesentet eas'. The intonation of the psalm tone is clearly shown at the start of the verse 'Hostias et preces tibi', and in the beautiful phrase set to the key words 'fac eas, Domine, de morte transire ad vitam'. There is a subtle apposition between the long note on the second syllable of 'morte' and that on the middle vowel of 'transire'. A perceptive choirmaster would see to it that such a point were made, but not emphasized.

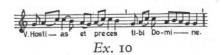

V. Hosti — as et preces ti-bi Do-mi —— ne.

Ex. 10

Fac e-as Do-mi—ne de mor-te trans-i——re ad vi-tam

Ex. 11

SANCTUS AND AGNUS DEI

The almost entirely syllabic settings of the *Sanctus* and *Agnus Dei* have the same melodies as Mass XVIII in the *Kyriale* (for Advent and Lent).

Sanctus, sanctus, sanctus, Dominus, Deus Sabaoth. Pleni sunt caeli et terra gloria tua. Hosanna in excelsis. Benedictus qui venit in nomine Domini. Hosanna in excelsis.	*Holy, holy, holy, Lord God of Hosts. Heaven and earth are full of Thy glory. Hosanna in the highest. Blessed is he that cometh in the name of the Lord.*

sanc-tus, sanctus, sanc-tus Dominus Deus, Sabaoth.

Ex. 12

Agnus Dei, qui tollis peccata mundi: dona eis requiem. (repeated).	*O Lamb of God that takest away the sins of the world, grant them rest.*
Agnus Dei, qui tollis peccata mundi: dona eis requiem sempiternam.	*O Lamb of God that takest away the sins of the world, grant them eternal rest.*

Ag-nus De-i, qui tol-lis pec-ca-ta mundi: do-na e-is re-qui-em.

Ex. 13

COMMUNION

The Communion chant, also syllabic, is one of the two in the Roman Gradual to repeat the last half of the antiphon after the verse. (The other is the processional chant sung during the distribution of the candles before the Mass of the Purification of the Blessed Virgin Mary.)

Lux aeterna luceat eis, Domine:	*Light eternal shine upon them, O*
cum sanctis tuis in aeternum,	*Lord, with thy saints for ever,*
quia pius es.	*because thou art gracious.*
V. Requiem aeternam dona eis	
Domine, et lux perpetua luceat	
eis. Cum sanctis tuis etc.	

The words of the Communion chant recapitulate the leading motives of the Mass—'Lux aeterna . . . lux perpetua . . . requiem aeternam', and the final 'Requiescant in pace. Amen,' sung in place of the usual 'Ite, missa est, Deo gratias' before the blessing of the congregation. No blessing is given in the Requiem Mass; everything is centred on the deceased person. The Absolution follows the Mass.

Ex. 14

Ex. 15

This title is not found before the fourteenth century but the ceremony dates from at least the ninth century when 'Subvenite, Sancti Dei, occurite Angeli Domini' ('Come to his assistance, all ye Saints of God, go forth to meet him, ye Angels of God', etc.) was sung. It was replaced, in about the fourteenth century, by 'Libera me de morte aeterna', the 'Subvenite' being said at the moment of death among the magnificent prayers under the title of 'Recommendation of a departing soul'. 'Libera me' is sung while the catafalque (the coffin set on a pedestal and covered with a black pall, on which is inscribed a golden cross) is aspersed with holy water and censed. This custom goes back to the early Middle Ages when the theology of penance had not been fully worked out, and it was thought that the dead could still be helped by sacramental absolution. If the coffin cannot be brought to the church the 'Libera me' is sung over an empty catafalque. This may seem odd, but it shows the church's care, in all circumstances, to help the departed soul. At the grave there is no more mention of 'dies irae': hope is now the dominant note, and the last prayer is preceded by the canticle of Zacharias 'Benedictus Dominus, Deus Israel' with the antiphon 'Ego sum resurrectio et vita' (I am the resurrection and the life).

Libera me, Domine, de morte aeterna in die illa tremenda: quando caeli movendi sunt et terra: dum veneris judicare saeculum per ignem.	*Deliver me, O Lord, from eternal death in that awful day, when the heavens and the earth shall be shaken, when thou shalt come to judge the world by fire.*
V. Tremens factus sum ego, et timeo, dum discussio venerit, atque ventura ira. Quando caeli movendi sunt et terra.	*V. I am seized with fear and trembling, until the trial shall be at hand, and the wrath to come: when the heavens and the earth shall be shaken.*
V. Dies illa, dies irae, calamitatis et miseriae, dies magna et amara valde: dum veneris judicare saeculum per ignem.	*V. That day, a day of wrath, of calamity and of misery, a great day and exceeding bitter, when thou shalt come to judge the world by fire.*
V. Requiem aeternam dona eis, Domine: et lux perpetua luceat eis. Libera me, etc.	*V. Eternal rest grant unto them, O Lord: and let perpetual light shine upon them. Deliver me, etc.*

The plainsong of the verse of 'Libera me' shows where the author of *Dies irae* and the makers of the melody derived their inspiration. 'Dum veneris', sung after verse two, is a repeat of the second half of 'Libera me'. Every word of it except the first is thrown into high relief by the music: then comes the quiet, low-pitched 'Requiem aeternam'. As the coffin is borne out of the church to the cemetery the choir sing the beautiful antiphon, 'In Paradisum deducant te Angeli', with its touching reference to Lazarus, the name of the beggar in Christ's parable of Dives and Lazarus (Luke 16: 19–31) who, after a life of poverty and disease, was carried by the angels to Abraham's bosom while Dives, prototype of the profiteer, suffered a just penalty for his lack of compassion.

In Pa-ra-di-sum de-ducant te An-ge—li

Ex. 16

CHAPTER FOUR

THE REQUIEM MASS TO THE END
OF THE SIXTEENTH CENTURY

1 Dufay, Ockeghem, Brumel, de la Rue

There is no mention of a polyphonic Requiem Mass in musical history before 1474, in which year the great Burgundian composer Guillaume Dufay directed in his will that one by him should be performed at his funeral. The score has unfortunately never come to light but the circumstances surrounding it are so moving and interesting that I shall discuss Dufay's will in detail in the course of this chapter.

One reason for the late appearance of the polyphonic Requiem Mass may be that polyphony came to be regarded as an additional element in ceremonial, a further means of festive adornment and elaboration of the ritual, and was felt to be out of place in the solemn circumstances of the Requiem Mass, for which the plainsong setting was considered to be the perfect vehicle.

The polyphonic music of the fourteenth century was, in the spirit of the period, called *Ars nova* (taken from the title of a theoretical treatise written by Philip de Vitry in about 1320) and was predominantly secular and church composers in their secular music could work and experiment free from ecclesiastical interference. It was, however, Guillaume de Machaut (c. 1300–c. 1370), the greatest French musician of the century, famous for his ballades, *rondeaux*, *virelais*, and motets—of which only six were in Latin—who produced, probably in the last years of his life, the first polyphonic Mass to be composed by one man.

This Mass, for four voices, is historically so important that something about it must be said here. It is a cycle of the five movements of the Ordinary to which is added a setting of the response 'Deo gratias', to the chanted words of dismissal 'Ite, missa est' that precede the blessing of the people at the close of the Mass.

The little figure below appears in all the movements, generally in the two upper parts, and is sometimes melodically varied. It may well have been suggested by the plainsong melody used in the tenor part of the *Kyrie*, which is subjected to a rhythmic pattern continually repeated throughout—a technique, prevalent in this century, known as isorhythm.

glo——ri-fi-ca-nus te.

Ex. 1

Other plainsong tenors are used in a similar manner in the *Sanctus* and *Agnus Dei*. The *Gloria* and *Credo*, on the other hand, do not quote plainsong—except for the priest's intonations at the start—and are set, for the most part, syllabically, one note to one word or syllable, in all parts. 'Jesu Christi' in the *Gloria* is set to chords with notes of the longest value used in the Mass, and so, in the *Credo*, are the words 'ex Maria Virgine'. This practice was to become a convention. These are some of the factors that were to influence composers of Masses throughout the Renaissance, although the isorhythmic technique gave way at the end of the fifteenth century to a less rigid method of presenting borrowed themes, sacred or secular, in Masses.

The idea of unifying the movements of the Mass by the use of a common motif, though Machaut's little figure is hardly significant enough to give more than an appearance of unity, is musical but not liturgical. It is true that the *Gloria* follows immediately after the *Kyrie* but the spiritual character of the texts is quite different—the latter is a prayer of petition, the former a hymn of praise—while the texts of the remaining chants are widely separated from one another both in character and in time.

For practical reasons we are compelled in the concert hall, on records, and over the radio, to hear the Ordinary of the Mass sung as a cycle of related movements, and no doubt people who have never attended the celebration of a Solemn High Mass in some great cathedral (in which of course the Proper is sung usually in plainsong, exceptionally in polyphony, and the Ordinary in polyphony) imagine that a Mass is a choral cycle made up of the texts of the Ordinary vaguely related to ritual actions of some kind.

After this digression I turn to Dufay's will. It is dated 8 July 1474; he died on 27 November of that year. He wished his obsequies to be celebrated in Cambrai Cathedral (of which he was a canon, as well as Master of the Music) with bells, bright lights and four candles to burn before the statue of St Anthony of Padua. The same day Masses were to be said for the repose of his soul. He asked that all those, great and small, who took part should receive a due reward from his estate and made provision for offerings of bread and money to the poor. 'For the hour of his agony' he made the following dispositions. After the last sacraments had been administered the hymn 'Magno salutis gaudio' was to be sung quietly by a group of eight choristers; the children of the choir would then start singing, with their master and two adult singers, his motet *Ave Regina Coelorum*, if his condition allowed. For the day after his obsequies he prescribed a Requiem Mass to be sung in the Chapel of St Etienne by a dozen of the best singers chosen from among the vicars-choral of high and low rank; the Mass over, they should, after the 'Requiescant in pace', perform a Sequence, chosen by them, then the *De profundis*.

Dufay expressly says 'Missam meam de Requiem' and this must be the '*Missa de Requiem compilata per M. G. da Fay, copiée par Simon Mellet en 1470*'. As the *Missa pro defunctis* was sung in plainsong almost up to the end of the fifteenth century it is tragic that Dufay's polyphonic setting has never been found. We do, however, have the beautiful four-voice motet *Ave Regina Coelorum*. It disappeared from Cambrai but was fortunately discovered in a codex in the chapter archives of St Peter's, Rome, unsigned but obviously, as will be seen, by Dufay.

The remaining works in the codex were by Loyset Compère, who had served as a choirboy at St Quentin and died there in 1518. The words of the second part of his motet *Omnium bonorum plena* ('Thou who art replete with good things') include a prayer to the Virgin Mary for the salvation of singers. 'First for Guillaume Dufay, moon of all music, light of singers, hear me, Mother' and later Johannes Ockeghem is cited. 'Moon of all music' is an apt poetical description of Dufay's gentle and lovely art.

Dufay's setting of the Marian antiphon, *Ave Regina Coelorum*, is a splendid example of a trope. The words added to the existing text are italicized. (The 'fire' is that of Purgatory, not of Hell.)

Ave Regina Coelorum,	Hail, Queen of Heaven,
Ave Domina Angelorum.	Hail, Mistress of the Angels.
Miserere tui labentis Dufay	*Have pity on thy dying Dufay*
Peccatorum ruat in ignem fervorum.	*Cast into the burning fire.*
Salve radix, salve porta,	Hail, root (of Jesse),
Ex qua mundo lux est orta.	Hail, gate by which light has entered
Miserere, genetrix Domini,	the world.
Ut poteat coeli debilem.	*Have pity, Mother of God, that*
	Heaven's gate may ope to the
	weak one.

27

The above is the text of the first of the two parts of the motet, which begins with two duets, scored respectively for the upper and the lower voices and covering the first two lines of the Marian antiphon. The top voice in each duet freely paraphrases the plainsong melody of the antiphon, and 'Ave' and the last syllables of 'coelorum' and 'angelorum' have beautifully balanced arabesque-like phrases. At the same moment as the second of the duets reaches its cadence point the tenor begins a repeat of the two lines of the liturgical text so far heard and so continues with it, keeping more closely to the plainsong melody, to the end of the motet. As the example below shows, the trebles suddenly enter on a high E flat (forming a chord of C minor with the other voices) with the first word of Dufay's personal prayer. The effect is most poignant.

Ex. 2

Dufay's request to have four candles burning before the statue of St Anthony of Padua shows that he had a special veneration for this saint and this is borne out by the frequent mention in his will of a Mass and two motets dedicated to him. The Mass, like the Requiem Mass, has not survived, but we know that in his will he left the book in which it was contained, together with the Requiem Mass and other Masses, to the Chapel of St Etienne. Now comes some detective work. In a Bodleian MS of the mid-fifteenth century containing works by English composers there are six leaves that contain the complete *Credo*, and parts of the *Gloria* and *Sanctus*, based on the plainsong Introit chant *Requiem aeternam* of the *Missa pro defunctis*, which is used as a *cantus firmus* throughout. Denis Stevens, the distinguished musicologist, tells me the style is in many respects akin to Dufay's, and that it would not be unusual to find copies of his work in English manuscripts. Indeed, such copies have been found by Stevens and Bukofzer. But, as I pointed out to him, no Requiem Mass would contain the *Gloria* and *Credo* and I cannot help speculating whether this *Requiem aeternam* cyclic Mass may not be the one dedicated to St Anthony of Padua, as a commemoration of his death. It is just possible. The plainsong theme of the Introit, placed in the lowest part, would have been played on a wind instrument. The illustration shows the end of the *Credo* and the final word ('eis') of the Introit.

Ex. 3

★

In default of the music of Dufay's Requiem Mass coming to light some day the one by Johannes Ockeghem (*c.* 1420–*c.* 1495) will remain the first known in the history of church music of the early Renaissance. From 1452 until his death Ockeghem was attached to the Royal Chapel of France, first as chorister, then as choirmaster, and served there under three kings, Charles VII, Louis XI and Charles VIII. He also had the high honour of being made treasurer of the Abbey of St Martin of Tours. Before discussing the work of this great Flemish composer, who was chaplain and composer to Charles VII in Paris, then treasurer of the Abbey of Tours, something must be said about the Mass itself as a medium for music in this period and down to the end of the sixteenth century.

In the thirteenth century the motet held a dominant position in church music composition but in the succeeding century, the period of the *Ars nova*, as I have said above, composers' attention was diverted to the numerous forms of secular music, particularly in France and Italy. With the return of interest in sacred music, and the emergence of the great Flemish school of composers, however, the motet took, in its refashioned form, second place only to the Mass. The Mass became, with this school, what the symphony was to be to composers in the eighteenth century, in the sense that it was the largest form for the exercise of their art: but whereas the symphony was intended to entertain and delight its cultivated audiences, the Mass was intended to interpret and adorn the liturgy. It was objective, and functional music, informed by liturgical ideals, however differently expressed. There has been only one composer since who could rise above the law and impose his commanding personality on the sacred texts with a Mass of the most profound spirituality, and that was Beethoven. His *Missa Solemnis*, heard within the context of the celebration of the Mass, as it occasionally is in Austria, does not dwarf the liturgy, even though it prolongs the service unduly, but it proclaims throughout a personal belief so God-centred, so enriching and sublime, that it enters into the universal and deepens the belief of the worshipping community.

The Requiem Masses to be dealt with in this chapter have, with one exception, no uniform pattern and this, as we have seen, is general until later years.

In France the *Dies irae* did not become an established section of the Mass until the mid-sixteenth century and so it is not set by Ockeghem. Instead of 'Requiem aeternam' (until the verse 'In memoria aeterna erit justus') as text for the Gradual, and 'Absolve Domine' for the Tract, as now, he uses 'Si ambulem in medio umbrae mortis' and 'Sicut cervus desiderat ad fontes aquarum', which I will identify later.

No one now mentions Ockeghem without apologizing for the foolishness of those who consider him to be, in Cecil Gray's words in *The History of Music* (Kegan Paul), 'a pure cerebralist, almost exclusively preoccupied with intellectual problems [who] goes out of his way to create difficulties for the pleasure of overcoming them. Expression was, for him, a secondary consideration, if indeed it existed for him at all.'

Ockeghem was an extremely learned composer, but if he is to be condemned for using and developing all the skills of his time, as in the too celebrated thirty-six voice canon, Tallis should also be condemned for writing his forty-two-part motet or, for that matter, Bach his *Art of Fugue*—which is absurd.

There is some evidence that Ockeghem studied with Dufay, and certain evidence in Josquin Des Prés' *Déploration* (Lament) 'Nymphes des Bois' of how much he was admired and mourned by his younger contemporaries. (*See* Chapter 16, pp. 213–14.)

In Requiem Masses composers quoted melodic material only from the plainsong Requiem. They would have considered it out of place to take, as they freely did in normal Mass settings, material from a secular or sacred piece of their own or anyone else's composition. Notes, of course, cannot be sacred or secular: they are indifferent sounds to be directed to whatever purpose the composer has in mind and they take on the associations of that purpose. And so Orlando de Lassus saw nothing irreverent in borrowing the melody of a French *chanson* 'Je ne mange point porc' ('I don't like pork') as melodic material in his Mass with that sub-title. He saw the possibilities in the melody and, so to speak, consecrated it to church use. His Mass does not smell of pork! The melody, moreover, if it was well known, would not necessarily have been recognized in its new rhythmic form and when put in the tenor part among, in this case, three other parts. On the other hand Taverner, in one of the earliest examples of a Mass in variation form, 'Western Wynde', keeps his borrowed melody almost unchanged in each section of the work, putting it either in the treble, tenor, or bass—but never in the alto—and if the beautiful melody was well known it would be easily recognizable. But any such borrowing from outside sources was clearly not held to be fitting in the solemn course of a Requiem Mass. The fact that the relevant plainsong is actually quoted or if not, its phrases are freely paraphrased, makes for an overall unity of conception proper to this Mass.

I have used the version of the Mass edited and transcribed by Bruno Turner, with his permission, for male voice choir, two bassoons, cor anglais, tenor trombone, and chamber organ. There is evidence that instruments were used in Requiem Masses in an account of the Mass sung on the death of Philip of Castille in 1507, and accompanied by 'en organis, trompeten, geigen und allerly saitenspiel': that is, 'with organs, trumpets, trombones, fiddles and other stringed instruments': but since composers gave no indication of what they had in mind—realizing that their requirements might not be uniformly available—an editor has to use his judgement. (I have omitted reference to the scoring as there are two recordings of the Mass now available which differ from each other and from Mr Turner.)

The Mass is scored for four voices but is predominantly in two and three parts, a fourth voice being added at the close of all the movements except the Introit.

INTROIT

'Requiem', intoned in plainsong. The voices enter on 'aeternam'. If the reader will turn back to the plainsong Introit on p. 13 he will see the correspondences and departures between it and from it in the top line of *Ex.* 4 on p. 32. The consecutive chords of the sixth at 'dona' in bars 7–9 are an expressive use of the faburden style. The start of the verse 'Te decet hymnus, Deus, in Sion' is sung to the psalm tone, all the voices enter at 'Et tibi reddetur votum in Jerusalem'.

Ex. 4

The words are treated chordally, as nearly always at such points in polyphonic requiems. The Introit is repeated at the end of the verse

Ex. 5

as the liturgy requires. Each part of Ockeghem's Mass, except in chordal sections which offer contrast of texture, has melodic and rhythmic independence, but each one is planned to make musical sense vertically as well as horizontally. The melodic parts each have their own 'lesser' rhythm, the whole texture being regulated by the 'great' rhythm of the chords they form vertically.

Kyrie Eleison. Kyrie 1 is in three parts, Kyrie 2 in two parts. Kyrie 1 is repeated. The plainsong is not quoted separately but freely paraphrased in the top voice of Kyrie 1, and simultaneously in the top part of Kyrie 2, with the lower part in notes of shorter length.

Ex. 6

Ex. 7

'Christe Eleison'. 1, in two parts; 2 in three parts; 1 repeated. Kyrie eleison 1 in three parts; 2 in two parts; 3 in four parts. These sections all continue to have the melody in the top part, but Kyrie 2 has one of the few canonic passages in the Mass. With the last Kyrie Ockeghem introduces his fourth voice. This gives a feeling of climax and the beautifully drawn-out cadence of finality.

Ex. 8

Composers knew nothing of our time signatures or bar lines; they had methods of indicating length of notes and the movement of the music far too complex to be dealt with here. Their music was called measured—*musica mensurabilis* as contrasted with *cantus planus*, plainsong, and that is indeed the origin of the latter term. There were, no more than in plainsong, no regularly recurring accents, strong and weak. Put into modern terms, a singer's entry could come on any beat of the bar and receive there a renewal of rhythmic energy. This is far removed from metrical rhythm. As Ernst Křenek puts it in his excellent book on Ockeghem, *Johannes Ockeghem* (Sheed & Ward, 1953): 'Every melodic phrase unfolds according to its own law, without any tone being automatically thrown into relief on account of a pre-existing pattern. Essentially all tones of the phrase are dynamically alike, but the long and high tones stand out by virtue of their being long and high, and thus gain weight, so that the articulation of the phrase is a result of the grouping of tones round such points of emphasis.' This is true of all the music in this chapter. The reader who plays the illustrations above on the piano can only get a faint idea, but still some idea, of the beauty of Ockeghem's music when sung. He will certainly note the splendid bass lines in the three- and four-part sections, and the 'colour' produced by the D flat in the second bar of Kyrie 1 (*Ex.* 6).

GRADUAL

The text for the Gradual consists of verse 4 of Psalm 22 in the Vulgate.

Si ambulem in medio umbrae mortis non timebo mala? Quonium tu mecum es, Domine. *V.* Virga tua et baculus tuus, ipsa me consolata sunt.	*What though I walk with the shadow of death all around me? I will not be afraid of harm, for thou, Lord, art with me. V. Thy rod, thy crook are my comfort.*

Gradual. 'Si ambulem': plainsong. 'In medio' to 'Domine': *a3*; V. 'Virga tua' to end: *a2* and *a4*.[1]

As a matter of cold statistics the Gradual runs to 110 bars as compared with the 60 bars of the Introit and this is accounted for by Ockeghem's first use of the long-drawn phrases characteristic of his art. They flow on step-wise, with infrequent skips, the latter most prominent in the middle part. As scored by Bruno Turner there are several sections for instruments only, and one at the end of the Gradual—that is, before the verse—of as much as five and a half bars. With a prolongation of final vowels most of these sections could, of course, be sung if voices alone were used throughout, but no doubt instruments were intended.

The melismatas, or floreating passages of plainsong—of which the most familiar is the vocalized final vowel of the Alleluia in the Proper of the Mass—are Ockeghem's model of continuous melody, but, of course, he uses a far greater variety of note values, ranging from a breve to a semiquaver (a whole note to a sixteenth note). However strange, even aimless these long melodic lines may sound to the unaccustomed ear—as the long sentences of Henry James seem to the unaccustomed eye—they are most carefully planned. The plainsong is so freely paraphrased as to rise very rarely to the surface.

The parts are increased to four from two for the moving repetition of the final words of the verse 'Consolata sunt' in which the first underpart moves up, all the others now having come to rest, to an expressive A flat.

TRACT

The text of the Tract comes from verses 2–4 of Psalm 42.

Sicut cervus desiderat ad fontes aquarum! Ita desiderunt anima mea ad te, Deus. *V.* Sitivit	*As a deer for running water my whole soul longs for Thee, O God. V. My whole soul thirsts for the living God.*

---

[1] *This is a useful convention to indicate the number of the parts.*

anima mea ad Deum vivum;
quando veneris, et apparebo
ante faciem Dei?
V. Fuerunt mihi lacrimae panes
die ac nocte, dum dicitur mihi
per singulos dies! Ubi est Deus
tuus?

*Shall I never again make my pilgrim-
age into God's presence? Morning
and evening, I have no food than
tears, daily must I listen to the taunt,
where is thy God now?*

Tract (no plainsong intonation), 'Sicut cervus': *a2*; 'Sitivit': *a2*;
'Fuerunt': *a3*; 'Ubi est': *a4*. Ockeghem follows the plainsong
much more closely here than in the Gradual. The music matches
the beautiful words.

The vocal lines are very long drawn in 'Sitivit anima mea';
eleven bars for the second syllable of 'vivum', eighteen for 'mea'.

Undoubted tone-painting comes into the next section on the
word 'lacrimae' (tears).

Ex. 9

At the end of the last words 'Ubi est Deus tuus?' the poignant
question is perfectly indicated by the movement of the parts at the
cadence. It will be noticed that the final cadence pause in the illustration is composed of open fifths (no interval of a third) for unison.
The major third came into use at the start of the sixteenth century,
but open fifths are to be found up to the end of the century and
beyond.

Ex. 10

OFFERTORY

The Offertory *a4* has the standard text 'Domine Jesu Christe, Rex
gloriae', with the first three words left in plainsong. With the repeat

of 'Quam olim Abrahae' it amounts to 140 bars of music and contains the most elaborate music in the Mass. In fact each of the three last pieces shows a gradual increase in elaboration. There is a striking passage for basses only, accompanied instrumentally, depicting 'the pains of hell and the deep lake', and in the section about Michael the Standard-bearer, the tenors rise up high above the other two parts as he appears and leads the departed souls into the holy light. The top part is in fact kept high for most of the time in the Offertory. This is the last part of the Requiem Mass set by Ockeghem.

If I have given a disproportionate amount of space to Ockeghem's beautiful Mass it is because it will be the least known of all the great Requiems and its idiom the strangest.

It should, ideally, be heard in a Gothic church, where its flowing melodic lines travelling down from choir to nave would suggest, in some manner, the tracings in the vaulted roof of, for example, Worcester Cathedral.

★

To unaccustomed and unobservant ears all church music of the polyphonic period may, as I have been told, sound alike. This is understandable as regards the latter half of the sixteenth century, when the musical language had become international, though hearing it unawares no one familiar with the music of Palestrina, Victoria, or Byrd would for long confuse the one with the others. Lassus, the most cosmopolitan of them all, is far less easy to identify. One reason for the ordinary listener's impression is that he probably only hears a High Mass at long intervals as a church sound, pure and beautiful (if the choir is good) and soothing to the senses, which was not altogether the effect intended.

I think, however, that even the modestly endowed listener will *see* in the musical illustrations the difference between Ockeghem's writing and that of Antoine Brumel, one of his pupils, to whose Requiem Mass *a*4 I now come.

Brumel (*c.* 1460–*c.* 1520) became heurier of Chartres Cathedral in 1483, a member of the choir at Laon in 1495, and Master of the Children of the Choir, and canon at Notre-Dame, Paris, between 1498 and 1500. He was one of the many Flemish musicians who were employed at the Papal Court and, to the mortification of their Roman contemporaries, sang in the Pontifical Choir Chapel. We hear of Brumel at the Court of Leo X in 1513. This is relevant information as Brumel includes in his Mass a setting of the Sequence *Dies irae* just then coming into use. (The first Missal containing the *Dies irae* in the Mass of All Souls Day was printed in Venice in 1493.) Brumel died in the service of the Duke of Ferrara.

In several of his normal Masses he used the already old-fashioned *cantus firmus* technique of putting the borrowed melody in the tenor in long notes, and this he does also in his Requiem. If the reader will turn back for a moment to page 32 and look at Ockeghem's Introit, and then examine Brumel's unadorned setting of it below, he will perceive the great difference of texture and, among other points, the bringing in of the voices, after the plainsong intonation, in imitation of one another, one by one, one of the most familiar usages in polyphony.

Ex. 11

Everyone is familiar with the pull of the leading note in our scale system: for example, if you run up the scale of C major and pause on B, the seventh note, you feel it must pull up to C. Now this progression existed in the fifth and sixth church modes beginning on F and C. (The opening section of the slow movement of Beethoven's String Quartet in A minor, 'A Song of thanksgiving to God on recovery from an illness', is in the fifth or Lydian mode), but 'Gregorian' composers usually avoided the progression of leading note to tonic, or key note, and used a whole-tone step to the tonic (or final, as it was then called) or approached it from above. In the course of the development of polyphony the half-tone steps between the seventh and eighth degrees of the scale became the general usage and the dominant, which is not invariably on the fifth degree of the mode in plainsong, was fixed on that degree in polyphony. Ockeghem uses the half-step, but in Brumel's Requiem, and thereafter, the harmonic sound is to modern ears akin to that in our major scale system.

The *Kyrie*, without any plainsong intonation, is very simply set, and as both it and *Christe* cover only one petition one supposes that the composer may have meant *Kyrie 2* and *Christe 2* to be sung in plainsong, with a return to the polyphonic sections for the third petitions. There is no added vocal part for the final *Kyrie*, or any other part of the Mass.

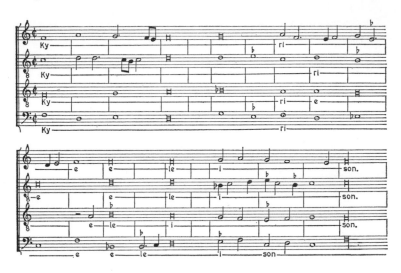

Ex. 12

This is a very austere Mass and if composed in 1500 it seems to indicate the composer had not yet felt the influence of the Italian sun, colour and music, which had so sweetened the art of Dufay. Ockeghem, as far as is known, never went to Italy or perhaps his 'brooding mysticism' might also have undergone a change.

Brumel sets the odd verses of *Dies irae* in polyphony, paraphrasing the plainsong melody in the top part, and leaving the even verses to be sung in plainsong. Later in the sixteenth century the opposite was usually the case, and this is liturgically and aesthetically preferable. Brumel repeats each polyphonic section, so that, for example, the music of Verse 3, 'Tuba mirum', is used again at Verse 9, 'Recordare Jesu pie', and Verse 5, 'Liber scriptus'. At Verse 15, 'Inter oves locum praesta'. Later settings made no such repeats, but suited the polyphony, with great restraint, to the varying emotions suggested by the text.

Brumel makes a most touching effect in the prayer at the close, drawing out the last vowels of 'Jesu' in the tenor and bass parts, 'Domine' in the alto and bass, 'Dona' in soprano, alto, and tenor, and so on to the 'Amen'.

Ex. 13

No light breaks in with the *Sanctus*, not even at 'Hosanna in excelsis', and 'Benedictus', treated very briefly, remains in the same austere style. A strange effect is made in both sections of *Agnus Dei* (the first would liturgically require a repeat) by the reiterated C's in the tenor part, which are like the tolling of a funeral bell—though no such thing can have been in the mind of the composer.

Ex. 14

There is a sense of light in the Communion, which begins with the plainsong intonation and here, as in the Introit, the voices come in one by one, in imitation.

Ex. 15

At the verse 'Requiem aeternam dona eis Domine', sung in plainsong, the response 'Et lux perpetua luceat eis' has a row of repeated C's in the *top* part, a subtle contrast with the bell-like sounds in *Agnus Dei*, for here they are full of light.

★

Pierre de la Rue, composer of the next Requiem Mass, was, like Brumel, a pupil of Ockeghem's, but shows his master's influence more clearly than Brumel, even though his style is as radically different. He is first heard of in November 1492, when he was engaged as a singer by Emperor Maximilian I. The greater part of his life was spent in the employment of Philip the Handsome and his sister Margaret of Austria at Brussels. He died at Courtrai in 1518.

His fine Requiem, a4, with sections a5, is composed at an extraordinarily low pitch. Even transposed a fourth higher, as it is in the published score, the bass is taken down to E flat below the stave, which in the original score would mean a further descent to B flat, defeating—one would imagine—even the most *profundo* of basses! This part would have been allotted to a trombone or a bassoon.[1]

He uses the plainsong intonations for the Introit and Offertory that became standard, but none in the *Kyrie* or Tract, and he omits the Sequence. De la Rue freely paraphrases the plainsong in all the movements except in parts of the *Sanctus* and *Agnus Dei*, where he uses the long notes of the *cantus firmus* style. In the Introit and *Kyrie* he writes effective antiphonal exchanges between upper and lower parts.

Ex. 16

Ex. 17

Ockeghem's influence is apparent in the long lines of the duet passages of the Tract. Here, de la Rue lightens the vocal texture by scoring for soprano, alto, and two tenors. One recalls Ockeghem

---

[1] *The French recording of this work has a solo vocal quartet (S.A.T.B.) and an instrumental ensemble of ten instruments, including two mediaeval harps. This effectively blankets the polyphony.*

again, at 'Fuerunt mihi lacrimae meae', in de la Rue's more dramatic and chordal treatment.

Ex. 18

The 'profundo lacu', in the duet section, for soprano and alto, with which the Offertory begins, takes the alto down to a low F— another instance of madrigalian tone painting.

The start of the *Sanctus, a5,* is beautifully imagined and there are exact quotations of the plainsong in the tenor part at 'Sabaoth', 'Hosanna in excelsis', and in the long notes of the bass part of the *Benedictus* at 'in nomine'.

For some obscure reason the editor has seen fit to print the two sections of *Agnus Dei a5* in reverse order so that when sung, 'requiem sempiternam', the proper ending, is heard first.

There is a subtle difference in the harmonic treatment of 'dona eis' in the two sections. *Agnus I* begins, as far as 'mundi', with heavy reiterated chords, underlining the 'bearing of the sins of the world'— compare this with Brumel's 'tolling bells' in his *Agnus Dei*—and at 'dona eis' the composer writes F, G, A in long notes in the baritone part. In the second section, in which the baritone sings the plainsong from the start, the notes at 'dona eis' are F, G, A flat, and this change of modality gives extra solemnity to 'sempiternam'—A flat appears in none of the other parts here which have A natural. In modern terms the music is in two keys at this point to the end, B flat and E flat, but this is church modal writing, not major-minor tonality.

At the Communion the four voices—the bass being omitted here —sing a radiant 'luceat eis, Domine', the soprano holding the C, the second vowel of 'eis', for a beat alone, all coming in at 'Domine', a lovely device.

Ex. 19

CHAPTER FIVE

THE REQUIEM MASS TO THE END OF THE SIXTEENTH CENTURY

2 Morales, Palestrina, Anerio, Asola, Victoria

The great Spanish composer Cristóbal Morales (*c.* 1500–1553) composed two Requiem Masses, one *a4*, one *a5*, of which the latter is the finer. Like all musicians of the period he made his way to Rome, as the centre of the Catholic Church, as soon as he could. As a boy he sang in the choir of Seville Cathedral —Seville was his birthplace—and then held a chaplaincy there as one of twenty beneficed priests engaged to sing at the services in the cathedral. It was in 1535 that he set out for Rome, after holding posts as chapel master at the cathedrals of Avila and Placencia. He arrived there on 1 September, the day Pope Paul III commissioned Michelangelo to paint the altar wall of the Sistine Chapel. As he was in Rome for ten years as a member of the Pontifical Choir it is tempting to imagine that Michelangelo's frightening Last Judgement had some influence on his impressionable mind when he was composing his Requiems. The character of his Requiem *a5* (in which a woodcut of a skeleton—spade in hand—digging a fresh grave, precedes the music) is graphically described by the Viennese musicologist and historian, A. W. Ambros.

> The *Missa pro defunctis*, though magnificent, inspires terror; one shivers in the presence of this sombre, nocturnal masterpiece. One feels as if one were wandering in dark hollows beneath leaden vaults supported by heavy pillars. In it all adornment has been stripped away, and everything is as plain as could be. Before the face of death all colours fade, and all gaiety ceases. Morales, the Spaniard, conceives death in all its terrible seriousness. . . . Coming from his Requiem immediately upon that of Palestrina, one is struck by the strange feeling that into the blackness of the graves has shot a ray of heavenly light, and that the stern messenger from an unknown land whom Morales presented to us has given way to an angel, serious but benign. One should always hear these two works in succession.

But one never will unless the B.B.C. undertakes the task. The professor certainly has a vivid imagination, coloured perhaps by his knowledge of the constant illnesses that dogged Morales and must have made his outlook on life far from happy.

In the dedication of his Second Book of Masses, Morales said, 'We musicians ourselves are aware that the spirit of the times constantly demands something new from us.'

One new thing, compared with settings in which the plainsong is used more or less exactly as *cantus firmus*, as is the case throughout this Requiem, is that Morales, unlike his Franco-Flemish contemporaries, nearly always ends the borrowed melodies in the same way as they end in the Roman Gradual.

Morales divides the Gradual 'Requiem aeternam dona eis Domine' into three sections, devoting the last entirely to the words 'Non timebit' ('evil tidings he shall not fear'). These words he repeats six times, putting a bare outline of the plainsong in the second alto part and in all the rest using fragments of it.

Ex. 1

The composer sets, and most beautifully, only the final prayer of *Dies irae* 'Pie Jesu Domine'. The serene vocal lines, and the gentle suspensions, in the tenor parts, give the lie to Ambros's picture of 'utter gloom'. The whole movement breathes consolation, hope and faith.

Ex. 2

The most sombre movement is the *Agnus Dei*. Here, as in the Requiems of Brumel and La Rue, is the same kind of chordal treatment, but with a subtle change of speed, made by different note lengths, in each section of the *Agnus Dei*. It does have a chilling effect.

★

We come now to what Ambros calls the 'ray of heavenly light' shed by Palestrina's Requiem Mass *a5*.

The original edition of Palestrina's Requiem Mass is dated 1554, when he was in about his thirtieth year—we do not know the exact year of his birth—and a member, by favour of Pope Julius III, formerly Bishop of Palestrina, of the Pontifical Choir. I say, 'by favour', because he was admitted without examination or assent of the singers, who naturally resented this breach of the rules. For the rest he was happy and, as his second wife had brought him a useful dowry, prosperous. During the series of severe epidemics that swept over Rome and the countryside of Central Italy between 1572 and 1580 Palestrina suffered the grievous loss of his two sons, two brothers, and his wife. Had he then, if he could have borne to do so, composed a Requiem Mass, it might have been a more deeply affecting one, perhaps embracing the whole text, than the early work we have. He sets only the *Kyrie*, Offertory, *Sanctus*, *Benedictus* and *Agnus Dei*, which is disappointing. There is, indeed, nothing to disturb here—there are none of the stark dissonances we find in the Morales Requiem. As always in his music Palestrina prepares these to secure not only harmonic tension but sweetness in the succeeding consonances whereas Morales, it seems to me, uses dissonance 'as a means of poetical expression, as a symbol of the emotions'.

In the first *Kyrie* Palestrina anticipates the plainsong melody in the soprano and alto voices before it comes in, four and a half bars later, in long notes. This is a distant foreshadowing of what Bach was so often to do in his chorale fantasias in the church cantatas.

Ex. 3

There is a lovely modulation, by means of the alto G flat in *Ex.* 4
below, as the final *Kyrie* reaches its climax. Imitation had been in
constant use by all composers since about the mid-fourteenth century, and in the hands of a master it never palls. One expects it, and
it always delights.

Ex. 4

In the singing of Palestrina's music by English choirs one misses
the virile Italian tenors and basses, so that, for example, the thrilling
entry of the basses with the plainsong 'Hosanna in excelsis' in the
Sanctus is apt to be robbed of its effect.

Palestrina rarely takes his sopranos above D and this gives a
restrained quality to his Requiem, but it also makes the higher notes
when used rather more telling, as in the example above from the
Kyrie, and again at the sudden rise to E on the repetition of 'sempiternam' at the end of the third *Agnus Dei*.

Ex. 5

★

From 1575 to 1579 there were among the choirboys who sang under Palestrina in the Julian Choir of St Peter's two brothers called Felice and Giovanni Francesco Anerio, the first and elder of whom succeeded, in April 1594, the lately deceased Palestrina as composer to the Papal Chapel, while the younger became Master of the Chapel at St John Lateran in 1600. Up to 1586 G. F. Anerio published no music and seems early to have been intended for the priesthood. He was, in fact, ordained in 1616. He died in June 1630, on a journey from Poland to Italy. His Requiem Mass *a4*, which was first printed in 1620, has recently been given wide currency in a splendid recorded performance under George Malcolm.[1] Anerio composed his Mass after the Council of Trent had concerned itself with the reform of church music at its twenty-second session, 17 September 1562. The decrees, put in very general terms, demanded the elimination of anything 'lascivious or impure', such as the use of secular melodies, associated with jocose or amorous words, which the Council Fathers thought might be recognized. There was, they considered, too much concern with the exhibition of technical skills, too little with the spiritual significance of the words set. In 1564, by a *motu proprio* of Pius IV of 2 August, two of the eight cardinals were charged with carrying out the resolutions regarding church music of the Council of Trent, which had ended eight months previously. One of them was the great Cardinal Borromeo, who commissioned a Mass from Vincento Ruffo 'which should be as clear as possible' and another from Don Nicola Vincentino 'who favours chromatic music' (the move away from the modes) 'thus by the comparison of the work of many excellent musicians we will better be able to judge this intelligible music. It must be serious and not greatly agitated, not based on secular themes which turn the temple of God into a stage where it is possible to perform every kind of music of a ridiculous and ludicrous buffoonery.' In other words the cardinals wished composers to return to a truly liturgical style and to give special attention to rendering the words intelligible and not to indulge in lengthy note spinning. In April 1565, the Papal singers came to the house of Cardinal Vitellozi to demonstrate to the assembly whether or not the words of the Masses sung to them could be understood. We do not know, unfortunately, what Masses they heard, but the presumption is that those by Ruffo and Vincentino and possibly Palestrina's 'Pope Marcellus' Mass were among them.

---

[1] *Since this book was written an admirable new edition of Anerio's Requiem Mass, edited by Anthony G. Petti, with a valuable seven-page introduction, has been published by Messrs J. & W. Chester Ltd. The illustrations I have used are taken from the faulty edition of 1865 edited by Joseph Schrems.*

A compromise had, of course, to be reached. Composers could not lay aside counterpoint and write more or less in block harmony. Palestrina's 'Marcellus' Mass is a miracle of verbal clarity achieved by making all voices predominantly sing the same syllables on the same notes, but even so he could not sustain this technique throughout, and he never wrote in so strict a style again. The compromise is well shown at work in Anerio's beautifully integrated Requiem Mass —the one form of the Mass that had never made use of secular themes or become the victim of technical skills. The Introit of this Mass is as good an example as any of the word correspondences and the concise and clear nature of the polyphony, which shows no loss of musical interest in any part. The plainsong is paraphrased in the tenor part—it begins with long notes in the traditional *cantus firmus* style, and then is freely treated. The psalm verse is, as almost invariably, in block harmony, the modified plainsong being now in the soprano part.

Anerio sets the Sequence, but not the Gradual or Tract. He leaves the odd verses of the Sequence in plainsong, instead of the reverse, as in Brumel's Requiem, and this ensures that the three different plainsong phrases are heard at 1, 'Dies irae', 3, 'Tuba mirum', 5, 'Liber scriptus' and so on. In the polyphonic sections, and thereafter, at the relevant even numbers, the plainsong is used usually very freely, often after a clear identification in the opening notes. After verse 9 ('Recordare, Jesu pie'), in plainsong, Anerio puts the third line of verse 10 at 'Tantus labor non sit cassus' into triple time, repeating the words twice. The use of triple time, here and in verse 14, 'Preces meae non sunt dignae', the latter half of verse 18, 'Qua resurget ex favilla', and at 'Dona eis requiem' before the 'Amen', gives special emphasis to the words.

Ex. 6

In the Offertory there is a splendid bit of pictorial illustration (a use of madrigalian technique) at 'ne cadant in obscurum', with a dramatic use of rests at the repetition of the two last words (*see Ex. 7*). The plainsong shines out clearly in the top part of the *Sanctus*, with the opening words extending over five bars in long held notes, the other parts moving beautifully below. Anerio sets the Absolution, *Libera me, Domine*, with hardly any reference to the plainsong intonation and at the close of the opening section brings

Ex. 7

his major third (G sharp) after the minor third (G) in the alto, into the treble part. This gives the word 'ignem' stern emphasis.

Ex. 8

The composer quotes the relevant plainsong phrase at 'Tremens factus' but not at 'Dies illa, dies irae', a nice avoidance of the obvious.

★

I must just add a word about the Requiem Mass *a*4 of Giovanni Matteo Asola, who held the position of Master of the Chapel at Treviso in 1578 and Vincenzo in 1581. In 1592 he was one of sixteen well-known composers who banded together to present a collection of settings of Vesper psalms to their great contemporary Palestrina, the dedication reading, 'To the most celebrated and pre-eminent head of the musical art'. The ageing composer—he died two years later—sent in return a motet on the text 'Ye are my friends, if ye do what I teach, saith the Lord', which discloses an unsuspected vein of humour in him. In respect of clarity of texture Asola certainly did what the master had taught in his music. This is the only Requiem Mass in this chapter to set *every* part of the Mass available for music and, if they knew it, it must have won the admiration of the Cardinals of the Commission. Tract and Gradual are treated chordally, and the composer takes care to make the words coincide in his four parts in the alternate plainsong and polyphony of the Sequence, which is modestly contrapuntal.

Asola's use of plainsong in the polyphonic sections is very similar to that of Anerio and he too ends the Sequence with an effectively placed major third in the tenor part of the last bar after a succession of bare fifth cadences.

★

Tomàs Luis de Victoria (c. 1548–1611) composed two Requiem Masses, one a4 in 1585 and the other a6 in 1603, modelled on its predecessor. The history of this last Mass is so interesting and so well documented by Robert Stevenson in his splendid book *Spanish Cathedral Music in the Golden Age* that I feel bound to add more biographical details than belong here in speaking of it. First of all it should be said that Victoria was born in Avila, the city of St Teresa, and in 1558, or thereabouts, became a choirboy in the Cathedral—Morales had been master of the chapel there from 1526 to 1530—and left there for Rome, when his voice broke, to study for the priesthood at the German College. This institution was founded by Ignatius Loyola in 1552 to train missionaries to bring back Germany to the Catholic faith, but it also admitted students of other nationalities, for their clerical training. On 28 August 1575, Victoria was ordained priest by Thomas Goldwell, the exiled Bishop of St Asaph, in the English Church of St Thomas of Canterbury, and nearly two years later he was admitted to a chaplaincy at St Jerome's, where for five years he lived on terms of daily intimacy with St Philip of Neri, founder of the Congregation of the Oratory, of whom it was said that 'his apostolate extends from the Pope to the smallest urchin'. In these sympathetic surroundings Victoria composed, and carried out his spiritual duties. His Second Book of Masses of 1583 carried a dedication to Philip II of Spain, in which the composer speaks of spending much time and effort in music over the past year in addition to 'other most noble studies' (theology, etc.) and adds, 'I worked most sedulously to perfect myself in that study to which as if by some hidden natural instinct I was drawn.' He goes on to declare himself exhausted from continuous musical toil and anxious to return home 'not empty-handed', he hopes, after his lengthy stay in Italy. Henceforth his goal will be a quiet life spent in the discharge of his priestly duties. Among the works he was bringing back was the Requiem a4, published in 1583. But did Victoria really mean to pronounce 'Requiem' over his creative genius, or was that remark the result of strain and overwork? However it might be, he arrived back in Spain about 1587 and from that date to his death in 1603 he was chaplain to the Dowager Empress Maria, widow of Emperor Maximilian II, daughter of Emperor Charles V, and mother of two emperors, a sonorous roll-call. This royal lady lived in retirement in the Convent of the Barefoot Nuns of St Clare, Madrid, in which order her daughter Margaret had professed solemn vows in 1584. It was a remarkable foundation, made in 1564, and liberally endowed by Joanna, sister of Philip II, who was devoted to music. She laid down, in the constitution, that 'the thirty-three rigidly cloistered nuns were to hear Mass in a small chapel attended by eight priests, all of whom (in addition to other requirements) were to be accomplished singers of plainchant and polyphony'. The nuns were separated, in the usual way in a strict order, from the priests and the outside world by a grille. The priests were to be over thirty years of age, Latin scholars, and of unexceptionable character. They were to have no other offices or duties and were never to remain overnight outside the chaplain's residency. They were to take their meals separately and each was to have his own servant (a very wise provision!). They were allowed one month's holiday a year. Their daily duties included the singing of two Masses—one a High Mass with deacon and subdeacon. Instrumentalists were to be engaged at Easter, Corpus Christi, and its Octave.

Philip II, in a new declaration of 1577, approved by Gregory XIII in 1578, increased the number of chaplains to twelve 'so that there could be three to sing each part'. (I do not see how this could be done at a High Mass requiring three of them as celebrant, deacon, and subdeacon.) Further details follow, including a rise in pay—which was doubled—and instruction about the duties of the post of chapel master, held by Victoria. A new ruling by Philip III added two more singing priests, chosen for specially good voices, and he increased the number of choirboys to six. It is interesting to read that a bassoonist was to be regularly employed 'who shall serve in the said chapel every day music is performed and assist the choir with his instrument'. One would have thought that a skilled choir would not need a bassoon player to double the bass voices. Many attempts were made to lure Victoria, as the most celebrated composer in Spain, away from the convent, but to no avail. He went to Rome once, perhaps twice again as, being private chaplain to the Empress and not one of the convent's priestly establishment, he could move about freely. At her death the Empress left him one of three chaplaincies she endowed in the convent. Victoria then retired from the post, which was unpaid, of chapel master, and simply became the convent organist. In 1605 he published his great *Officium Defunctorum* at Madrid, which includes the Requiem Mass a6, dedicating it to Princess Margaret with a clear statement that he composed it for 'the obsequies of your most revered mother'. She had died on 26 February 1603 and was buried in the convent cloister on 1 March, but the Mass and its attendant pieces were most probably sung in the commemoration ceremonies in the Jesuit Church of Sts Peter and Paul (on the present site of the Cathedral of Madrid), which had been magnificently endowed by the Empress. Vespers for the Office of the Dead was sung on 22 April, the Requiem Mass the day after, followed by a panegyric delivered by Padre Jeronimo de Florencia, a famous preacher of the day. As the Jesuit Fathers had enjoined every father with talent 'to write poetry and compositions of all sorts in praise of Her Majesty', Victoria, who had had such close associations with the Society of Jesus for so long, would be certain to have been asked for a special contribution. Lack of time might have caused him to base his Requiem Mass on the earlier one. In the dedication he called the Mass a 'swan-song', a term that has usually been taken to mean that he would not compose any more, but it is clear he meant a swan-song for the Empress. He did not in fact publish any more works, but he had no reason to suppose he would die, as he did, at the age of sixty-three on 27 August 1611, in the chaplain's house adjacent to the convent.

This long introduction to the two Requiems will have given some idea of the closing years of the last great composer of liturgical Requiem Masses. Palestrina and Lassus had died in 1594, Byrd—who never composed a Requiem Mass—died in 1620 and so ended the glorious golden age of Latin church music. Victoria and Byrd were both deeply spiritual men and both have left some idea of their views on music. Mr Stevenson prints a catena of phrases, made by Dom David Pujol, O.S.B., taken from Victoria's dedicatory prefaces to his works 'to form something of a coherent aesthetic philosophy'. Among these the following are of particular interest. 'Music, because instinct with rhythm and harmony, describes the very being of God—Creation itself testifies to the divine harmony—Music is not man's invention but his heritage from the blessed spirits—Music can affect for good or ill the body as well as the mind—Music of the right stamp serves not only to enhance the splendour of the cult but also to excite the faithful.' In his Requiem *a*4 of 1583 Victoria, like Morales, put the *cantus firmus* in the top part and in long notes—by then a very old-fashioned device—and in a low key. The Offertory, scored for altos, tenors, baritones, and basses (no sopranos) is the most sombre and dramatic piece, with great emphasis laid on 'de poenis inferni et de profundo lacu', which takes the basses down to a low G at 'profundo'.

The change from four- to three-part writing comes in 'Libera me, Domine' at 'Tremens factus sum ego'; in this brief section the music is identical with that at the same place in the 1605 Requiem *a*6. Comparison of the two works, which can only be made by the individual, is fascinating. The cadences remain, in the later work, as always with Victoria, clean cut and unadorned but the vocal lines are now more eloquently drawn. For example, in terms of measures (bars) the 1583's first *Kyrie* has 17 bars to 46 in the 1605, and the last one, 18 to 8. The *cantus firmus*, fined down here, is in the soprano (cantus 2) throughout and, as Mr Stevenson says, the addition of another soprano as a counterpointing voice *above* the plainsong-bearing voice is a master stroke, lightening the whole texture, and notably also in the Gradual, which was so sombre in the 1583 Requiem. All these factors and the higher pitch remove the gloom that overshadows the earlier work. Victoria is greatest in his motets as Palestrina is greatest in his Masses, but there is no doubt that his 1605 Requiem is superior to Palestrina's, or anyone else's: it is indeed a masterpiece. In both Victoria's Requiems plainsong intonations are used in full except in the *Kyrie* and the Responsory 'Libera me, Domine'. The verse of the Gradual is taken in plainsong as far as 'aeterna' ('In memoria aeterna'), the choir entering very effectively to complete the line with 'erit justus'. 'Hostias et preces tibi', the verse of the Offertory, is left wholly in plainsong, and 'Quam olim Abrahae' has only 7 bars of music to the 25 of the earlier work. In the Responsory at the Absolution Victoria changes his dispositions, bringing in plainsong, after the polyphonic start 'Libera me', for 'de morte aeterna in die illa tremenda', so that there is an extra interpolation of plainsong which makes a well balanced pattern of interchanges. Most significant is the treatment of the verse 'Requiem aeternam, Domine' in the two works. The serenity in the 1605 Mass is absent in the 1583. Because the liturgy requires a repeat of 'Libera me, Domine' up to the words 'quando veneris judicare saeculum per ignem' this serenity is disturbed by the thought of the judgement of the world by fire, but the peaceful 'Kyrie eleison, Christe eleison, Kyrie eleison', radiantly set, restores it. Victoria also set one of the lessons from the Book of Job (10: 1–7), 'Taedet animam meam vitae meae' ('In my soul I am weary of my life'), which forms the second lesson in what is called *The Dirge* (that is, Matins of the Office of the Dead) and from the same source (Job 30–31: 7–16) the motet 'Versa est in luctum cithara mea' ('My harp is turned to mourning'). The first of these, for four voices, has an interesting example of what are technically called 'secondary seventh chords', used also in several places in the 1605 Requiem.

Ex. 9

In the motet, 'The voice of them that weep' is made especially poignant by the use of an augmented fifth chord on 'flentium' (weeping).

Ex. 10

★

A Requiem Mass *a*4 attributed to Josquin Des Prés by some historians is in fact a motet called 'Requiem', composed by a Dutch contemporary, Jacob Obrecht, on the death of his father. It has a secular text. A 'six-part' Requiem in fourteen sections appearing under Josquin's name in Leyden is of doubtful authenticity. As Gustave Reese observes, if it is by the composer it would be the only Mass of his in more than four parts.

Another great composer, Orlando de Lassus (*c.* 1532–1594) is also absent from this chapter, but this is simply because I cannot summon up any enthusiasm for his Requiem Mass *a*5, which has a prevailingly dense texture. It is regarded as a model of the contrapuntal technique of the Netherland School, and as such is to be admired, but it is in Lassus's motets, not his Masses, that his true greatness is to be found.

It may be of interest to mention a Requiem Mass *a*6 by Jean Richafort (*c.* 1480–*c.* 1547) in the course of which two tenors sing in canon the Sarum chant to words of Verse 5 of Psalm 17 'Circumdederunt me gemitus mortis' ('Death's terrors were near at hand') and also reply to one another, as if with exclamations of personal sorrow, to the melody of the first words of Josquin's chanson *Faulte d'argent*, 'C'est doleur non pareille' ('It is unheard-of grief'). During this the other voices sing the liturgical words, the top voice having the relevant plainsong. The 'Circumdederunt' melody, a favourite one of Josquin's, was used by Gombert in his lament on the death of Josquin and Richafort's Requiem Mass would seem to be intended for the same purpose.

It is a strange thing that there is no known Requiem Mass by an English composer to add to the list, and this in spite of the many mentions of bequests and directions for such Masses to be celebrated. I take the following particulars from Dr F. Harrison's admirable book *Music in Mediaeval Britain* (Routledge, 1958)—which in fact takes in the sixteenth century, and so the liturgical and institutional changes brought about at the time of the Reformation. Dr

Harrison considers that 'the transition from medieval to Renaissance concepts of structure and style, which took place on the Continent in the fifteenth and early sixteenth centuries, was not fully accomplished in England until after the mid-sixteenth century'. At Worcester Cathedral the choirmaster, John Hampton, appointed in 1486, instructed in plainsong and polyphonic music the eight choristers who sang the Marian-Antiphon daily after Vespers and a Requiem Mass four times a year in the Lady Chapel built by Bishop Alcock. Again under the statutes (1507) of the Guild of Jesus at St Paul's, drawn up by Dean Colet, 'a Requiem Mass was to be celebrated incontinently after . . . the Masse of Jesu ended'. Finally in 1504 Jaxon, a chaplain, noted in a book of *cantus fractus* (part music) a Mass *Lux aeterna*, without naming the composer, which has, in spite of its title, never come to light! It might be a case similar to the *Requiem aeternam* Mass of Dufay mentioned on p. 28.

The losses of English manuscripts, noted as existing, have been very great, but the reason for the non-mention of a polyphonic Requiem remains obscure. One must conclude that plainsong was invariably used and at other times the many Masses for which bequests were left were said, not sung.

CHAPTER SIX

THE REQUIEM MASS IN THE SEVENTEENTH CENTURY

When, if ever, the history of the Requiem Mass comes to be written, the author will encounter formidable difficulties in dealing with the seventeenth century, and not least in seeking out and transcribing unpublished material which is to be found in monastic and other libraries all over Europe. It is possible that among the results of such labour would be the discovery of some Requiem Masses of perhaps greater musical interest than the few that are to be found in the available collections of church music. Of those I was able to examine, the one by Giuseppe Pitoni (1657–1743) has a strikingly dramatic treatment of *Dies irae*.

The prime difficulty, in general, presented by the seventeenth century, lies in its being a time of transition, a period of a more revolutionary character even than that which introduced polyphony into church music about the ninth century, and with more widespread results.

This book is not intended to be a history of music, but it is obvious that some indication should be given here of the contrast between the styles of the Renaissance and those of the Baroque period which lasted up to the time of Bach and Handel. I cannot do better than quote the admirable summing-up of the brilliant discussion of the matter—to which the interested reader should turn—which Manfred Bukofzer gives in his invaluable book *Music in the Baroque Era* (Dent, 1948), p. 16.

Renaissance	*Baroque*
One practice, one style.	Two practices, three styles.
Restrained representation of the words, *musica reservata* and madrigalism.	Affective representation of the words, textual absolutism.
	Polarity of the outermost voices.
All voices equally balanced.	Diatonic and chromatic melody in wide range.
Diatonic melody in small range.	
Modal counterpoint.	Tonal counterpoint.
Intervallic harmony, and intervallic dissonance treatment.	Chordal harmony and chordal dissonance treatment.

Chords are by-products of the part writing.	Chords are self-contained entities.
Chord progressions are governed by modality.	Chord progressions are governed by tonality.
Evenly flowing rhythm regulated by the *tactus* [up and down beat].	Extremes of rhythm, free declamation and mechanical pulsations.
No pronounced idioms, voice and instrument are interchangeable.	Vocal and instrumental idioms, the idioms are interchangeable.

Such a summary is a generalization, but it serves to indicate the way matters were developing. 'Musica reservata and madrigalism' need a word of explanation; '*musica reservata*' seems to mean a faithful observance of word values and 'madrigalism' their pictorial representation: this sometimes found its way into motets of the Renaissance era. 'Textual absolutism' poses the problem Richard Strauss dealt with in his opera *Capriccio*. 'Prima la musica' or 'Prima le parole': which should have primacy, words or music? The 'first practice', a phrase coined by Monteverdi, was known as the *style antico*; in other words the Palestrinian style, which came to be identified with the *a cappella* (or unaccompanied) writing of the Roman school of composers, and especially with the practice of the Pontifical Choir.

The 'second practice', the *style moderno*, embraced all the newly emergent forms of sacred and secular music of church, chamber and theatre: that is to say opera, oratorio, cantata, sonata, *concerto grosso*, and so forth. In all these forms, the *basso continuo*, with which, as Bukofzer says, the Baroque era practically begins and ends, played an outstanding part. It was no longer a matter of instruments merely doubling the bass part of a vocal piece; it reflected the harmonic implications of the complete vocal texture, and so led to the figured bass. This was a kind of musical shorthand which gave the continuo players on the organ or harpsichord an easy clue to the harmonic foundations of the piece. This *basso continuo* gradually developed independence of the other parts; and, in the hands of an imaginative player, added its own contribution to the ensemble. All this is familiar enough to us in, for example, performances of Bach's Passions and Church Cantatas. In the seventeenth century, composers, whether or not they composed Requiem Masses in the manner of the first practice, unaccompanied or with instrumental doubling, or the second practice with *basso continuo*, or in polychoral style, seem to have preserved much of the restraint implicit in the liturgy, though their treatment of *Dies irae* is naturally more dramatic than hitherto.

The plainsong intonations appear, as before, in all or some of the movements, but are not so frequently used as thematic material, though there is often a flavour of plainsong in the vocal parts. Chromatic passages occur which are absolutely foreign to the style of Palestrina and his school but familiar enough in madrigal compositions of the last quarter of the sixteenth century. In prevailing diatonic surroundings we find, for example, this commonplace passage in the Offertory of the Requiem Mass *a*4 of Claudio Casciolini, a minor Roman composer born *c.* 1670; it recurs again at the words 'Calamitatis et miseriae' in his setting of the responsory, 'Libera me, Domine, de morte aeterna'.

Ex. 1

Counterpoint is more subservient to harmonic writing in this and other Requiem Masses of the period I have examined than in those of previous centuries. The Mass, in general, during the seventeenth century, lost its place for ever as the chief form for the exercise of a composer's art. The new-style motet, the cantata, the opera, the sonata, offered more exciting possibilities.

No better example could be given of the change that had come over music as early as the first decade of the seventeenth century than Monteverdi's *Vespers* of 1610, composed when he was in the service of the Duke of Mantua and, we must presume, performed in the Ducal Chapel of Saint Barbara. Monteverdi dedicated the Vespers, the four Motets 'intended for princely chapels and apartments', and a Mass *a*6 to Pope Paul V, composing the latter work, perhaps as a wise precaution, in the Palestrinian style. It is thought probable that he submitted the collection to the procurators of St Mark's, Venice as a 'test piece', when, on the death of G. C. Martinengo in 1613, the post of *Maestro da Cappella* of St Mark's fell vacant.

Rome had now yielded to Venice as the centre of musical activity. Nietzsche wrote in *Ecce Homo* 'If I try to find a new word for music I can never find any other than Venice', though he does not reveal how well he was acquainted with the works of its greatest composers, Adrian Willaert, his pupil Andrea Gabrielli, and the latter's more celebrated nephew, Giovanni, and Claudio Monteverdi.

These predecessors of Monteverdi, and above all his contemporary Giovanni Gabrielli, had made full use of the opportunities of polychoral writing offered by the two choir and two organ galleries in the magical cathedral, a fact Palestrina took note of in his later Masses, and above all in his motets.

Monteverdi said that the modern composer must build on the foundation of truth and in his church music that meant the introduction when he so desired, of the 'agitated style' (*stile concertato*) of which he speaks in the celebrated preface to his Eighth Book of Madrigals to which he gave the revealing title of *Madrigali guerrieri et amorosi*. His 're-discovery of the warlike genius' found vivid expression in this very varied book, especially in the dramatic cantata *Il combattimento di Tancredi e Clorinda*.

Subjective expression, in ever-increasing measure, now invaded sacred music. The words were to be the mistress of the harmony. Precise declamation was to be preferred to the interwoven vocal lines of the polyphonic art of the past. How then would such ideals consort with the composing of a Requiem Mass? It was open to a composer to treat the text in the reserved Roman style, unaccompanied or with a 'following bass', or in polychoral style, with a *basso continuo*, or with an independent figured bass accompaniment, and to single out 'Dies irae' for specially dramatic or emotional treatment. This was to be done in various sections of the normal Mass, in the way familiar to us in later years, and reaching its apotheosis in Beethoven's deeply personal confession of faith, the *Missa Solemnis*.

Counterpoint was weakened by a new relationship between bass and treble, leaving the latter to pursue its ways without the need to consider the other voices as it had been bound to do when there was equality between all parts. We find, therefore, in Monteverdi's *Vespers*, the old and new combined. In the *Magnificat* the old *cantus firmus* practice of putting the quoted melody—in this case plainsong—in long notes is maintained, and in the psalms the ancient psalm tones, more freely treated, run like a golden thread. Instrumental *ritornelli* and every vocal effect known to the time are frequently introduced. The Vespers and the motets are indeed a compendium of Baroque practice. The 'word', however, is by no means always 'mistress of the harmony', as may be seen, for example, in the remarkable *Sonata sopra Sancta Maria*, an instrumental piece with an obbligato vocal part, a plainsong phrase, coming in at irregular intervals, from the Litany of the Blessed Virgin Mary.

In 1621, Monteverdi, then Master of the Music at St Mark's, Venice, was one of the composers commissioned by the Florentines living in Venice to compose music for the memorial service for the late Duke of Tuscany. All of it is most unfortunately lost, but Giulio Strozzi, a Florentine poet, and librettist of two of Monteverdi's operas (also lost), has described the composer's contributions in a pamphlet about the occasion. The Requiem Mass was preceded by 'a plaintive *sinfonia* which brought tears to the eyes', after which the composer's son, Don Francesco, 'sang with the sweetest voice "O vos omnes attendite".' The words are those of the second responsory from the Second Nocturn of Matins of Holy Saturday, 'O vos omnes qui transitis per viam, attendite et videte si est dolor sicut dolor meus' ('O all ye who pass by this way, see if there be any grief like unto my grief'): words exquisitely set by Victoria in his Office of Holy Week, published in 1598. The Sequence *Dies irae* was the only section of the actual Mass contributed by Monteverdi, but as Strozzi mentions 'responsories' it is possible that he set *Libera me* from the Absolution. The other piece was Psalm 100, 'De profundis clamavi ad te, Domine' ('Out of the depths I have cried to thee, O Lord') which comes in the Office of the Dead. Strozzi describes it as 'delicate . . . as it were a dialogue between souls in purgatory and angels visiting them.'[1]

These descriptions show how grievous is the loss of the music. The *De profundis* was obviously in the 'modern style' of the motets in the *Vespers*. *Dies irae*, being within the Mass, and lengthy, would no doubt have alternated plainsong and polyphony in the old style, but we can only make vague guesses about the treatment of the other two pieces and must remain unaware of the identity of the other composers contributing. Monteverdi dominated vocal music in the first half of the seventeenth century, Alessandro Scarlatti (1660–1720) the end of it and into the eighteenth century. E. J. Dent describes one of his two Masses with orchestra (1720) as a worthy ancestor of the Masses of Bach and Beethoven. The remaining eight out of Scarlatti's ten extant Masses are in the Palestrinian *a cappella* style, well made but unremarkable music. One of them is a Requiem Mass (date unknown) and one must regret that it is, as a whole, so unrepresentative of the genius of this great composer.

---

[1] *Monteverdi by Denis Arnold (Master Musician Series), Dent, 1963.*

CHAPTER SEVEN

THE REQUIEM MASS FROM THE EIGHTEENTH TO THE TWENTIETH CENTURY

1 Michael Haydn and Mozart

It is one of the pleasures in writing this kind of book that one comes across works hitherto known only by name, if at all, and not explored. A foreign record catalogue put me on the track of the Requiem Mass by Michael Haydn (1737–1806), younger brother of Joseph Haydn (1732–1809), which proved to be not only a fine work but one which evidently had some influence on Mozart's Requiem.

During the time the Haydn boys sang in the choir of St Stephen's Cathedral, Vienna, Michael, then eight years old, appeared to be the more gifted of the brothers. His beautiful voice is said to have had the astonishing compass of three octaves, and when the Empress complained of Joseph 'crowing like a cock'—presumably when his voice was breaking—the solos were turned over to Michael. He became also so proficient on the organ as to be able to act as deputy, on occasion, for the cathedral organist. Another of his activities was to start a club among his fellow choristers for the detection of plagiarisms in their compositions! Michael's superiority was still evident in his seventeenth year when his brother, still poor and unknown, was acting as accompanist and valet to the famous, and notoriously bad-tempered, singing teacher Nicolo Porpora in order to study his method and earn some money. Michael, meanwhile, had gone in 1757 as musical director and concert master in the service of the Bishop of Grosswardein in Hungary, and there composed a full-length Mass.

Haydn composed his *Requiem Solemne* for the funeral of Sigismund von Schrattenbach, Archbishop of Salzburg, which took place in December 1771, the year in which he also suffered the loss of his young daughter. (The 'solemn' in the title merely indicates the more elaborate ceremonial attached to the funeral service of a prelate.) The Mass is scored for two oboes, two trumpets, three trombones, timpani, two violins, cellos, and double basses, S.A.T.B. soloists and choir. The omission of the violas is curious. It seems to have been a Salzburg custom not to use them, or at any rate, not to score for them, for Einstein thinks they may have played the bass part an octave higher. The length of the Requiem, fifty-one minutes, would not have pleased Archbishop Colloredo, who insisted, as Mozart tells us, that even a Pontifical Mass should be despatched in three-quarters of an hour, and not one moment more.

I was immediately struck by the composer's fine sense of form. He unifies Introit and *Kyrie* by the recapitulation of the second and third of the three contrasted themes set forth in the ten bars of the orchestral prelude to the Introit. Of these (a) and (c) have the tread of a solemn march—an Introit, as has been said, is a processional piece —(b), with trumpets sounding below, is quietly expressive.

Ex. I

The chorus, beginning with the basses, enter with a new theme, to a syncopated orchestral accompaniment, distributed successively over the four parts. The first four notes clearly derive from those of the plainsong Introit.

The choral entries of 'et lux perpetua' and the psalm verse 'Te decet hymnus' are preceded on the orchestra by (b) and (c) respectively. Haydn quotes the plainsong psalm tone for the verse. From this point the one weakness of the Mass begins to be evident, a certain poverty of invention in accompanimental figures and their harmonies. The vocal parts, however, are so well designed that one soon ignores this.

At this time brother Joseph, then thirty-nine, had composed only three Masses, the youthful Mozart—he was then fifteen—five short ones and one of full length. Mozart was eager to see all Michael's church music, and Joseph considered it surpassed his own. This, however, is certainly not true of his last six Masses which are nearly all musically, if not liturgically, of far finer character; indeed they are among his greatest works.

Haydn's *Dies irae* is all-of-a-piece, with built-in solo sections, but never a pause in its on-going rhythm until *adagio* is marked in the penultimate bar. The accompaniment up to the soprano solo 'Mors stupebit' has a fortuitous resemblance to the flute melody of Bach's 'Badinerie' from the B minor Orchestral Suite, with the gaiety removed by the tempo direction, *Andante maestoso*. Haydn makes no attempt to dramatize 'Tuba mirum' but Death's and Nature's stupefaction at the sight that met their eyes after the sounding of the last trump is depicted by a shuddering little figure in the orchestra, the voice part here having (c) from the prelude to the Introit.

Ex. 2

This fine and dramatic soprano solo ends with a sudden rise of an octave at 'unde mundus judicetur', the alto soloist then following with an exact repetition, at a lower pitch, of the soprano's first eight bars, but then going on to the same octave rise. The tenor solo 'Juste judex ultionis' is even more remarkable, repeating the phrases used in the chorus's 'Tuba mirum' and then by two-phrase repetitions at the same pitch emphasizing the prayer 'supplicanti parce, Deus'.

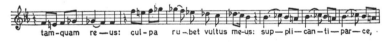

Ex. 3

'Confutatis maledictis' derives its force from the low-pitched choral part, the flames being suggested by a very mild orchestral accompaniment. The composer is more imaginative, orchestrally, at 'Lacrimosa dies illa', in which he gives a sobbing figure to the strings; the choral part, too, is most expressive. Haydn ends with a fugal 'Amen' into which is woven the quiet prayer 'Pie Jesu Domine, dona eis requiem', set to a phrase derived from the first bar of *Ex. 3*.

This seems to me an extraordinarily well-integrated setting of the Sequence, and in point of form it is much to be preferred to the breaking-up of the poem into distinct sections. Haydn gives the opening words of the Offertory 'Domine Jesu Christe' to the solo tenor—with a clear reference to the plainsong intonation at this point—and, after the chorus complete the sentence with 'Rex gloriae', he writes a beautifully moulded four-bar phrase that deserves quotation. The key here changes to G minor, from the C minor before prevailing.

li-be-ra, li – be-ra a-ni-mas omni – um fi – de-li-um, fi – de — li-um de – func-to-rum

Ex. 4

Haydn's orchestral part is distinctly more ambitious in this piece and he vividly illustrates in this and the vocal parts the 'pains of hell', the 'deep lake' and, with constantly repeated triplet figures on the violins, the prayer to be delivered from the 'mouth of the lion', repeating also 'ne cadant in obscurum' no less than seven times. This throws into high relief the lovely soprano solo 'Sed signifer sanctus Michael' which brings the Archangel Michael, the Standard-bearer, on to the scene to lead the souls of the departed into the 'holy light'.

sed sig — ni—fer sanc-tus, sanc-tus Mi-chael repraesentet   e-as in lu-cem sanctam,

Ex. 5

By a now established convention 'Quam olim Abrahae promisisti et semini ejus' is treated fugally; the fugue subject is given character by its last two bars.

Quam o-lim   A-bra-hae pro-mi-si — sti,

Ex. 6

The *Sanctus*, basically in E flat major, begins, surprisingly, in F minor, goes through C and G minor at 'Pleni sunt coeli et terra gloria tua' and then, for 'Hosanna in excelsis', into E flat major. As in the fugue subject of 'Quam olim Abrahae', an unexpected rise of a seventh gives character to the phrase.

Ho – san-na ho—san-na

Ex. 7

This seventh interval is brought into the opening bars of the orchestral introduction to the brief *Benedictus*, given, as by custom, to the solo group.

As in the Offertory, the *Agnus Dei*, briefly treated, begins with an expressive prelude for the strings. The movement leads straight into the opening of the Communion, 'Lux aeterna luceat eis, Domine', which is begun by the solo soprano, with accompaniment for violins only, in thirds, for one and three-quarter bars. Then the same words are repeated by the solo group to the same phrase to which they were set at the repeat of the Introit, another instance of purposeful planning. 'Cum sanctis tuis' is treated, again according to convention, as a fugue, but this time with a rather weak subject. The beautiful return to the 'Requiem aeternam' for soloists, marked *adagio*, with the Introit phrases mentioned above, and in the orchestral part (b) of *Ex*. 1, makes one wish the work had ended here—but the liturgy requires the repeat of 'Cum sanctis tuis', and so the fugue has the last word in this fine work.

*

On 4 April 1787 Mozart, hearing that his father was 'really ill', wrote him the often-quoted letter in which he expresses his thoughts about death.

> As death, when we come to consider it closely, is the true goal of an existence, I have formed during the last few years such close relations with this best and truest friend of mankind, that his image is not only no longer terrifying to me, but is indeed very soothing and consoling! And I thank my God for graciously granting me the opportunity (you know what I mean) of learning that death is the *key* which unlocks the door to our true happiness. I never lie down at night without reflecting that—young as I am [he was thirty-one]—I may not live to see another day. Yet no one of all my acquaintances could say that in company I am morose or disgruntled. For this blessing I daily thank my Creator and wish with all my heart that each one of my fellow creatures could enjoy it . . .

Mozart's attitude to death, in this touching letter, is completely in accord with Christian teaching, but the obvious reference to Free Masonry ('you know what I mean') shows that he had heard at the Lodge he attended an exposition about man and death more appealing to him than the prevailing Catholic teaching. At this period many priests, and many of the laity, including as an example to others the Emperor Joseph II, were Masons without ceasing to be Catholics. They merely ignored the official ruling.

A little over four years later, in the last year of his life, Mozart wrote, as some have alleged, a letter to da Ponte in response to a suggestion that he should leave Vienna and seek employment in England. This letter—a transcript, not an autograph—is dated simply September 1791, written in Italian, and has no addressee named and no signature.

My dear Sir,
I wish I could follow your advice, but how can I do so? I feel stunned, I reason with difficulty and cannot get rid of the vision of this unknown man. I see him perpetually; he entreats me, presses me, and impatiently demands the work. I go on writing because composition tires me less than resting. Otherwise I have nothing here to fear. I know from what I suffer that the hour is come. I am at the point of death: I have come to an end before having had the enjoyment of my talent, life indeed was so beautiful, my career began under such fortunate auspices; but one cannot change one's own destiny. No one can measure his own days, one must resign oneself, it will be as providence wills, and so I finish my death-song. I must not leave it incomplete.

The unknown man, Jahn says, was the 'stranger, a tall thin grave-looking man dressed from head to foot in grey who, in July of this year, had presented Mozart with an unsigned letter asking him to name his price for composing a Requiem'. He was, in fact, the steward of Count Franz von Walsegg, a minor nobleman and an even more minor composer in the habit of passing off works by other hands as his own.

The letter, purporting to have been discovered by Ludwig Köchel in London, and the property of a Mr Young, was included, as being the last one extant of the composer in Nohl's edition of Mozart's letters (1865) but it is rejected by Emily Anderson, in her splendid three-volume edition *The Letters of Mozart and his Family* (1938) as being a patent forgery. She asserts that at the time Mozart was in good spirits. However, the date in September is not given and there is another mystery to come to terms with, in the theory that Mozart was poisoned. This is given credence by May and Vincent Novello, who base their account on information imparted to them by Constanze Mozart in July 1829. 'I know I must die,' he exclaimed some six months before he actually did, 'someone has given me *accqua toffana* and has calculated the precise time of my death, for which they have ordered a Requiem, it is for myself I am writing this.'

Acqua toffana, a poison named after a Neapolitan woman called Toffana, was brought first to the notice of the police in 1659 when an increase in the number of widows became a scandal. Why, one asks, should anyone have forged the da Ponte letter, unless for gain after Mozart's death? It does contain one or two things Mozart might have said. He became unwell when in Prague on 6 September for the first performance of *La Clemenza di Tito* (written as a festival opera for the coronation of Leopold II as King of Bohemia) and returned to Vienna in the middle of the month a very sick man. The letter reflects a distressed condition of mind, but the phraseology, especially in the closing sentences, seems contrived. The poison theory involves Salieri, who was supposed to have said the day after Mozart died, 'Good riddance, too, otherwise we would all have been dead.' But, though Salieri was so jealous of Mozart, his confession when dying that he had poisoned his rival was, according to Mozart's son, the ravings of a man whose whole life had been so full of cabals and intrigues that in his last fevered hours he imagined he had done this terrible thing.

What is more important is a diagnosis published in 1963 in *Acta Mozartiana*, Vol. 1, by Dr Dieter Kerner of Mainz, based on a very thorough analysis of known symptoms which, in the doctor's view, shows that Mozart did not die of a protracted and infectious kidney ailment but of chronic quicksilver poisoning. The details of such a poisoning have only in the last half-century been clinically investigated, but they all fit the classical picture of mercurial poisoning. This diagnosis, however, was rejected out of hand by Professor Otto Deutsch, and so we are still left guessing as to who could have wanted to poison Mozart. Franz Niemetschek, in his biography of 1798, wrote, 'Mozart also had enemies: many relentless enemies who pursued him even after his death.' If only the author could have been more explicit and given his sources: but, of course, only seven years after the composer's death those enemies would probably be alive—and active!

It is distressing to read in one of Mozart's many pitiful letters to his faithful friend Michael Puchberg, begging for yet another loan, that after sending round a list for subscribers to a series of concerts to be given in Vienna, he had received, after a fortnight, only *one* reply, and that was from Baron von Swieten. This was in July 1789. In March 1784 the list for his concerts had covered eight printed pages. It seems also that Leopold II, who immediately dismissed da Ponte on his succession, took against Mozart, for what reason is not known, and that the Empress described *Tito* at its first performance as a *porcheria tedesca* (a German swinishness), while among the Court 'a strong distaste for Mozart's composition was shown'. Another document in the Prague Central Archives substantiates that Mozart became ill just when he had to compose the last part of his opera *La Clemenza di Tito*.

The conjectures and rumours, the fact and the fiction, that cloud

Mozart's last years, with the substratum of truth in them, make one's heart bleed for the great little man, but one is glad to remember one happy spell when *Die Zauberflöte* (*The Magic Flute*), which he conducted at its first performance on 30 September, had such a great and continuing success. When the illness that had attacked him in Prague returned as he set to work again on the Requiem and he had at last to take to his bed he would follow the performances, we are told, with his watch and now and then sing bits of what was being sung at the time on the stage of the Theater an der Wien.

In 1825 Georg Nissen, a Danish diplomat, who married Mozart's widow, asked her sister Sophie Haibl to send him an account of her brother-in-law's last illness for the biography he was writing about him. It is a lengthy and garrulous document but it was accepted as true by Constanze, and gives the only information we have. The last section is relevant to this chapter. I have incorporated the correct spellings of proper names as made by Else Radaut in her article in the American journal *High Fidelity*, March 1965.

> Süssmayer was at Ms bedside, the well-known Requiem was on the bedspread and Mozart was explaining to him how he ought to finish it after his [Mozart's] death. . . . The doctor Closset was looked for all over, till they found him at the theatre: but he had to wait till the piece was over—and then he came and ordered *cold* [stress original] compresses to be put on [Mozart's] feverish brow, and these provided such a shock that he did not regain consciousness again before he died. The last thing he did was to imitate the kettledrums in his Requiem.

Niemetschek writes that 'the doctors were not agreed as to the exact nature of his illness'. He died at fifty-five minutes after midnight on 5 December and at three o'clock in the afternoon on 6 December, his coffin was blessed in the Crucifix Chapel at the north side of St Stephen's Cathedral. He was alone in death, as he had virtually been in life: neither his wife nor sister, nor any of his friends were present and no one, but a small dog—if we are to trust the lithograph recording the scene—followed the coffin to its resting-place in St Mark's Cemetery. As Miss Radaut says, 'To an 18th century Viennese death and burial were unimportant things' but Constanze, in later years, found it necessary to excuse her absence on account of her 'grief and youth'. 'I just didn't think to have the grave marked,' she said. In fact, as Mozart died in debt, a third-class funeral was all she could afford and no doubt she would have felt ashamed to be present. In the Central Cemetery today, opposite the space in which are the graves of Beethoven, Schubert, Brahms, Hugo Wolf, and Johann Strauss, there stands a small granite monument in memory of the man who died so untimely, with a world of music still in his brain; the man who was to awaken, still does awaken, and always will, such deep and abiding love and reverence.

In a brilliant article contributed to *The Musical Quarterly*, Professor Friedrich Blume examines all the evidence that has come to light about the composition of the Requiem and disposes of a large number of unacceptable theories. He rightly entitles his article 'Requiem, but no peace', because the whole truth may never be known. In a reprint of the article in the book *The Creative World of Mozart*, edited by P. H. Lang (Norton, 1963) Blume records an important discovery, made in 1962 by Wolfgang Plath, of Augsburg, of a sheet of sketches for the Requiem which contains one for 'Rex tremendae majestatis' from the *Dies irae*, together with the exposition of an 'Amen' fugue (not used in the Requiem) perhaps intended to form the close of the Sequence. This, though Blume does not mention it, might well show that Mozart had studied Michael Haydn's Requiem of 1771, in which the 'Amen' is treated at least in a *fugato* style. On the same sheet there is a fragment for *The Magic Flute* and so it can be dated September–October 1791 and settles the question of the approximate date of the composition of the whole work. It also confirms the view that Süssmayer completed the composition with the aid of Mozartean sketches which he destroyed after use. The essential point is how much of the work is authentic Mozart. The autograph gives the complete Introit and *Kyrie*, the first five movements of the Sequence, the *Lacrimosa* (up to bar 8) and the Offertory *Domine Jesu Christe* and its verse. It may well be, as Vincent Novello, no mean judge, thought, and had confirmed in his conversation with Constanze, Eybler, and Stadler, that Mozart had composed, in essentials, the *Sanctus*, *Benedictus* and *Agnus Dei* even before the Offertory—or at least prepared outlines of these. Constanze said repeatedly that Süssmayer had only done 'what anyone could have done', that is, to fill out a design already in existence. It seems to me extraordinary that no real research seems to have been undertaken about Süssmayer's competence as a composer of sacred music. Vincent Novello doubts it, and so must have examined the evidence, but his choral music cannot all have vanished! Blume's conclusion, however, is that, unless proved to the contrary, Mozart, not Süssmayer, must be considered in all essentials the composer of the *Sanctus* (with 'Pleni'), *Benedictus*, *Hosanna*, and *Agnus*. Süssmayer filled in 'what anyone could have done'.

The instrumentation raises another problem. Mozart, apart from the strings, gave only the following indications:

Introit and *Kyrie*: two basset horns, two bassoons, two trumpets, timpani
Tuba mirum: trombone solo up to bar 18
Recordare: two basset horns.

Blume believes the composer did not mean the orchestration of the Introit to be applied, as Süssmayer has applied it, to the whole work. He compares the result to 'a thick grey crust, comparable to the layer of whitewash that was plastered over the naves of the Gothic churches in the Restoration'. The omission of flutes, oboes, clarinets, and horns is certainly in opposition to Mozart's practice, and no other Mass of his has such a uniformity of colour. Is it just possible that Mozart, ill and depressed, felt that basset horn tone-colour expressed the feelings of a man in mourning for his life? Certainly he uses the instruments only four times in *The Magic Flute* and once in *Tito*, but he does so throughout the brief *Mauerische Trauermusik (Masonic Funeral Music)* (K. 477) except when the plainsong psalm tone is quoted by oboe and clarinet. Sir Thomas Beecham, in the course of a telephone conversation about other matters, once asked me suddenly, 'Who was that fellow who orchestrated Mozart's Requiem?' I replied: 'Süssmayer', and when I asked him why he wanted to know, he said, 'Oh, I'm now orchestrating it myself.' That is one solution and preferable, perhaps, to those who dislike the extant score.

The Introit theme which is foreshadowed in Mozart's setting for chorus, organ and orchestra of a psalm verse 'Misericordia Domini cantabo in aeternum' (K. 222) is based on the same section in the Requiem Mass by F. L. Gassmann (1729–1774), a Bohemian composer who had studied with Padre Martini (for whom Mozart wrote 'Misericordias' in the strict ecclesiastical style 'to the Abbé's delight') and who took an important part in the life of Vienna as composer, conductor and teacher when he came to live there in 1764; but the theme itself is said to be a traditional one.

Ex. 8

The first of the subjects in the double-figure of the *Kyrie* is identical with that of the double-fugue 'And with His stripes we are healed' in Handel's *Messiah*, and was used by Bach in No. 20 of the '48 Preludes and Fugues', Book 2, by Haydn in the last movement of his string quartet in F minor, op. 20, No. 6, by his brother Michael in much the same form in 'Cum sanctis tuis in aeternum', the last section of his Requiem Mass, and by Mozart in the psalm 'Laudate pueri Dominum' from his *Vesperae Solennes de Confessore* (K. 337), composed eleven years before the Requiem Mass. Such themes were

Ky-ri-e e —— le-i-son

Ex. 9

common property in days when thematic originality was not considered to be of such prime importance as it came to be in the succeeding centuries.

Knowing all we do about the tragic circumstances surrounding Mozart's Requiem it is easy to read too much into the heavy tread of the strings and organ accompaniment (cello and double-basses double the bass of the organ part all through the Introit except where marked otherwise) to the mournful theme sung by bassoons and *corni di bassetto*, the stern entry for trumpets and timpani, before the wailing descending octaves on the violins that continue up to 'et lux perpetua', where another and flickering figure breaks in, not one of heavenly light.

The view of death expressed in the Introit is far removed from the serene approach to the dark angel Mozart so beautifully expressed in the letter to his father quoted on page 64. It brought into my mind the fevered beauty of the final movement (Allegretto ma non troppo) of his String Quartet in D minor (K. 421)—that quartet of tensions and poignancy in all its movements—especially the coda with its cries as of a frightened child. It is a movement like a dance of death.

There came into my mind also Schubert's song, one of his greatest, *Der Tod und das Mädchen* ('Death and the Maiden') and the cry of the stricken girl who suddenly opens her eyes and sees and recognizes the dread stranger by her bedside.

> Pass by me, pass me by.
> Go away, wild skeleton,
> I am still young—go, dear Death,
> And do not touch me.

'I am still young', and that sentence in the unauthenticated letter to da Ponte, 'I have come to my end without having had the enjoyment of my talent', here haunts the mind. In the song, it will be remembered, Death calms the anguish of the girl. 'I am your friend . . . be comforted. I am not wild, you will sleep gently in my arms.' That comfort, one would like to think, came to Mozart when he composed the verse 'Hostias et preces tibi' section of the Offertory, with its promise that the souls of the departed would be led from death to life. As the prayer for the 'lux perpetua' ends, and for a moment the opening theme of the Introit returns, the solo soprano sheds light in the prevailing darkness with the psalm verse 'Te decet hymnus, Deus, in Sion'. Michael Haydn, at this point, used the psalm tone of the plainsong setting, one that Mozart used in his *Masonic Funeral March*, but here the tone which all commentators simply call 'an ancient Gregorian chant', or something similar, is in fact the *tonus peregrinus*, the 'stranger tone', associated with Psalm 113, 'In exitu de Egypto Israel', in the Vespers of Sunday.

Ex. 10 and 11

Mozart had used this tone, twenty years before, in the concluding chorus of his oratorio *La Betulia liberata* (the libretto, on the story of Judith and Holofernes, is by Metastasio), a chorus in praise of God's giving victory over the enemy. In the Requiem the chorus repeat the tone after the soprano, at 'exaudi orationem meam', with a decisive accompaniment that leads into the repeat of 'Requiem aeternam'. The double fugue of the *Kyrie* bears witness to Mozart's close study of both Bach and Handel. It is, for a Mass meant for liturgical use, too long and elaborate, but one casts aside such considerations in view of this agitated appeal with its near-note of hysteria. 'Kyrie eleison' is set to the first fugue subject, 'Christe eleison' to the second, the two texts, therefore, running simultaneously. This is an original conception to which I know of no parallel. Towards the end the music reaches a terrifying climax. The *Dies irae* begins with the familiar rhythm ♩♩♩♩ the melody rising effectively in pitch during the course of the first seven bars, followed by a resounding fanfare sequence. The repetition of the words so far (verses 1–2) is demanded more by the need of the music to expand than by the dramatic situation, except that it gives the composer a chance to depict the 'tremor' ('quantus tremor est futurus') by voices and orchestra (all parts).

The tension so far established is completely dissipated in 'Tuba mirum' by the notorious trombone solo, unaccompanied, succeeded by gentle phrases on the solo instrument after the second bar of the entry for solo bass: these phrases, arpeggios, and scale runs continue, in the autograph, to bar 18 where 'Mors stupebit' begins. But Süssmayer adds the trombone to the autograph in bars 24–34, giving it a most tame close in the last two of those bars.

It has always seemed to me extraordinary that Mozart, with his sense of drama, should have scored what is a climactic verse in this way, nor would it be any better if Mozart had meant to use the bassoon from bar 5 onwards, as one copy shows. Sir Thomas Beecham's substitution of the full brass blazing away in the first three bars, and cellos playing the succeeding passages, at least avoids the bathos otherwise inevitable. Is this not a case of a mere sketch which Mozart would have filled out if he had lived to complete and revise his score? Tension returns with 'Cum vix justus sit securus', which splendidly leads up to the great outburst of 'Rex tremendae majestatis', a most powerful movement into which the trumpets and drums added by Süssmayer erupt with thrilling effect: but, as Blume points out, in the last two bars, at the words 'Salva me fons pietatis', marked *piano*, and with a whole bar rest in the first of these, Süssmayer ignored Mozart's obvious intention to have the prayer sung unaccompanied by orchestrating these bars. This effectively destroys the poignant appeal of the prayer.

Blume says about the long flowing 'Recordare, Jesu pie' in which Mozart had written out the opening measures for the basset horns and the following string introduction up to bar 14, 'What could have been more natural than to let the strings rest at the entrance of the chorus and have the basset horns go along with its upper voices? . . . it is only when the chorus resumes the principal motive at the words "preces meae" it suddenly occurs to Süssmayer to have the basset horns go along now—a wholly Mozartean inconsistency. The fact that he took over all the faults from Eybler is little excuse for him.'

'Recordare, Jesu pie' ends with music of heavenly melodic and harmonic beauty set to the prosaic verse in which the poet prays to be given a place among the sheep on Christ's right hand and well away from the goats. It is interesting that both Verdi and Britten bring a similar note of sweetness into the closing phrases of their settings of these words.

'Confutatis maledictis' ('All the wicked are confounded'), the following movement, is a marvellous conception. Tenors and basses loudly declaim the stern words, underlined forcibly by bassoons and trombones, while the strings relentlessly repeat in rapid notes a one-bar phrase which rises in pitch at each repetition. When the trembling spectator of this terrible judgement now makes his humble plea 'Voca me cum benedictis' ('Call me with the blessed'),

Mozart, with a simple modulation from A minor to C major, completely changes the climate. The prayer, intoned by sopranos and altos, is accompanied by a lovely, aspiring melody for violins only; and then, after a repeat of 'Confutatis maledictis', with different melodic lines, some changes in orchestration and now in G minor, the consequent modulation to 'Voca me cum benedictis' takes the music into A minor. The prayer is doubled in length and also made more urgent by a higher rise in pitch than before and more poignant in its descent to the key-note. 'Oro supplex et acclinis' ('I pray, kneeling in supplication') is given to the whole chorus, accompanied by an agitated orchestral accompaniment that ceases only at the penultimate bar of the movement.

Mozart then leads the music, by means of two chords separated by a rest, from F major into the D minor of the profoundly affecting 'Lacrimosa dies illa' ('Lamentable is that day'). There is a desperate pathos in the rising chromatic scale passage at 'Judicandus homo reus' ('The guilty man rises to be judged'). At the climactic point on the word 'reus' Mozart's autograph ends. Blume says that a copy of the score, in Stockholm, belonging to F. S. Silverstolpe, a nineteenth-century musician, 'specifies quite definitely' that the 'Lacrimosa' and the 'Domine Deus Jesu Christe' are exclusively by Mozart and 'completely worked out by him'.

Ex. 12

In the Offertory, the sequences of falling sevenths at the line 'Ne absorbeat eis Tartarus, ne cadant in obscurum' ('lest Tartarus swallow them, lest they fall into the darkness') are vividly descriptive. The entrance of Michael the Archangel, which sheds a lovely light on the scene, is followed by the obligatory fugue at 'Quam olim Abrahae promisisti' ('which thou didst once promise to Abraham'). This fugue is, of course, repeated after the verse 'Hostias et preces tibi Domine' ('To thee, O Lord, we offer praises and prayers') which is full of exquisite serenity. That serenity floods into the

'Benedictus' for solo quartet after the exultant 'Sanctus' and a 'Hosanna' that is too commonplace to represent more than a rough sketch—if that—of what Mozart would have made of it.

The *ostinato*-like violin and viola accompaniment in *Agnus Dei* (D minor again), relaxed at the prayerful phrases of 'Dona nobis requiem', rising to a higher pitch of emotion in the next petition, and higher still before 'Requiem sempiternam', gives a great urgency and pathos to the movement. After it, in the Communion 'Lux aeterna luceat eis, Domine', the music returns to the music of the psalm verse 'Te decet hymnus' in the Introit, and then sets 'Cum sanctis tuis in aeternum' to the *Kyrie* fugue. There are precedents for this in Mozart's earlier Masses (K. 220 and 317) and it was on this basis that Süssmayer claimed he devised it: but it is a disappointing conclusion.

So, at any rate, ends the 'Requiem—but no peace'. It would be unfair to dismiss Süssmayer's part in the work only with contempt, for without him we might have been left with much less than has survived and though the great beauties of the work that are unmistakably Mozart's make his 'vulgarizations' regrettable, they are not as disastrous as they might perhaps have been.

CHAPTER EIGHT

THE REQUIEM MASS FROM THE EIGHTEENTH TO THE TWENTIETH CENTURY

2 Cherubini and Berlioz

Luigi Cherubini was born on 14 September 1760, ten years before Beethoven came into the world, and died on 15 March 1842, four months before Wagner's twenty-first birthday. The inscription on the plaque placed on the wall of the house in Florence where he was born speaks of him as one 'who, supreme in the mastery of harmony, creator of sublime religious melodies, restored every kind of musical style, and though a wanderer among strangers, preserved in all that concerned his art the glory of Italian primacy'.

This panegyric is more patriotic than precise, in view of the work of Haydn, Mozart, Beethoven, and Schubert alone, but, though little of his huge output is performed today, it should be remembered, or realized, that in his eight serious Paris operas—out of the twenty-six he composed—many of which are in one act and of little account—Cherubini carried on the reforms of Gluck. Beethoven is reported to have said to a friend, 'Cherubini is among all living composers the one who merits the most attention. Even with his conception of the Requiem I can entirely associate myself and I shall, if I should ever have occasion to write one myself, take over much exactly as he has written it.' This was the Requiem in C minor, the first of the two Cherubini composed: the D minor was not completed until eleven years after Beethoven's death.

It was Cherubini's preference for heroic and noble characters in his operas that appealed so greatly to Beethoven and notably influenced his choice of *Leonore*, or the Faithful Wife (the first title of *Fidelio*, his only opera), the story of which is closely allied to that of Cherubini's finest opera, *Les Deux Journées*, the works having the same librettist.

In June 1805 Cherubini accepted an invitation to compose a work for the Vienna Opera. He had been upset by Napoleon's continual complaints about his music being all noise. What the Emperor liked were the soothing strains of Italian opera, above all those of Paisiello, his chapel-master at this time. When the latter retired in 1804, Napoleon, passing over Cherubini, offered the post to Méhul (whom we know mainly as the composer of *Joseph and his Brethren*), whereupon that humble and delightful man suggested he should share the post with Cherubini. Napoleon's answer to this proposal was, 'Do not speak to me about that man. I want a maestro who will make music, not noise.' Before he left Paris, in very low spirits, Cherubini undertook, as a labour of love, the first performance in the city of Mozart's Requiem, which made a profound sensation and had to be repeated. Napoleon, who probably kept away, would have called it 'tudesque', the epithet he always used for the German music he so much disliked.

In Vienna, after calling on Haydn, whom he loved more than any other living composer, Cherubini met Beethoven for the first time, and here the latter was able to hear Cherubini's *Les Deux Journées*, which was enthusiastically received. It is possible that Cherubini would have settled in Vienna had war not broken out between France and Austria, a war which led the French Emperor to take up his residence at Schönbrunn. In a mood softened by the successful outcome of the war, the Emperor sent for Cherubini and asked him to direct his concerts in Vienna. He soon complained again about too much noise in the orchestra, so the composer had all *forte* passages played *pianissimo*, a mortifying resolution for the man Haydn called 'the greatest living musician' and Beethoven 'the greatest dramatic composer of the age'.

On returning to Paris in April 1806, Cherubini found conditions very unsettled after the war. He left Vienna, it is said, after being greatly distressed at not being able to find Mozart's grave, or any memorial to him, and also because he did not wish to come into competition with Beethoven, whose genius he fully recognized, but whose music he found 'harsh'. Cherubini was soon again in disfavour with Napoleon and was passed over when honours were distributed to Méhul, Gossec, Grétry and Lesueur, composers whom he could not but regard as inferior to himself. He practically ceased to compose, and for eighteen months fell into a state of deep depression. It was even reported in Vienna that he was dead. His occupations for most of the day were drawing and botany, to which he had once before turned when things were going badly. He felt the need of a complete change and rest and at the invitation of his friends the Prince and Princess of Chimay, he went in 1808 to their castle in Belgium, accompanied by Auber, for an indefinite stay. It was all these circumstances that led to the extraordinary second spring of religious music that was to close his long and great career.

A short while before the Feast of St Cecilia, 22 November, a deputation from the music society in the village of Chimay plucked up courage to ask the famous composer in their midst to receive them and when in his presence to ask, through their president, if he would write a Mass for them to perform on the day of the Feast. 'No,' Cherubini brusquely replied, 'it's impossible', and returned to his botany, leaving them to make as graceful an exit as possible. Madame de Chimay, who was in the plot, made no comment but cunningly put a sheet of music paper on his table and covered it with some rare plants. When he returned from his walk Cherubini, also making no comment, began to compose the first of the eight Masses—and other pieces of sacred music—he was destined to write up to seven years before his death.

He had composed three Masses in his teens, and none thereafter until now, but during his student days at Bologna his stern teacher, the famous Giuseppe Sarti, had required him to write twenty motets in the style of Palestrina, a composer to whom the boy, at this time, was not attracted. To get the right atmosphere Sarti made him and his fellow pupils do these exercises at night in a large unfurnished room, illuminated only by a lamp suspended from the ceiling! But the contrapuntal discipline he learnt there, and had never really forgotten, now came to his aid. A few years later, before composing his first Requiem Mass, he made an intensive, and this time ardent, study of the great Roman composer, with such effect that Adolphe Adam said, 'If Palestrina had lived in our own times he would have been Cherubini . . .'

The Requiem Mass in C minor was commissioned by the government in 1815 for the commemoration, in the following year, of the execution of Louis XVI, and was first performed on 21 January of that year in the crypt of the Abbey Church of St Denis. It is scored for mixed chorus—there are no soloists—and an orchestra consisting of two each of oboes, clarinets, bassoons, horns, trumpets, three trombones, timpani, gong, and strings.

Michael Haydn and Mozart's Introits, in their Requiems, are both in the well-tried polyphonic style of successive imitative entries from bass to treble, but Cherubini, who so easily might have begun in the same way, chose chordal treatment of the text and maintains this not only to the end of the Introit but throughout the *Kyrie* as well, avoiding any repetition of words except in the latter where the music compels it. The frequent use of pause marks at cadence points, the constant *pianissimo* markings in the Introit, save for one *crescendo* to *sforzando* at the end of 'Exaudi orationem meam', sustain the atmosphere of solemnity and mourning created by the omission of violins from the score of the movement, which gives the top string line in the six-bar orchestral introduction to the dark-toned violas.

Ex. 1

Behind this restraint lies the hand of a master dramatist but one who is respectful of liturgical considerations here and throughout the Mass. It is absurd for an otherwise admirable critic such as the late Eric Blom to say in his *Stepchildren of Music* (Foulis, 1924) that 'if in Cherubini's church music we look for the intense human emotion of Bach's *B minor Mass* or Beethoven's *Missa Solemnis*, we shall inevitably be repelled almost as if we had come into personal contact with his brusque and irritable nature'. This is reading the man, and only a part of him in any case, into the music with a vengeance. Bach's work is not a Mass at all but an oratorio, or—if you like—a series of church cantatas. Beethoven has told us in what style he would have composed a Requiem if he ever did so, and it was the style of the present work. One does not look for human emotion in a Requiem Mass for liturgical use nor 'melodic warmth to stir the heart', and if it is true that 'a curious chill' pervades all Cherubini's Masses, except, Mr Blom allows, his second Requiem— it is a chill that the sight of the coffin on the black and gold draped catafalque in the sanctuary, the black vestments of the sacred ministers, also produces in the congregation. One may regret that death may be thus presented—I have already said that I do so—as it has been since the eleventh century but it was not for Cherubini to challenge tradition, even if, *per impossibile*, he had wished to do so. The burden of sorrow is, in fact, lifted in the higher-pitched phrases at 'et lux perpetua', and at the repeat of 'Requiem aeternam', etc., after the verse, there are extended polyphonic vocal phrases, of great and consolatory beauty.

The syncopated accompaniment (violas, bassoons) to the *Kyrie* lends urgency to the prayer and in the last 'Kyries' we reach the first *forte* markings. Then, *pp*, as predominantly before, the violas again repeat the opening bars of the Introit and the music sinks quietly to rest on a C major chord.

Cherubini, still omitting the violins from the score, sets the Gradual in straightforward and brief chordal measures, there being

the lengthy Sequence, *Dies irae*, to follow. Violins are now introduced into the score and the whole orchestra comes into play.
In the sixth bar of the short orchestral introduction the composer
brings in a stroke on the gong: this was considered an error of taste,
theatrical. Spontini had been one of the first to use this instrument
in his opera *La Vestale* in 1807 and perhaps Cherubini made a note
of its dramatic effect. Elgar, in the Prelude to *The Dream of Gerontius*
and, less probably, Britten at the start of his War Requiem, may,
in their turn, have noted Cherubini's use of it.

The chorus sings *Dies irae*, etc., in canon, to the same rhythm as
Michael Haydn and Mozart. The orchestral basses, after the gong

Ex. 2

stroke at the start of *Dies irae*, pound away softly on C, then G,
with a *crescendo*, from 'Quando judex', for thirty-one bars. Trumpets
sound and drums roll as the chorus burst out, in fanfare-like phrases,
with 'Tuba mirum'.

Cherubini perhaps gave a hint to Verdi for his vivid and imaginative treatment of 'Mors stupebit et natura', words Mozart passes over
quickly.

At 'Liber scriptus' Cherubini resumes the canonic treatment at the
start of the Sequence up to 'Nil inultum remanebit'. 'Rex tremendae',
a fine stirring contrast, with trumpets sounding, is followed by the
lovely entry of the sopranos and the other voices, *pp*, with 'Salve
me'. There is no chill about this heartfelt response to the words.
The composer allots 'Recordare, Jesu pie' to the sopranos and altos,
'Quaerens me sedisti lassus' to the tenors, 'Juste judex' again to
sopranos and altos, and 'Ingemisco, tamquam reus' to the basses.
From 'Qui Mariam absolvisti' he builds up to the full chorus entry,
in canon once more, at 'Confutatis maledictis'. Almost all through
this section the orchestra have a flickering figure (strings), as a kind of
blending material. This is the least inspired part of the Requiem and
one feels the composer is covering the ground too obviously. The
climate changes at the hushed 'Voca me cum benedictis'; the following words 'Ora supplex et acclinis' are preceded by pulsating quiet
notes on the upper strings. 'Lacrimosa dies illa', in slow time, has

nearly every syllable marked *fp*, and the final prayer 'Pie Jesu Domine, dona eis requiem. Amen' is treated with touching simplicity.

The best moments in the Offertory are the dramatic outburst, with heavy chordal support in the orchestra, at the words praying that the souls of all the faithful departed may be freed from the 'poenis inferni', followed by the hushed singing of 'et de profundo lacu', and an equally vivid illustration, which the Joseph Haydn of the *Creation* would have appreciated, of the lion ('libera nos de ore leonis').

Ex. 3

The scoring for violins only, *tremolandi*, at the prayer 'ne cadant in obscurum', was another of the things in the work that gave rise to charges by some of the composer's contemporaries, and their immediate successors, that he was too 'theatrical' in the Mass. Michael the Angel enters imaginatively in B flat major. After this point I part company with the 'Quam olim Abrahae' fugue that follows, on a very commonplace subject which not only goes on far too long but is succeeded by a prolonged kind of *stretto* in quicker time. And all of this after the verse 'Hostias et preces tibi' has to be repeated. It was a charge against Cherubini that he over-extended himself in his operas: certainly here his architectural sense has deserted him. The *Sanctus* is commendably brief, but generally immemorable. Its most interesting moment, for purposes of comparison, comes in the detached notes, choral and orchestral basses, of the *Benedictus*—an effect Berlioz possibly copied in his Introit (p. 89). The composer, after the *Sanctus*, inserts a short motet with the last words of the Sequence 'Pie Jesu Domine dona eis requiem', a prayerful, chordal piece with a beautiful ending.

The *Agnus Dei* and Communion, are, like the Introit and *Kyrie*, combined in one movement. We are spared another fugue at 'Cum sanctis tuis in aeternum' and are given in *Agnus Dei* a marvellous movement that could only have been written by a great composer. Into the poignant aspiring figure that pervades the orchestral part for about half of the time Cherubini builds a demisemiquaver which gives a particular urgency to both vocal and instrumental parts.

The jagged figuration leaves the music at the word 'sempiternam'. Everlasting rest? The prayer here is anguished, as if uncertain of the answer. From this point to the end, the composer writes at his highest level of inspiration vocally and orchestrally, and every bar is quotable.

There is a brief crescendo as the prayer is repeated, with strings *tremolandi* and a completely unexpected chord just as the *tremolo* ends and the voices slowly descend the scale.

The opening figure of the *Agnus Dei* returns but on the strings, as the Communion begins, in F minor. After 'cum sanctis tuis in aeternum', the chorus sing 'Requiem aeternam', etc., *only* on the note C, in unison (ranging over two octaves) right up to the end of the Mass with the orchestra in every bar reiterating the figure mentioned above over pedal C. And so the music reaches at last the peace of the full C major chords, the key which F minor has been masking all this time.

Ex. 4

Cardinal Newman, deeply moved by this wonderful setting, spoke of 'the lovely note C which keeps recurring as the Requiem approaches eternity'. Berlioz paints a very unpleasing picture of Cherubini in his *Memoirs*, and in their encounters when he was at the Conservatoire, and after, it is always he who scores off the peppery old man. There was another and much more attractive side to Cherubini, but from the start the very sight of the wild and lawless young man—as he saw Berlioz—drove him into a rage or (which Berlioz considered more dangerous, always scenting a plot against him), into a deceptive sweetness. But, in a generous mood, Berlioz could write of his 'enemy': 'The Requiem Mass in C minor is on the whole, to my mind, the greatest work of its author. No other production of this grand master can bear any comparison with it for abundance of ideas, fulness of form, and sustained sublimity of style. The *Agnus Dei* in *descrescendo* surpasses everything that has been written of the kind. The workmanship of this portion, too, has an inestimable value: the vocal style is sharp and clear, the instrumentation coloured and powerful, yet ever worthy of its object.'

Early in 1836 Cherubini, in his seventy-sixth year, began work on a second Requiem Mass, this time in D minor, and scored for three-part male chorus (T.T.B.) and orchestra. Such a combination in a work of any length offers difficult problems of balance and contrast, and the reader may wonder what led the composer to choose it. He intended the work to be performed at his own funeral—which took place at the Church of St Roch in April 1842—and according to Ferdinand Hiller, he wished to avoid the painful incident that had occurred at Boldieu's funeral in 1834, when the rector of the Madeleine Church refused to admit female singers—whether as being incapable of exercising an ecclesiastical office, according to Canon Law, or because of being operatic artists, Hiller does not say —and so the composer decided on male voices only, but why he chose three I do not know. At any rate Cherubini handles the medium with great skill and entirely avoids monotony. Except for one bad patch in the Sequence, the music, taking the work as a whole, moves at a higher level than in the C minor, though it contains nothing so sublime as the *Agnus Dei* in that Mass.

Cherubini again sets the Gradual, and 'Pie Jesu' as a Motet after the *Sanctus*. He had made no allusions at all to plainsong in the C minor but he begins the D minor with the four time-honoured notes at the start of the plainsong Introit, distributed between cellos and wind. The choral entry, unlike the C minor, is imitative in style, bass, tenor 2, tenor 1 in succession. The dynamic scheme is different; there is already a *crescendo* from *pp* in the eleven bars of the orchestral introduction, leading to a *sforzando* chord in the bar before the voices come in. Violas as well as violins, this time, were excluded from the scoring in the movement.

Ex. 5

The second tenors begin the verse 'Te decet hymnus' accompanied only by the cellos, and as they end the orchestra are given a rhythmic figure with a 'built-in' demisemiquaver that invades chorus and orchestra, *pp*, at 'Exaudi orationem meam' and remains till the end of the verse. It returns in the *Kyrie* and, as presumably intended, creates a sense of urgency in this prayer.

The Gradual, except for the four opening bars for bassoons and string basses, sung unaccompanied, is a fine piece of polyphonic writing and greatly superior, musically, to the rather dull setting in the C minor. The fully scored *Dies irae* is given the same rhythm and much the same imitative treatment as in the earlier work, and the more imaginative orchestral accompaniment is all the more effective for bursting out after the quiet ending of the unaccompanied Gradual.

'Mors stupebit' is also more imaginatively handled than in the C minor. The staccato exchanges between the voices do give a feeling of Death's and Nature's stupefaction, and the F octave on the oboes, repeated an octave lower by the clarinets, is dramatic in itself and technically a splendid way of taking the music into B flat major at 'cum resurget creatura', leading to a big climax at 'judicanti responsura'.

Ex. 6

There is a pause after 'cum vix justus sit securus', then the tempo quickens as the orchestra flashes up the chord of A major and the chorus thunder out 'Rex tremendae majestatis', the demisemiquavers figure in the choral and orchestral parts here underlining the majesty of the passage. The music quietens for the lovely phrases of 'Salva me, fons pietatis' and it is now, after all this fine music, that Cherubini makes, for him, an inexcusable blunder. This scrupulous composer sets the three lines of each of the six verses from 'Recordare, Jesu pie' to 'Preces meae non sum dignae' simultaneously, a different verse on each of the three voices up to 'Inter oves locum praesta', the verse praying to be found among the sheep, not the goats—where, musically, Cherubini here deserves to be. This quick covering of the ground, in *Glorias* and *Credos*, was one of the things the Council of Trent's commission had denounced, as Cherubini must have known.

He recovers his true form at the change of tempo to *presto* and the powerful confounding of the wicked, 'Confutatis maledictis'—a stirring, flaming passage in octaves—and in the touching unaccompanied 'Voca me cum benedictis'. 'Lacrimosa dies illa' begins in octaves for the voices with a poignant figure on the violins, also in octaves, separating the opening words and then, with the flute prominent in the orchestra, we come to the final prayer, 'Pie Jesu Domine, dona eis requiem', eloquently repeated in broad lyrical phrases. The Sequence closes in D minor as, indeed, does the whole work, for Cherubini will not admit the major third.

He moves swiftly and dramatically over the opening section of the Offertory, reflecting its changing moods as far as the words about Michael the Standard-bearer. The music shudders into the darkness of 'ne cadant in obscurum' and then the flute rises to a

Ex. 7

G *in alt*, the clarinets descending, the oboes rising, as Michael appears. This is the high point of a superb setting, superior in almost every way to that in the C minor. The inevitable fugue, *Allegro molto*, follows at 'quam olim Abrahae'. It is very brief at this point but considerably lengthened at the repeat after the verse 'Hostias et preces tibi'. Demisemiquavers come into their own again in the grand *Sanctus*, and with electrifying effect at 'Hosanna', where they are followed by a long note.

Ex. 8

In the beautiful motet 'Pie Jesu' the orchestra is confined to three-bar phrases for woodwind designed perhaps to help the singers to maintain the pitch. Cherubini leaves 'dona eis requiem' in *Agnus Dei* unaccompanied but brings in the orchestra at 'sempiternam', repeating that word three times, and with especially moving effect in long notes over a pedal A, with arpeggios rising up above. The opening words of the Communion 'Lux aeterna', shine out radiantly and are followed by a moment of silence: then one after the other, from the first tenor to the bass, and accompanied separately only by oboe, clarinet, and bassoon doubling the vocal parts, the chorus sing 'quia pius es'. This, as the liturgy requires, is followed by 'Requiem aeternam', etc., the chorus here singing a monotonous bare fifth (D–A) for fifteen bars up to the repeat of 'luceat eis', where a radiant D major chord suffuses voices and orchestra with light. It quickly fades and the final orchestral chord, emphasized by six repetitions, is in D minor.

✳

Six months after Cherubini completed his D minor Requiem Mass Berlioz received a definite commission from the Minister of the Interior, who wished to raise the standard of sacred music in France, to write a Requiem to be performed at the Government's expense on the day of the service annually celebrated for the victims of the Revolution of 1830. He composed the work, he tells us, ardently and with great rapidity.

> For a long time the text of the Requiem had been to me an object of envy, on which I flung myself with a kind of fury when it was put within my grasp. My head seemed nearly to burst with the pressure of my seething thoughts. No sooner was one piece sketched than another presented itself. Finding it impossible to write fast enough I adopted a sort of shorthand, which helped me greatly, especially in the *Lacrymosa.* Every composer knows the anguish and despair occasioned by forgetting ideas which one has not time to write down, and which thus escape for ever.

Berlioz's *Memoirs* must always be read with caution but there is no reason to disbelieve his story that the Director of Fine Arts was opposed to the Minister's scheme and arranged for the ceremony to take place without music, for in fact this did happen and it was the Minister of War who gave Berlioz the opportunity for a performance of the Requiem. On 13 October General Danremont lost his life in capturing Constantine, a city in Algeria, and so a Requiem Mass was to be celebrated for him and those of his men who had fallen with him, in the Church of the Invalides. This news, according to Berlioz, 'put Cherubini into a perfect fever', and that might well be so. He was the most celebrated composer in France and his C minor Requiem had been used for national ceremonies before. He now had a new one ready, the D minor, and he was to be passed over 'in favour of a young man who had introduced heresy into the schools'. It was a severe blow to his pride and was resented by his friends and pupils. But the Minister of the Interior told Berlioz, who had written a sympathetic letter to Cherubini, that if he gave way he would never speak to him again. And so Berlioz stood firm. His Requiem was performed on 5 December 1837 before a very distinguished congregation, with a large representation of the press, French and foreign, and as many of the general public as could be accommodated. It was essential for Berlioz that his work should succeed in full measure. Failure was unthinkable.

'The windows of the huge Chapel of St Louis at the Invalides were blocked, the walls draped in black. Around the coffin flickered 600 candles and incense boats; 4,000 other pinpoints of light dotted the gloomy shell. Major Lehoux headed the cortège with 24 muffled drums beating in the name of the 12 Paris legions, and Séjean played the organ for the service.'[1]

Berlioz had heard Mozart's Requiem at the Madeleine Church and Cherubini's C minor at Les Invalides and taken close note of the acoustics of both churches. He decided he would need 190 instruments and 210 voices, with four brass choirs, each with timpani, in addition to the full orchestra.

He had studied with Lesueur who, during the Revolution of 1790, had written a choral ode for a huge choir accompanied by four orchestras, surpassing Méhul, who had used three in his triumphal *Hymn*. It was a time of gigantism. Berlioz now used five orchestras! He had one great anxiety, the conductor. The Director of Fine Arts, perhaps out of malice now that Berlioz was to have his Requiem performed, insisted that F. A. Habeneck, then fifty-six, should conduct. In spite of previous disagreements between him and Berlioz on various occasions all went well at rehearsals, but when

---

[1] Berlioz, G. *Jacques Barzun* (*Gollancz*). *The author seems unaware that it is the thuribles into which the incense is put that might show a flicker, not the boats!*

the time came to cue in the four brass sections stationed at the four corners of the main orchestra—the one absolutely indispensable cue in the whole work—Berlioz writes, 'Habeneck puts down his baton, quietly takes out his snuff-box, and proceeds to take a pinch of snuff.' Berlioz, lynx-eyed, had been watching this and leapt on to the rostrum, stretched out his arm, and marked the four great beats of the new movement, conducting it to the end. This almost incredible story, related in the *Memoirs*, has been questioned. Charles Hallé, who was there, supports it. Osborne, a friend of Charles Hallé, who was also there and sitting in the nave with Berlioz, not only denies it, but when he asked the composer why he put such a wholesale piece of invention on record he burst out laughing and said it seemed too good a story to be lost. The fact that Habeneck subsequently rehearsed this section so intensively leads me to suspect that Berlioz was speaking the truth, even if he exaggerates the details.

With Berlioz we come, for the first time among these composers of Requiem Masses, to a man whose creative imagination in setting the text was neither here, nor in his *Te Deum*, nor in his 'Sacred trilogy', *L'Enfance du Christ*, for which he wrote the libretto, illuminated by faith. On the first page of his *Memoirs* he describes his position in regard to the Church with delightful sincerity. It reads like Bernard Shaw.

> I need scarcely state that I was brought up as a member of the Holy Catholic and Apostolic Church of Rome. Since she has ceased to inculcate the burning of heretics, her creeds are charming. I held them happily for seven years; and though we quarrelled long ago, I still retain the tenderest recollections of that form of religious belief. Indeed, I feel such sympathy for it that had I had the misfortune to be born into the midst of one of those ponderous schisms evolved by Luther or Calvin, my first rush of poetical enthusiasm would have driven me into the arms of the beautiful Roman faith.

He goes on to describe his feelings on receiving his first Communion, on the same day as his eldest sister, in the Convent of the Ursulines. The nun's choir sang a Eucharistic hymn.

> At the sound of those virginal voices I was overwhelmed with a sudden rush of mystic passionate emotion. A new world of love and feeling was revealed to me, more glorious by far than the heaven of which I had heard so much. . . . This was my first musical experience, and in this manner I suddenly became religious, so religious that I attended Mass every day and took Communion every Sunday, and my weekly confession to the director of my conscience was *'my father, I have done nothing'*, to which the worthy man always replied 'go on, my child, as you have begun'; and so I did, for several years.

How could one not love such a man! He is indeed one of the most lovable of all composers. It was the vision, the experience of the artist he was born to be, he describes; but even more than that I think. In the exquisite epilogue at the end of *L'Enfance du Christ*, when the narrator (a solo tenor) begins with the words 'O my soul, bow down in contemplation, sink all thy pride in humble adoration before so great a mystery', the master of the orchestra laying aside all instruments but the human voice, and bringing in the chorus, it is as if Berlioz had instinctively fallen on his knees. And as the 'Amens' of angels ever receding into the distance, and echoed by mankind, die away, I am left in tears, as I am by the 'Requiescat in pace' at the end of Britten's War Requiem. Berlioz too tells us that his *a cappella* chorus 'drew tears from many. I am happy when I see my audience weep' and, writing to his life-long friend Humbert Ferrand, he said, 'It seemed to me to contain a feeling of infinite, of divine love. I thought of you as I listened to it.' I do not wish to claim more than that both here and at the end of the Offertory in his *Grande Messe des Morts*, there revived in Berlioz for the moment something of the emotion he felt at his first Communion, something of the innocence and beauty of a child's faith. 'The ceremony of innocence' was drowned all too soon by the harsh realities of life, the all too human failings of the Church and its administrators. This is not a digression, it is a refutation of the view, held by several of Berlioz's biographers, that his Requiem Mass is devoid of religious feeling, that it is merely a dramatization of the melancholy end of man, unlit by any gleam of hope. He was always at the mercy of his moods, and speaks in one of the closing paragraphs of the *Memoirs* of music and love as 'the two wings of the soul', but the lonely and suffering man ends the book with Macbeth's grim words that 'Life is a tale told by an idiot, signifying nothing'.

There is no need, at this time of day, to defend Berlioz's Requiem against the superficial charge of its being, basically, a succession of loud assaults on the ear and of odd instrumental experiments. If one cared to do the reckoning I dare say there are more double *forte* passages in Verdi's Requiem than in Berlioz's. Neither composer indicated triple *forte*; that is left to conductors.

Liturgical considerations were not in Berlioz's mind. This work, like Verdi's, is essentially meant for the concert hall rather than the church; these are not functional Masses. Berlioz, as I mentioned before, had heard Mozart's Requiem in the low-vaulted Madeleine Church and Cherubini's C minor in the Invalides Chapel, and noted the different acoustics for the planning of his orchestration. There is a certain similarity between the three rising phrases at the start of the Introit in both works, but quite a different scale of dynamics.

Ex. 9

The composer may also have taken a hint from Cherubini in the use of detached notes in the counter-melody first sung by the tenors as the basses end the first words. Note, also, the solemn reiterated rhythm of the orchestral basses, which continues up to the repeat of the opening words.

Ex. 10

There is an Italianate flavour in the 'dona eis' phrases sung by the tenors, with a graceful vocalization on 'dona' above. The repeat of 'Requiem aeternam' is altogether more forceful than at the start, but yields to a lyrical treatment of the psalm verse 'Te decet hymnus'. Berlioz repeats the Introit words a third time, changing the words to 'Requiem aeternam dona defunctis, Domine', a quiet choral passage, and this time the 'lux perpetua' does shine out in the very soft octaves for flutes and clarinets accompanying the chorus. Yet again Berlioz repeats the Introit words, but now the woodwind wail above the free recapitulation of the choral music heard at the start, and the emphatic bass has vanished.

Ex. 11

A lovely modulation, as the chorus reiterate 'et lux perpetua luceat eis' leads, after ambiguous tonality, to a burst of light on 'luceat', a D major chord, followed by very soft repetitions of 'eis'.

One of the great pleasures and excitements of music is the unpredictable—though there are times when one is irritated by the avoidance of the opposite—and there is a number of unpredictables in Berlioz's Requiem. The first is his very soft and bare setting of the greater part of the *Kyrie*, with pauses after each petition. Tenors and basses murmur 'Kyrie eleison' after sopranos and alto have sung 'Christe eleison' to a humbly beseeching phrase, accompanied only by cellos; tenors sing the next 'Christe', accompanied only by bassoons, answered by basses only on a low G, all the entries being followed by a pause, as if a reply was awaited. Then, in succession, from the basses upwards (but altos still with sopranos) the beseeching phrase is followed by repetitions of 'Kyrie eleison' in crescendo to a discordant *ff*, diminishing at once to *p*; the final chorus chord is inconclusive: the lower strings bring the movement to a solemn end. This imaginative conception is unequalled in any other orchestral Requiem Mass known to me.

Ex. 12

Berlioz tells us that he wanted the *Dies irae* to strike terror into the hearts of his hearers and, to this end, he does not—like Verdi—at once summon up an apocalyptic vision of the Last Judgement but moves towards it in a controlled crescendo, with three premonitory swirls up the scale, the last of which runs into the huge E flat chord which signals the sounding of 'Tuba mirum'. The really unpredictable thing lies in giving the opening words of the Sequence *pp* to the sopranos, accompanied by flutes in octaves. The four brass orchestral groups and the huge array of timpani added here to the main orchestra cannot fail to produce the stunning effect desired, but as music Verdi's 'Tuba' is more subtly designed and more effective and the attention of the audience is not deflected by what they see going on. Berlioz closes the section with an even more massive E flat chord and maintains that key without anti-climax when the basses begin 'Tuba mirum', their utterances punctuated with heavy brass chords. 'Mors stupebit', with the tenors striking through the choral texture with descending whole bar notes, is very effective. The dominant chord of E flat announces the dramatic 'Liber scriptus' (basses only again) and once more Berlioz ends in E flat, and then continues in much the same way as before, still in that key. The sopranos rise to a great cry on the penultimate syllable of 'creatura' in the repeat of the 'Mors' verse—but the movement ends quietly. Berlioz sees to it that enough alien harmonies are introduced to mask E flat sufficiently up to the three last bars.

'Quid sum miser' is for tenors only, until the last bars when the basses are brought in to close this third unpredictable piece. The orchestra here recapitulates the opening themes of *Dies irae*.

Ex. 13

The tenors are directed to sing 'with an expression indicating humility and fear' and that is exactly what the scoring suggests.

Something must here be said about Berlioz's juggling with the text, not only in the Sequence, but in the remaining numbers, Offertory, *Sanctus*, and *Agnus Dei*. His biographers usually mention it in passing but, not having studied the liturgy, make no further comment. The fact is that sometimes the composer's omissions and rearrangements do not make any sense at all. In 'Quid sum miser', verse 7 of the Sequence, he cuts to verse 9, 'Recordare Jesu pie' and then to verse 17, 'Oro supplex et acclinis'. This can just pass. No. 4, 'Rex tremendae majestatis', verse 8, follows in its proper place, but 'Confutatis maledictis' in verse 16 is broken into twice with the exclamation 'Jesu' and ended with the first two words only of the last line, 'Voca me cum benedictis'. 'Voca me'—'call me', to what? With a complete disregard of grammar and sense, Berlioz now lifts the words 'et profundo lacu' out of the Offertory and continues from the same movement into 'Libera *me* [not 'nos'] de ore leonis' to 'ne cadant in obscurum ne absorbeat *me* [again] Tartarus'. The only thing one can say with justice is that in the frenzied hurry to get his music on to paper Berlioz fell into 'the deep lake' of obscurity. In No. 5 he goes back on the tracks of the poem and inserts verses 12–13, 'quaerens me sedisti lassus', etc., with some running together of different lines. In No. 6 he is so wholly concentrated on verses 18–19, 'Lacrimosa dies illa' up to 'homo reus', that he repeats them no less than thirteen times, omits 'huic ergo, parce, Deus' (spare him, Lord) but does get in 'Pie Jesu, Domine, dona eis requiem. Amen', the final line of the Sequence. This appears, however, in the wrong place, about three-quarters of the way through, and therefore he leaves out the 'Amen'!

This juggling and mangling of the texts, of which there is a good deal more, should not, I think, be excused even in an obviously non-liturgical work but, as I have suggested, one does excuse it because of the fine quality of so much of the music. The only other composer who treated the Mass (not the Requiem Mass) in so cavalier a fashion was Schubert, and the music of the sections in which he does this does *not* excuse him. To return now to Berlioz's music.

No. 4, 'Rex tremendae majestatis', opening with huge chords of E major, C sharp minor, A major (going down the scale) and great cries of 'Rex' bringing in nearly as large forces as in 'Tuba mirum', is indeed a majestic and thrilling utterance, with which the lyrical phrases of 'qui salvandos salvas gratis, salve me, fons pietatis' are well contrasted. The tempo quickens as the composer repeats 'Rex', etc., in successive entries at a low pitch, with a crescendo through 'Recordare Jesu, pie' to the cry of 'Ne me perdas illa die'. Now comes 'Confutatis maledictis' *ff*, and 'Jesu' *pp*, the whole immediately repeated. What is the point of breaking the tension with 'soft' chords and the interpolated soft exclamation? I can only think that Berlioz had 'Recordare, Jesu pie' in mind here, and the exclamation means 'let me not be included amongst the cursed'. But the break at 'Voca me', the long pause marked, after the vivid depicting of the 'flammis acribus', and the *sotto voce* 'et' (a whole bar) 'de profundo lacu', accompanied only by a deep bass note on the orchestra, is harder to explain. Why did those words and those that follow, from the Offertory, come into Berlioz's mind at this point? I just do not know. He ends, reasonably from the point of view of design, by repeating 'qui salvandos salvas gratis', an outburst of 'Rex tremendae majestatis', with quiet responses of 'salve me', and closes beautifully with 'fons pietatis'.

No. 5, 'Quaerens me', is an unaccompanied setting of the text which is a relief to the previous assault on the ear, but calls for no further special comment. And so we come to the final section: No. 6, 'Lacrimosa dies illa'. This is a masterpiece of invention and emotion.

As I have said, the text is repeated thirteen times. The first utterance is punctuated by a poignant cry, a wail of sorrow, from the orchestra. This continues through two repetitions of the text, the fourth being given a vivid representation of 'that day'.

Then the music quietens to a most moving setting of the words, emphasizing 'lacrimosa' rather than 'judicandus'.

Lovely, too, is the appeal to Jesus, 'Pie Jesu Domine'. We now have the seventh repeat of the text, and a recapitulation of the music as first heard, followed, at the ninth repeat, by the music of the fourth reaching a huge climax, with 'Qua resurget judicandus homo reus' in resounding octaves for chorus and orchestra. This, as it continues, is the peak and climax of the movement and Berlioz has still enough ammunition in reserve to carry it through successfully. In a short coda, chorus and orchestra sing, with full force, and again in octaves, 'Lacrimosa dies illa' with brass blazing and timpani rolling. It is remarkable that for the greater part of the movement the altos sing with the sopranos—the composer favours this three-part writing almost throughout the *Mass*, only dividing the parts where the line goes too high to be practical for the altos.

No. 7, the Offertory, is the superlatively unpredictable movement in the work, and as Schumann said, it surpasses everything else in it. The only parallel to it I can think of, and that remote, is the *Sonata sopra Sancta Maria* in Monteverdi's *Vespers* of 1610. Berlioz mentions Monteverdi in his *Treatise on Orchestration*, and the first modern edition of the *Sonata*, with other fragments of the composer's church music, was published in 1834, but it is exceedingly unlikely they were known to Berlioz. In the *Sonata* the chorus reiterate, to a single phrase of the plainsong Litany of Loreto, the words 'Sancte Maria, ora pro nobis' at varying intervals, as a kind of vocal counter-melody to the orchestral part, which carries the main burden of expression. So here the chorus, in unison throughout, chant the words of the Offertory to one constantly reiterated phrase, variously spaced out, the orchestra providing a kind of fugal sonata expressive of the hushed prayer, a 'Litany' to Jesus Christ sung by the souls in purgatory—the title Berlioz gave to the movement.

Ex. 14

Woodwind are added to the strings, and then brass, preceding the section that speaks of 'the pains of hell' before Berlioz adds the words that specify what they are. This brings a crescendo to the first climax, with the trumpet ringing out and the lower strings shudderingly descending. The violins introduce a touching variant of the fugal theme, the string basses replying to each vocal phrase 'de poenis' with a sinister murmur. After the words 'profundo lacu' the music seems to be expiring but the orchestral basses begin their solemn tread once more and there are premonitory signs, over a pedal D, of the appearance of Michael, whose arrival is signified by very loud chords on the brass. There is a gradual diminuendo and during the chorus's whispered chanting of 'Quam olim Abrahae et semini ejus' the orchestra becomes silent. But on the last syllable of 'ejus' a flute, high up, begins the gentle descent of a radiant chord, with voices and woodwind, of D major, note by note (A, F sharp, D, A, F sharp, D). The effect is indescribably beautiful, especially after the long reign of the minor key, and what follows is equally inspired and best left to the illustration below, which shows the fugal theme in a heavenly light.

Ex. 15

No. 8 is the too celebrated 'Hostias', with the tuba below and three flutes high above punctuating the unaccompanied vocal entries. The essential thing here is the right acoustic to give the impression not of an eccentricity of scoring, but of —*pace* the Bishop of Woolwich—the depths of the earth and the heights of heaven. It expresses, as I see it, the sense of the words Berlioz omitted, 'de morte transire ad vitam'—but this may seem fanciful.

No. 9, *Sanctus*. Berlioz is able here to give his lovely melodic vein full play in the delicately expressive tenor solo responded to by the women's voices in three parts. Those who have been puzzled by the technical term 'enharmonic modulation' can hear, without pains, what a beautiful thing it may be. The Sanctus is in D flat major, the G flat of that key becomes the F sharp of the modulation to D major, as the tenor ends and the women come in.

Soprano and altos in unison again are joined by men in the commonplace 'Hosanna in excelsis' fugue. Berlioz omits the *Benedictus*, and the one petition of *Agnus Dei* he sets is preceded by six eight-part chords for woodwind and horns, softly echoed by violins in four parts, with lovely effect: he then punctuates the choral entries with the wide-spaced orchestration (3 flutes–tuba) he used in No. 8, 'Hostias'. After this imaginative section it is disappointing to find the composer recapitulating, without change, the music of the Introit, beginning with the psalm 'Te decet', a sign, no doubt, of the hurry he was in. But at the sentence from the Communion 'cum sanctus tuis in aeternam' (accompanied by deep bass chords) he once more becomes inventive, and closes with a serene 'Amen'.

CHAPTER NINE

THE REQUIEM MASS FROM THE EIGHTEENTH TO THE TWENTIETH CENTURY

3 Verdi and Dvořák

In the course of a letter to Camille Bellaigue, Verdi's French biographer, Arrigo Boito described the great composer's religious beliefs in terms so unequivocal that they give the final answer to misdirected attempts to present him as a 'good Catholic'. That vague term—for a 'good Catholic' can be a bad Christian—is usually taken to mean a man of a conservative habit of mind who accepts without question what the Church requires his assent to in matters temporal as well as spiritual. No one who has studied Verdi's political creed and activities, his passionate desire to see realized the ideal of a free and united Italian republic, could possibly squeeze Verdi into the conventional 'good Catholic' category.

In 1872, seven years before he brought himself to be married in church to Giuseppina Strepponi, the latter made a revealing comment on his agnosticism to a Neapolitan friend: 'this *rascal* claims, with a calm obstinacy that infuriates me, to be, not an outright atheist, but a very doubtful believer'. Her own views, quoted in George Martin's *Verdi* (Macmillan, 1965) were not exactly orthodox. 'There is no doubt that religious belief (not priestcraft) and the Gospel doctrine of grace and charity lead the spirit to regions of great calm and serenity where one finds the faith to walk with rectitude. Where too, one learns forgiveness for sinners and the charity to bring them back to the fold. . . . For some virtuous natures belief in God is a necessity: others, equally perfect, while observing every precept of the highest moral code, are happier believing nothing. Manzoni and Verdi! These two men give me food for thought—my imperfections and my ignorance, alas, leave me incapable of solving so obscure a problem.' Verdi never at any time made any published pronouncements on his agnosticism. He would drive his wife, in these earlier years, to the door of the church for Mass, but would not go in. It seems clear, also, that discussion of religion, even with friends, was distasteful to him.

This is not the whole of the story, and I come now to Boito's letter to Bellaigue.

This is the day of all days of the year he loved the most. Christmas Eve brought back to him the marvels of childhood, the enchantments of faith which is only truly heavenly when it encompasses miracles of belief. That belief, alas, he had lost, like all of us, early on. But he retained more than we did perhaps, a poignant regret for this all his life. He gave us an example of Christian faith by the moving beauty of his religious works, by the observance of certain rites (do you remember his fine bowed head in the Chapel of Saint Agatha?), by his splendid homage to Manzoni, by the dispositions he left for his burial in his will. 'One priest, a candle, a cross.' He knew that faith is a solace to men's hearts. To the labourers in the fields, the unhappy, the afflicted who surrounded him, he offered himself, without ostentation, humbly, austerely, as an example to their burdened consciences. . . . In the ideal sense, moral and social, he was a great Christian: but one must guard against making him out to be a Catholic in the political and strictly theological sense of the term: nothing could be further from the truth.

There are two things to be added to this moving testimony. Verdi ends his Requiem with the first words of the Absolution. 'Libera me, Domine, de morte aeterna in die illa tremenda. . . . Libera me, libera me.' Commentators who have not studied the liturgical text have emphasized that this is a prayer for the living, not the dead. 'Verdi has his singers and audience praying for peace and light, not for the dead, but for themselves the living.' That is not quite true, as the words of the verse show, but the liturgy requires a repeat of 'Libera me' after the verse 'Requiem aeternam dona eis, Domine, et lux perpetua luceat eis' and this repeat, therefore, ends the Absolution with the words 'Dum veneris judicare saeculum per ignem' ('Thou will come to judge the world by fire'). A composer who sets only the Absolution and not the antiphon 'In Paradisum', sung as the body is taken from the church to the graveyard, or— which is the end of the Office of the Dead—the canticle Benedictus with its antiphon, 'Ego sum resurrectio et vita' ('I am the resurrection and the life') is faced with a stern conclusion. Verdi chose to repeat the most personal part of the Absolution.

Twenty-four years after the first performance of the Requiem Verdi, then eighty-five, returned to the setting of sacred texts, but not as church music. He took pains to study the history of the *Te Deum*, the third in order of composition of his *Four Sacred Pieces*. He never intended these to be sung as a whole, in fact he said he meant to publish none of them, and it was only because Boito had, without consulting Verdi, made an arrangement for them to be performed during Holy Week in Paris—a strange choice—that the composer felt bound to give way.

Verdi realized the significant change that comes in the *Te Deum* after the lines 'Te ergo quae sumus, tuis famulis subveni, quos pretioso sanguine redemisti. Aeterna fac cum sanctis tuis in gloria numerari'. The verses that follow from 'Salvum fac populum tuum, Domine, et benedic hereditati tuae' ('O Lord save thy people and bless thine inheritance') to the end are an addition to the original text—they are verses from various psalms—and as Father Joseph Conolly says, in *Hymns of the Roman Liturgy*, they give the *Te Deum* an air of supplication and a penitential character. It seems that in the Middle Ages it was chanted in times of great calamity, whilst on joyous and solemn occasions the *Gloria in excelsis* was sung.

Verdi did not know this, but he realized that these last verses had very little to do with military victories or coronations, etc., with which the canticle was ordinarily associated. 'The end is a prayer, "Dignare, Domine, die isto sine peccato nos custodire", which is sorrowful and moving to the point of terror,' he said. He noted the introduction of the first person singular in the last line. 'In te, Domine, speravi, non confundar in aeternum' ('In thee, O Lord, have I hoped, let me not be confounded for ever') and he also noted that the mood was very similar to that of 'Libera me, Domine, de morte aeterna', but how different his music is! The chorus (divided into eight parts) sing, 'In te, Domine, speravi' in massive chords rising to a great climax at 'speravi', but then at once softening to low-pitched chords for 'non confundar in aeternam', with three warning notes for the horns sounding above the dark string tremolo. There is a whole bar of silence. Then the upper strings play a most expressive phrase (heard earlier in the work), after which a sustained trumpet note shines out and a solo soprano sings 'In te, Domine'. The pattern is repeated twice, with increasing volume of tone, the soloist adding 'speravi', and the chorus coming in with the soloist the third time, all attaining the great climax previously heard. The violins are left alone on an E at the top of their compass, just audible, far away, while the woodwind play very quiet and sombre chords, below, but near. There is a huge empty space as if between heaven and earth. As the harmonies become unmistakably minor, the high violins note ceases: a moment of silence, then a deep low octave E in the orchestral basses. It *is* 'moving to the point of terror'. Does heaven return no answer to the humble and four times repeated prayer, the prayer of the individual soul and of the multitude? Could that last octave imply a chord of E major? We cannot know just what was in Verdi's mind. We do know that he asked that the manuscript of his *Te Deum* should be placed under his pillow when his last hour came and this, we may be sure, was done. He left the world with a plea for mercy. When reading Boito's letter, written on Christmas Eve, there came into my mind one of Thomas Hardy's most moving and beautiful poems, *The Oxen*, one that I think Verdi, who so dearly loved his farms and the countryside, would have appreciated, and which perhaps sums up his 'hope that it might be so'.

Christmas Eve, and twelve of the clock,
   'Now they are all on their knees,'
An elder said as we sat in a flock
   By the embers in hearth-side ease.

We pictured the meek mild creatures where
   They dwelt in their strawy pen,
Nor did it occur to one of us there
   To doubt they were kneeling then.

So fair a fancy few would weave
   In these years! Yet, I feel,
If someone said on Christmas Eve,
   'Come; see the oxen kneel

In the lonely barton by yonder coomb
   Our childhood used to know,'
I should go with him in the gloom
   Hoping it might be so.

Rossini's death in Paris on 13 November 1868 caused Verdi to lament, 'His reputation was enormous, the most popular in our time and a glory to Italy! When that other who is still alive [Manzoni] is no more what will remain? Our Ministers and the exploits of Lissa and Custozza.' (The ironical reference in the last sentence is to the humiliating defeat of the Italian navy at Lissa, and part of the army at Custozza, in the Austro-Prussian War of 1866.) Five years later Alessandro Manzoni died in Milan on 22 May 1873, at the great age of eighty-nine. He had slipped on the steps of the Church of San Fedele as he was going in to early morning Mass and was carried home unconscious. His death, therefore, was not unexpected. It affected Verdi so deeply that he did not feel able to attend the funeral. He wrote to Contessa Maffei, 'Now all is over! and with him ends the most pure, the most holy, the greatest of our glories. I have read many papers. Not one speaks fittingly of him. Many words, but none deeply felt. There is no lack of gibes. Even at him? Oh, what a wretched race we are.'

It is difficult for us, even if we have read and admired Manzoni's great novel *I Promessi Sposi* to understand Verdi's extraordinary reverence for the poet. Verdi had read the novel when he was sixteen and summed up the deep impression it made on him in a letter to a friend. 'It's that this is a *true* book; as true as the *truth*.' There is a very interesting account of the importance of the book to Italy in George Martin's admirable biography of Verdi.

In 1827 [he says], there was no *national* Italian language; the basis of what ultimately became one was still only a dialect, the Tuscan, descended from the language of Dante, spoken in and around Florence. Elsewhere different areas and even towns each had its own dialect . . . the court and official languages of the various Italian States at the time were French, Latin (in the Papal States) and German. Manzoni chose the Tuscan dialect as the richest and most beautiful for his novel, but had to begin with a mixed vocabulary of Lombardy, Tuscan, French and Latin with made up words derived from one or the other by analogy or extension. In succeeding editions up to the definitive one of 1840 he substituted more and more Tuscanisms which gave rise to the quip that he had 'washed his linen in the Arno'. . .

The book became almost a primer and dictionary of the emerging Italian language and from the first schools used it as such. Verdi admired Manzoni as a political figure, but even more as an artist, and as a man, modest and retiring. The two great men at last met in 1848, through the agency of Contessa Maffei, prompted by Verdi's wife, and there is a charming tradition that their conversation—of which there is no record—consisted simply of Manzoni saying, 'Verdi, you are a great man' and Verdi replying, 'But you are a saintly man.' Verdi, however, described his impressions of their meeting in a letter to the Contessa, also quoted in George Martin's biography.

'What can I say? How to describe the extraordinary, indefinable sensation the presence of the saint, as you call him, produced in me. I would have gone down on my knees before him if we were allowed to worship men. They say it is wrong to do so and it may be: although we raise up on altars many that have neither the talent nor the virtue of Manzoni and indeed are rascals.'

All that he felt, all his reverence for the 'saintly man' is expressed in the Requiem. As I have said, Verdi had not the heart to be present at the funeral but, he wrote to Giulio Ricordi, his publisher, 'I shall come soon to visit his grave, quite inconspicuously and perhaps, after I have thought it over and measured my strength I shall propose something to honour his memory.'

There is no doubt that he had had it in mind for a long while to add to the setting of the Absolution ('Libera me, Domine') which was his contribution to a proposed Requiem Mass for Rossini, the various sections of which were to be composed by a number of Italian composers. The project ran into difficulties and was abandoned, but Verdi kept his setting by him and now came the opportunity to add a setting of the Mass texts themselves. It is understandable that Verdi felt it necessary 'to measure his strength'. *Aïda*, which had been produced for the first time in Italy at La Scala, Milan, in 1872, just over a year before Manzoni's death, had shown a great advance in his art but a large-scale choral work needed a different orientation. Chorus work, in opera, has to be on broad lines: ensembles often deal with conflicting emotions of the characters, solo singers must have arias. If in fact the 'Libera me' fugue is all that survives of the Rossini contribution—a point that, in default of the manuscript, can never be known, but which seems probable—there was a formidable task before him, but to carry it out there was the burning desire to give of his best, to overcome obstacles, to the honour of his great friend.

Verdi's Requiem is the first of those dealt with in this book that was intended, from the start, for the concert hall, not the church. This enabled the composer to deal more freely with the text than would otherwise have been the case. In actual fact Verdi is very much more respectful of the liturgy than Berlioz, whose cavalier way with it I have described. One can only conclude that the ecclesiastical authorities in Paris either did not pay attention to this or chose to ignore it. Verdi does not give the opening movement 'Requiem aeternam' its liturgical title, Introit, but observes the repeat after the psalm verse 'Te decet hymnus' and dovetails the movement with the *Kyrie*. In the Sequence he repeats 'Dies irae' briefly after 'Liber scriptus', more fully before 'Lacrimosa'. This was something new. In the Offertory he repeats 'Quam olim Abrahae' and follows Cherubini in uniting *Sanctus* and *Benedictus* and he makes various repetitions of the text in the Communion and in the Absolution.

The working out of the chosen scheme is that of a master dramatist and a melodist at the height of his powers. Verdi always spoke of himself as 'an unlearned composer', but this is far from the truth. Manzoni chose the Tuscan dialect, full of popular expressions, for his novel: Verdi, following Rossini, also far from 'unlearned', chose to subordinate learning to give the Italian people popular opera, giving full rein to the native genius for lyricism which, from the sixteenth century, had taken the chill off the music of the Netherlanders and given grace to their melodic lines. But all the time Verdi's musical learning was brought ever more conspicuously into play, culminating in the Requiem, *Otello*, *Falstaff*, and the *Four Sacred Pieces*.

As a young man he had studied with Vincenzo Lavingna, *Maestro al Cembalo* at La Scala, professor of composition at the Milan Conservatoire, and a first-rate musician. Lavigna put him through a course of harmony, counterpoint, and fugue, taking examples from the works of Palestrina, Marcello, Bach, Haydn, Mozart, and Beethoven. His master, in a leaving certificate, declared his pupil to be 'equal in ability to any accredited *Maestro di Cappella*'. By his bedside, on the top shelf of a small standing bookcase, Verdi kept small bound volumes of the complete string quartets of Mozart, Haydn, and Beethoven, and he used to slip one into his pocket whenever he went out. When asked by Boito to make suggestions for the curriculum of a proposed state school of choral music he made out a list of Italian composers which had Palestrina's name at the head and in brackets 'first and foremost'. Verdi passionately desired that young Italian composers should be true to their heritage and not go a-whoring after Wagner. In answering an effusive letter from Hans van Bülow who, influenced by Brahms, had changed his biased and harsh opinion of the Requiem, Verdi quoted Wagner as saying that everyone should maintain the peculiar characteristics of his own nation. 'Happy you, who are the children of Bach! And we? We, children of Palestrina, once had a great school—and today? Perhaps it is corrupt and in danger of falling into ruin. If we could only turn back to the beginning.' This letter was written in 1892, the year of the completion of *Falstaff*.

Verdi kept faith with the past and so, in his way, did Puccini. It is reasonable to suppose Verdi studied carefully the Requiems of Mozart, Cherubini, and Berlioz. He was critical of the French composer, considering that he was 'without restraint and lacked the calm and equilibrium which produces perfect works of art'. That is a perceptive remark, for Berlioz was at the mercy of his impulsive temperament, but Verdi fully recognized his genius.

Verdi's Requiem is undoubtedly the most beautiful setting that had ever been, or ever will be, composed. The opening bars of the Introit, for muted strings, breathe the very spirit of the words 'Requiem aeternam' murmured by the chorus in a manner unapproached before. Who can ever forget the gentle crescendo of the cellos, to the lovely phrase expressive of the 'lux perpetua', moving the music from A minor to A major?

Ex. 1

There is a flavour of plainsong in the psalm verse 'Te decet hymnus', for unaccompanied chorus: but with the *Kyrie* Verdi gives hostages to fortune. This is a solo tenor lead not marked *forte* until the last bar of 'eleison', but Italian tenors, and others, sing the passage as if it were 'Recondita armonia' from Puccini's *Tosca*! Not a strange harmony of contrasts, but a discordance! In the hands of a perceptive conductor and a soloist who is an artist the lead is never vulgarly belted out. It is an urgent prayer, not a melodramatic one, but if the other three soloists take their cue from the tenor, he can lead them all into error!

Dyneley Hussey, in his excellent book on Verdi (Master Musicians Series, Dent, 1940), points out that in nearly every bar, where there is accompaniment at all, the voice parts, solo or choral, are doubled by some instrument, thus reinforcing the vocal tone. This is Verdi's general practice and often lends a specially beautiful colour to the vocal lines.

Verdi ends the *Kyrie* significantly, I think, not with 'Kyrie eleison' but with 'Christe eleison' and sets its last repetition to the wonderful progression from A major, through two chords for voices in eight parts—disposed to obtain the fullest but quiet sonority —and orchestra, of F major, B flat major, and so back to A major. Then the violins, repeating two octaves higher the phrase just played by violas and cellos, carry the prayer, so to say, up to heaven. It is a perfectly fashioned movement and the serenity, the solidity of these chords, render the cataclysmic outburst of *Dies irae* all the more startling. Verdi may have taken a hint, perhaps, from the hammer blows of the primary accents of the octosyllabic lines of the poem when he wrote the pounding chords on the orchestra that announce the Day of Judgment. His accentual patterns for the chorus are much more forceful and dramatic than those of Mozart and Cherubini and the chromatic melismas for second lines of sopranos, altos, and tenors with first sopranos and basses sustaining a 'pedal' G all through are a brilliant inspiration.

The scheme demands the separation of 'Dies irae' from 'dies illa' with the orchestra surging on between. It is here that the composer directs that the cords of the bass drum should be well stretched so that its notes, on off-beats, will sound dry and strong. The anguished cries die down, ending 'not with a bang but a whimper', and with some of Verdi's most imaginative orchestration. In scoring *Aïda* Verdi had discovered the effective use to which flutes in a low register could be put, as in the aria 'Celeste Aïda', the duet with the voice, and then a long trill, and he uses it here in a series of trills, with short chromatic phrases below for woodwind (oboe/clarinet, clarinet alone, clarinet and bassoon successively). In the hands of an imaginative conductor this scoring produces a sinister effect of dissolution.

The distant but sure approach of the dread Judge 'Quantus tremor est futurus, Quando judex est venturus' is marvellously depicted: the menacing 'footfalls', incisive figures on woodwind and solo horn, underlined by the timpani, the 'tremor' a semiquaver figure on violins echoed by cellos—this brought to my mind a similar obsessive figure in the dramatic scene in *La Traviata* (Act 2, second finale) when Alfredo flings his winnings at Flora's feet—and on the double-basses, pizzicato, the theme of 'Dies irae'. How often the genius of these pages goes unnoticed. There can be no doubt that Verdi's approach to 'Tuba mirum' is superior to that of Berlioz, in spite of the larger resources the latter demanded.

Berlioz begins, *ff*, in an emphatic E flat major; Verdi's trumpet fanfares, echoed 'off-stage', make a gradual crescendo to the great E flat, chord for all the brass. Berlioz's sudden D flat is undeniably effective but the return to, and full close on, E flat just before the basses sing 'Tuba mirum' reduces the tension built up. Verdi continues in A flat minor and brings his chorus basses in, without pause, on the dominant seventh chord of that key. The subsequent treatment of the text in the Sequence differs too radically to make comparison possible or at least profitable. Verdi's remarkable setting of 'Mors stupebit' shows his advance in subtlety of harmony and orchestration. The *pizzicato* on the double-basses is the essential bass of the whole movement and implies the key of D minor: but when the soloist ends 'Judicanti responsura' on a high and loud E flat, woodwind and horns, marked *frizzante* (a word not found in Scholes's *Oxford Companion to Music* or *Grove*—a 'stinging F sharp'), indicate G minor: but after a bar of silence, the voice sings and the rest of the strings play D, starting that spine-chilling chromatic descent to the dominant chord of D minor.

Ex. 2

That A major chord is in our ears as Verdi starts the mezzo-soprano solo 'Liber scriptus' unaccompanied, on A, but holds her off from the key chord of D minor until she comes to 'Unde mundus judicetur', so that the words shall be given the full force of the now established key. There is nothing here that any intelligent music-lover with a vocal score could fail to see and it is the realization of such fine planning that deepens appreciation of a composer's genius. I do not propose to work through the score in this way, although I hope some readers have done or will do so, but I must point out Verdi's treatment of 'Nil inultum remanebit', just before he brings the chorus in with a partial repeat of 'Dies irae'. The passage for the mezzo-soprano is similar to the solo bass's 'Mors' (stupebit), but here it is utter desolation, not amazement, that the words describe, with the strings alone accompanying the voice. Notice the quick notes on the first two syllables of 'remanebit', the darkening tonality and the horror expressed—at least if sung by a singer who is an artist—on the final 'Nil'. *Nothing* will remain hidden.

Ex. 3

The accompaniment to the mezzo-soprano's 'Quid sum miser tunc dicturus?'—in which she is later joined by tenor and bass—is another imaginative piece of scoring. There is no warmth in the clarinet's thirds and a sense of utter misery in the bassoon figure with its first note marked *staccato*. That can go for nothing in the hands of a less than front-rank player.

I would dearly love to know if Verdi had in mind Michelangelo's painting of the Last Judgment over the altar in the Sistine Chapel when he set *Dies irae*. That stern implacable figure of a youthful unbearded Christ, with right hand menacingly held aloft over the damned writhing below, is in accord with the literal interpretation of His words in St Matthew's Gospel, but it is far from the whole truth unless we accept that these poor creatures have pronounced their own doom. Beside the vengeful Christ His Mother averts her face. Verdi has shown us something of this Christ, but now reveals the Saviour of Mankind whom Michelangelo had, in this painting, not chosen to depict. The 'Rex tremendae majestatis' is also the fountain of grace ('fons pietatis') and the emphasis is now on 'Salva me', a direct appeal to a King whose prerogative is mercy. The prayer draws exquisite music from Verdi. How could the sacred heart of Jesus not be touched by the appeal to Him to remember that He bore the sins of the world, the bitter pains of the Crucifixion, for the sake of sinful mankind whom He loved? Through much of the tenderly beautiful duet for soprano and mezzo-soprano the woodwind reiterate a rhythmic figure which seems to utter 'salva me'. Into this duet, in a completely natural way, Verdi introduces a very short cadenza for the soloists. This is a test for the soprano who has, after a rest of only one beat, to pitch a high B flat *pp*. A composer has always to remember practical considerations, and so Verdi has now to serve his tenor and bass soloists. The tenor who follows Verdi's directions implicitly in 'Ingemisco, tamquam reus', etc., is a rare bird indeed, and it is in fact possible to hear them *completely* ignored. In the latter part the singer pleads to be placed at the right hand of the Lord among the sheep and not among the goats; but it is, on artistic grounds, among the goats, that those belong who use this beautiful solo as a vehicle for the display of their admired voices.

Verdi, who always scrutinized his libretti carefully, sees at once that the 'Ingemisco' verse must be treated as *arioso*, the verse with the touching reference to Mary Magdalene, lyrically. In the *arioso* 'parce Deus' is marked *ppp*. Verdi at least expected *p*. 'Qui Mariam absolvisti' with its last phrase echoed by solo flute, oboe, and clarinet, is to be sung *dolce con calma*, and though the singer has a chance to open up to a limited extent—there is no *f* marked—in the rising scale passage to a high B flat, 'spem dedisti' is marked *pp*. The 'Statuens in parte dextra' is marked *f* and needs volume, but once again the cadence is meant to be soft. The contrasts for the bass 'Flammis acribus addictis', *ff*, 'voca me cum benedictis', *dolce cantando*, are too obvious to be missed: but often too much voice and too little feeling are used for the prayer asking to be called to the assembly of the blessed.

Those who examine the full score of the Requiem will see how carefully Verdi supports the voices in the superb and finely built-up ensemble in 'Lacrimosa' for the whole forces. The short unaccompanied passage for the solo quartet 'Pie Jesu Domine' has a Palestrinian purity of texture.

Verdi surpasses the effect he made with the 'Christe' chords at the end of the *Kyrie* in the last bars of *Lacrimosa*. He moves from a lightly scored chord of B flat to a full chord of G with *every* instrument brought in, from piccolo to double bass, as the chorus sing 'Amen', the whole *pfp*; the orchestra alone returning to the B flat chord now also fully scored. The effect of that G major chord, preceded, by this master dramatist, by the chord of B flat–D, on violins only, is of a sudden gleam of heavenly light, an answer to the prayer, 'Pie Jesu Domine, dona eis requiem'.

Ex. 4

In the concert hall an interval follows at this point. When another work is included this is understandable but not otherwise. Verdi's Requiem is about the same length as Britten's War Requiem and that is always performed without a break. Verdi himself releases the tension built up in the long setting of the Sequence with the gracious phrases of the Offertory. Here the *locus classicus* is the entry of the soprano as Michael the Standard-bearer appears shining in the heavens. The soprano sings only the word 'sed' to a long-held note lowered a semitone from E to E flat in the last two bars. During this, which in the hands of an artist makes a magical effect, two violins very high up play the phrase the soprano will sing after the change of key '(sed) signifer sanctus Michael repraesentet eas in lucem sanctam . . .' 'The holy light'—that is what the violins have caused to shine. Verdi, as I have said earlier on, only makes a feint at a fugue at 'Quam olim Abrahae', for which relief many thanks.

Then comes 'Hostias et preces tibi, Domine, laudis offerimus' (with the right accentuation, *pace* Berlioz). This exquisite melody has the economy and the texture of plainsong—it moves wholly within the compass of five notes and brings out to perfection the spiritual significance of the words—perhaps even more than Verdi realized. The accompaniment is equally perfect. A *low* tremolo on violins and violas, and an imitative phrase on the cellos ending with a low *pizzicato* C. Who but Verdi would have thought of this?

The music continues to develop beautifully as the other soloists come in and one feels that the prayer for the holy souls that may pass from death to life has been fully understood by this great composer and by none other before. Another lovely use of the flute here, as the solo quartet murmur 'fac eis, Domine', etc., playing in its highest register the 'Hostias' melody.

The prayer, after the 'quam olim Abrahae' repeat and an effective passage in octaves for solo quartet and orchestra, is taken up to heaven by the soprano. It is a passage sopranos dread, for it is unaccompanied and ends in a soft floating A flat above the stave (one recalls the easier end of the Ave Maria in *Otello*) which has to receive a gentle crescendo as the other three singers join in.

The self-styled unlearned Verdi brings off a very successful double fugue for double chorus in the Sanctus. The sopranos of both choruses have the subjects but the second of these does not long survive, the other is all-conquering and cleverly characterized by accents on the weak beats. Palestrina again comes to mind when Verdi puts his main fugue theme into long notes in the chorus; there he surrounds them with flickering points of light (staccato arpeggios on first violins and cellos, violas and cellos pizzicato). The last Hosannas are illuminated by the blazing light of a great orchestral swirl up and down the scale.

Plainsong and Palestrina, in letter as well as spirit, colour the *Agnus Dei*. It was a bold thing to give the melody first to soprano and mezzo-soprano in octaves, starting 'cold', that is, unaccompanied from the beginning. The effect, provided their intonation is perfect, is most lovely, the silver tone of the soprano bordering the purple of the mezzo's tone. The chorus and orchestra repeat the melody in unison throughout. The movement is perhaps the most original thing in the work, as divinely simple as it is beautiful. For the second petition Verdi puts the melody into the minor, keeping his soloists in octaves as before but in counterpoint with solo flute and clarinet, violas—following the melody line—and cellos. With the chorus entry the melody, now harmonized, returns to the major key, and so it remains to the end. For the third verse the soloists are accompanied by three flutes twining garlands of sound round the voices. Finally Verdi unites soloists, chorus, and orchestra. The soprano sings 'Dona eis' in unison with the mezzo-soprano in the closing bars, but an octave below at 'requiem sempiternam', adding, with the darkened tone, a greater poignancy to them.

Verdi, continuing to be liturgically minded, sets the Communion 'Lux aeterna' as a separate movement, not as in the Mozart and Cherubini Requiems joining it on to *Agnus Dei*. (Berlioz, it may be remembered, simply repeated the Introit at the end of his *Agnus Dei*, beginning with the psalm verse 'Te decet hymnus'.)

Until recently when a sung Requiem Mass was celebrated, no opportunity was given to the members of the congregation to go to Holy Communion. Today it is a general custom except on some State occasion. 'Up to the fourth century it was not only a rule that the faithful communicated at every Mass, but Communion was even more frequent than the celebration of Mass, which was usually restricted to the Sunday.' (*The Mass of theRoman Rite*, Joseph J. Jungmann, p. 408.) The text of the Communion, in such circumstances, forms a very special prayer. But Verdi, writing for the concert hall, may well have had in mind the sorrowful breaking of his communion of fellowship with Manzoni, for there is a moving intimacy about this beautiful movement. Twelve first and twelve second violins divided into three groups of four—

each have three note chords—halo the mezzo-soprano soloist with shimmering sound (all playing tremolando) as she sings 'Lux aeterna luceat eis, Domine, cum sanctis tuis in aeternum: quia pius es'. Then the grievous loss breaks in on the composer once more, the halo is withdrawn and the bass soloist intones a funeral chant to 'Requiem aeternam dona eis' punctuated by sombre chords on bassoon, trombones, tuba, with drums rolling. To this the other soloists respond in gently appealing measures. The use of the three soloists but no chorus, throughout, intensifies the intimacy of the music. The three voices unite in a brief and exquisite unaccompanied section. Then with different orchestration, the 'funeral march' (as it sounds to me) is resumed. The love in Verdi's heart for his friend suffuses with warmth the beautiful melody now begun by the mezzo-soprano at the repetition of 'Et lux perpetua'. This, too, has a most imaginatively scored accompaniment. The flute—in a low register—doubles the soloist's melody, the piccolo flickers above in quick staccato notes, doubled by first violins at the same high pitch, second violins are tremolando below.

When the soloist reaches the word 'aeternam', on which a crescendo is marked, the whole of the strings have a loud and abruptly broken off chord (*tronca*) that gives an impression of the absolute finality of death. Then, as if it had not happened, the gentle music is resumed, only to be halted once again by that chord, after which all is peace, light, lovely arpeggios for flute and clarinet soaring above 'Domine', the last word of the text, with the flute alone continuing up to a note at the top of its compass, sustained almost to the end of this most perfect movement. I could almost wish that Verdi had ended here, even sacrificing the beautiful unaccompanied section of solo soprano and chorus fashioned out of the orchestral start of the Requiem, for the agitated recitative for the soprano comes surely from Verdi's contribution to the abortive Rossini Requiem. Much of it has a faintly theatrical flavour that jars. But there are treasurable moments, other than the one I have mentioned. The sudden irruption of 'Dies irae' in its original key of G minor just after the soloist's whispered 'Tremens factus sum ego et timeo', tapering off into silence on a C major chord, is a fine dramatic stroke, and this recapitulation heightens the beauty of the heavenly quintet 'Requiem aeternam' which recapitulates the music of the Introit. It is really the jaunty fugue 'Libera me, Domine' that sticks in my gullet! But the magician casts a spell with the expressive 'Libera me' phrases that follow later on, and one can't help being thrilled with the huge climax, 'Domine, Domine, libera me de morte aeterna', taking the solo soprano up to a resounding top C. By the time the tumultuous prayer dies away, leaving the soloist, then the chorus also, to whisper the key words, one has capitulated. The widely spaced final chord is of C major. And so we leave Verdi 'hoping it might be so'.

If Verdi's Requiem is not the work of a truly religious and spiritually minded man then I do not know the meaning of those words.

*

I find it hard to believe that, in 1943, I described Dvořák's Requiem Mass, in my biography of the composer, as 'a masterpiece', but I suppose writing the book on fire-watching nights at the top of one of B.B.C.'s many buildings—for, as a sufferer from claustrophobia nothing would induce me to go into the underground shelter—may have affected my critical judgement, especially when the particular judgement was so often threatening!

If, however, Dvořák's Mass is unsatisfactory as a whole, it does not deserve the trouncing Bernard Shaw gave it on the occasion of its first performance in Birmingham on 9 October 1891, and at greater length and in more stringent terms at the mere announcement of the London performance a month later which he declared he would rather die than attend! 'Mechanically solemn, trivially genteel, very careful and elaborate, and beyond belief uninspired' are some of his milder comments. They come after a description of the Brahms Requiem, considered equally deserving of censure, as 'so execrably and ponderously dull that the very flattest of funerals would seem like a ballet, or at least a *danse macabre* after it'. In later years Shaw apologized 'for failing to recognise and appreciate Brahms's "unfamiliar idiom"'—surely not so unfamiliar as all that in 1891—though, with his detestation of nineteenth-century oratorio I doubt he would have altered his opinion about Brahms's Requiem or felt he had been unfair to Dvořák, every one of whose works mentioned in *London Music* (1888–89) and *Music in London* (1890–94), whether vocal or instrumental, he dismisses with contempt, even the great D Minor Symphony (No. 7). Shaw put his point of view about religious music in the latter half of the nineteenth century forcefully in one of the monthly notes he contributed in 1885 to a magazine called *Our Corner*. His corner was 'Art'.

. . . nowadays religious music means either a legend from scripture, melodramatically treated exactly as a legend from Hoffmann or an opera libretto would be, or else a Mass in which the sensuous ecstasies of devotion and adoration, the hypnotic trances and triumphs which make religion a luxury, are excited in a refined fashion by all the resources of the accomplished musician, just as they are in a cruder way by the tambourines and cornets of the Salvation Army. Gounod's *Mors et Vita*, like Rossini's *Stabat Mater* and Verdi's *Requiem*, belongs to this class: but in it there is also some of the descriptive melodrama of the modern oratorio.[1]

In an earlier paragraph he suggests, in speaking of Berlioz's Requiem that 'to a genuinely religious man the introduction of elaborate sensational instrumental effects into acts of worship would have seemed blasphemous'. But one cannot blaspheme about something in which one does not believe. Berlioz certainly did not regard his Requiem as 'an act of worship', nor did Verdi. Suppose that a ninth-century Benedictine musician-monk had been able to listen to Victoria's Holy Week *Responsories*, would he not have been shocked at the composer's lack of restraint, which could only have seemed to him vulgar, if not blasphemous? And what would Fra Angelico have thought of El Greco? Great religious music, in the Catholic and liturgical sense, came virtually to an end at the close of the sixteenth century, having miraculously avoided the secular spirit of the Renaissance and the early Baroque. After that composers who set liturgical texts must be taken on their own terms. They may, if Christians, produce pale models of the past or, as Fauré, Duruflé, and Pizzetti did, re-create the past, or, like Verdi, be touched to greatness by reason of their being great composers and compassionate human beings.

Dvořák was a very simple and God-fearing creature, deeply religious, profoundly influenced by Brahms, whose friendship for him and championing of his music seemed a sort of miracle. He wanted his music to cross the frontiers, for the honour and glory of the country he so devotedly loved, and he succeeded in this where Smetana had failed. But he paid the price in his religious music, most of all in his Requiem but also in *Stabat Mater*, of conforming to the English tradition of oratorio. That is what his Requiem is, not a Mass but a full-length, dangerously extended oratorio. Free of that burden he showed how originally and delightfully he could write in his short setting of *Te Deum*, composed in 1892 for the quincentennial celebration of Columbus's discovery of America. This is a little masterpiece, a lovely expression of his faith and love of nature—for his beloved birds come into it to praise God with men. It is a Franciscan conception.

Shaw missed entirely the original things in the Requiem—it may be that the indifferent performance at Birmingham masked these as much as the equally indifferent first performance of Elgar's *Dream of Gerontius* was to do at a later date. The leading motif of the work, which for brevity's sake I shall call 'motto', used in a

---

[1] *Bernard Shaw*, How to Become a Music Critic. *Ed. Dan H. Laurence* (*Hart-Davis, 1961*).

manner Dvořák had learnt from Liszt, is finely imagined and one can find in it the lineaments of the first phrases of the plainsong Introit. It is scored, as first heard, for muted strings.

Ex. 5

At the repeat the flute, playing this motto, sheds a gentle light over the prayer for rest. The psalm verse, loudly declaimed, is empty music and not made any more acceptable, at the entry of the four soloists, by the repetitiveness that is a major weakness in the work, as in numerous others of the nineteenth and twentieth centuries. The music comes alive again at the *Kyrie* introduced by the motto high up on the violins. In this prayer, treated with the same simplicity as in Berlioz's Requiem, the motto on flute and oboe separates the vocal entries.

Dvořák sets the Gradual with some imagination, but an irritating immediate repetition of each sentence adds nothing. The imagination lies in the unaccompanied start, for solo soprano, with the first phrase of the motto, woodwind and horns coming in at 'aeternam'. After 'et lux perpetua luceat eis' for sopranos and altos unaccompanied, the composer repeats the whole section half a tone higher. Then he does his duty to his soprano and gives her a lyrical, but for him, an uninspired, solo, to an unvarying chordal accompaniment. Tenors and basses in four parts, unaccompanied, close the movement.

The Sequence is the weakest part of the work. Dvořák was not one to depict the terms of the Day of Judgement or the lake of fire—the devil in his comic opera *The Devil and Kate* is a very likeable fellow—and the best he can do is to make a march-like figure the basis of the *Dies irae*, placing it over pounding bass notes and a prolonged tremolo on the lower strings, and subjecting the music to a drawn-out crescendo followed by an inevitable diminuendo. At the end of all this—covering nine pages of vocal score—he has despatched only two verses of the Sequence.

He starts 'Tuba mirum' in an original way by presenting the motto, four times, starting on B flat with three rises of a semitone thereafter (B natural, C, C sharp). Verdi and Puccini both use this device, Verdi in the temple scene in *Aïda* at the priests' summons to Radames, Puccini in the last and climactic section of Turandot's aria in Act 2, 'In questa reggia'. I wonder if these composers, all born Catholics, remembered the plain chant triple Easter 'Alleluia', or the Good Friday 'Ecce lignum crucis', in each of which the pitch is twice raised at these dramatic moments.

The first three entries in this movement, for trumpet, close with a ghostly chord on horn and woodwind that brings to mind a similar effect at the start of the *Agnus Dei* in Berlioz's *Requiem*. This striking start is followed by an alto solo, declaiming 'Tuba mirum' to a figure of accompaniment, for woodwind, that is maintained through the choral repetition of the words (tenors and basses) and again through the solo bass's 'Mors stupebit'. Anti-climax hangs over these vocal parts. The brief and modal tenor solo 'Liber scriptus', with a picturesque figure for oboe, in detached notes, as a pendant to each vocal phrase, is Dvořák in good form again, but one's heart sinks as he recapitulates 'Dies irae', taking in also 'Tuba mirum'.

'Quid sum miser tunc dicturus?', for solo quartet and chorus, is a well-devised movement with an imaginative use of the motto, which one must suppose always to represent the main concept of the movement in which it appears.

All through this section of the movement both the orchestral and vocal parts are very expressively handled, so much so that the verbal repetition for once sounds inevitable and not forced. After the chorus sing the opening words again, to the motto, there is a direct lead into 'Rex tremendae majestatis', forcefully treated in the conventional manner and giving the solo soprano a most effective and sudden entry, at 'Salve me', rising to a climactic top B natural. The coda, too, is excellent, solo soprano and alto, the chorus responding, singing very softly and prayerfully 'Salve me, fons pietatis'.

'Recordare, Jesu pie' for solo quartet, in Dvořák's lovely lyrical vein, is really moving and there is quite a subtle use in the solo bass's 'donum fac remissionis', and the orchestral parts, of a little motif before set to 'ne me perdas illa die'.

In 'Confutatis maledictis' Dvořák resorts to very conventional rushes up the scale, clinched with a *sforzando* chord in each bar of the accompaniment; and after expressive low-pitched unaccompanied phrases for full chorus at 'voca me cum benedictis' he uses these again in exactly the same way at the repeat of the words. The motto, prominent in 'Lacrimosa dies illa', is heard on horns and trombones beneath a pulsating upper part, and its use at 'Pie Jesu Domine, dona eis requiem' is particularly well judged.

Dvořák invents memorable phrases for the words at the start of the Offertory 'Domine Jesu Christe, rex gloriae', which are preceded by a short orchestral prelude of no particular significance. These phrases are sung by the chorus basses—it is the closing one that is so attractive.

Do —— mine Je —— su Christe, Rex glo —— ri-ae, Rex glo —— ri-ae

Ex. 6

The solo alto sings the same words, with muted violin and harp accompaniment, to a contrasting phrase. The conventional orchestral shudder comes in at 'de poenis inferni' but Dvořák skates lightly over the 'profundo lacu'! There is a considerable amount of declamation in the movement and use of a pulsating bass to represent 'ne absorbeat eas Tartarus, ne cadant in obscurum'. Michael makes an unmemorable entrance—eight bars in all—and then comes an equally unmemorable and lengthy fugue at 'Quam olim Abrahae'. The subject is said to be of Czech folk-song origin, but that doesn't make it a better fugue. It gives the chorus a good sing, but that is about all.

The composer introduces 'Hostias et preces tibi' by repeating, words and music, the 'Domine Jesu Christe, Rex gloriae', here for solo bass, and music only, at 'Tu suscipe pro animabus illis, quarum hodie memoriam facimus', etc. This is a well devised kind of repetitiveness that does make sense and does not irritate. It is followed, however, by the dread *dal segno al fine*, the thirteen dull pages of the 'Quam olim Abrahae' fugue. The *Sanctus* starts charmingly with a folk-song-like melody by the solo bass, answered by a semi-chorus of altos, marked *andante maestoso*, but the significance of the latter word is only later revealed. When the full chorus enter Dvořák summons up the trombones to blaze out the last three notes of the melody, violins tremolando above.

The 'Benedictus' is in Dvořák's most attractive melodic vein, of which there is all too little in this work, and its pastoral-like theme, anticipated before at the final repetition of 'Pleni', etc., is very well worked out and goes through some beautiful modulations. The climax grows naturally out of the melody.

Be—ne-dic—tus qui ve—nit in nomine Do — — — — mi-ni,

Ex. 7

The resemblance between Dvořák's setting of 'Pie Jesu' and Cherubini's in his D minor Requiem, in key and design not in thematic material, is so marked that it can hardly be fortuitous. In both cases the vocal parts are left practically unaccompanied, but whereas Cherubini had only three male chorus parts in his work Dvořák has four soloists and full chorus. In his 'Pie Jesu', however, he gives the first and last sections to male voices (tenors and basses, each in two parts), the chorus altos joining in the final 'dona eis requiem sempiternam'—and the middle section to soprano, alto, and tenor soloists—an effective contrast of vocal colour. The motto comes into all of the orchestral entries except the last and into all but the last vocal section. This is a very moving motet. The high level of the 'Benedictus', and of this movement, is maintained in *Agnus Dei*, in which only the last petition (with 'sempiternam') is set. The motto is of course prominent and there is a welcome touch of modal harmony in the chorus's response to the solo tenor. It is a pity it wasn't carried through to the cadence.

The anticipated crescendo begins with the words of the Communion 'Lux aeterna luceat eis', to lead to the climax demanded by the tradition of English oratorio. Cherubini avoided this in both his Requiems—church works—and so did Verdi. Dvořák spares us a fugue, and after the big climax at 'cum sanctis tuis in acternum quia pius es' he gives the motto to the solo alto and then, unaccompanied, to the solo soprano. The work ends with the four soloists' quiet singing of 'lux perpetua luceat eis', the horns responding. At the repeat of the words the soloists are in unison *pp*—the chorus responding with the full chord of B flat. The last word is with the motto, which gently travels down the scale, *ppp*, as if whispering 'dona eis requiem'.

Dvořák has been charged with going astray in the thematic working out of the single numbers inasmuch as 'he often develops his thematic material in a way that suggests his being guided by purely musical, or to be more precise, melodic considerations. He frequently resorts to such technical devices as the splitting up of a vocal melody into its constituent motives with which he plays about in the manner of an instrumental development.' (*Men and Music*, Mosco Carner: Joseph Williams, 1940.) If this is true, and I think it certainly is, it calls to mind the essential problem in both polyphonic and orchestral Masses. Where the words are few musical development requires their repetition and this is most conspicuous in countless settings of 'Benedictus qui venit in nomine Domini', Beethoven being the prime 'offender'! The length of this movement was, however, also dictated by the congregation's dislike of a long period of silence at a High Mass. Dvořák had to consider the provision of a work, with an interval, that would last the time of a full-length concert. Verdi avoided the development of small motives by writing the full-blooded and well defined melodies that characterize each section of his great work. But Dvořák's repetitiveness is not development, it could more easily be borne if it were, and if his Requiem is to survive some bold spirit—one of his countrymen—should go to work with a blue pencil.

CHAPTER TEN

THE REQUIEM MASS FROM THE EIGHTEENTH TO THE TWENTIETH CENTURY

Fauré, Duruflé, and Pizzetti

Gabriel Fauré composed his Requiem Mass in memory of his father, who died in 1885, but by the time it was finished his mother had also died and so it commemorates both of his parents. It was first sung at the Madeleine Church, Paris, in 1888. At this time the composer was assistant organist, only succeeding to the post of chief organist eleven years later when he had at last achieved the small measure of recognition—mainly through the Requiem—his country, and the musical world, gave him.

A wide gulf separates his attitude to the liturgical texts from that of Berlioz and Verdi. To him the Berlioz work was one in which 'a taste for big dramatic effects, and an indifference towards what concerns religious music—or, for that matter, music pure and simple —may find equal satisfaction'. To a man of such exquisitely refined sensibility as Fauré, Berlioz could only appear as vulgar and Verdi over-emotional. He did not, as his music shows, wish to astonish or dramatize; the key-note of his work lies in the emphasis he puts on the first word of the liturgy, 'requiem', which he makes its last. At the same time his omission of the Sequence is in itself no clue to his theological beliefs, or lack of them. It is open to a composer writing for church use, as Fauré admittedly was, to leave out this tendentious poem which, as I have said before, has no proper place in the Mass for the Dead but, as Fauré knew, the Sequence would have to be supplied in plainsong. He chose to set, as a motet after the *Sanctus*, the last lines, 'Pie Jesu Domine, dona eis requiem' and in this he had many predecessors from Morales onwards. He chose also to set the Absolution, from which the words of the Sequence partly took their inspiration, and therefore he has to deal with 'Dies illa, dies irae, calamitatis et miseriae', but having despatched that quickly, in a powerful passage, he omits the repetition of 'Dum veneris judicare saeculum per ignem', but not the verse 'Requiem aeternam', before returning, as is required, to the repeat of 'Libera me'. No doubt his wish to set the antiphon 'In paradisum' and to end on that note influenced him in including these portions of the funeral rites.

Michael the Archangel is eliminated from the Offertory and the words 'ne cadant in obscurum' are left over for the repeat which, in its turn, eliminates 'de ore leonis'! These sort of omissions, which are not serious but need to be mentioned where a liturgically planned work is in question, may well arise from purely musical reasons. A musical phrase may reach its end having failed to accommodate all the words. A notable instance occurs in Mozart's *Ave verum* where the music of the climax comes—in slightly altered form—from the 'writing' quintet in Act I of *Così fan tutte*. This, the composer felt, is where I must end, and so he omits the beautiful prayer at the close of the received text 'O dulcis, o pie, o Jesu, filii Mariae', which is the true climax of the motet. Byrd did the opposite and added to these words a coda, 'miserere mei', an unprecedented personal appeal.

More serious and inexplicable is Fauré's omission of the *Benedictus* after the *Sanctus*, for it would have been simple to add the brief 'Hosanna in excelsis' to a setting of the few words. Fauré was not on easy terms with scoring for orchestra and much of the work here, as also in his opera *Penelope*, and the incidental music to *Pelléas et Mélisande* (from which the *adagio* of Mélisande's death scene was played as his coffin was carried out, after his Requiem had been sung at the funeral in November 1924) was done by colleagues. I imagine his collaborators obtained from the composer a clear idea of what he wanted. Violins are omitted entirely from all the numbers except the *Sanctus*, *Agnus Dei*, *Libera me* and *In Paradisum*, and only briefly intervene in the *Sanctus*. The dark tones of the viola are therefore prominent. The score provides for flutes, clarinets, bassoons (double woodwind), four horns, two trumpets, three trombones, cymbals and two harps, strings, and organ, but page after page of the staves accommodating the woodwind and brass are left empty.

Only a great composer could have achieved memorability with such simple means. This is at once apparent at the start of the Introit: the double *forte* unisons (woodwind, horns, strings) that separate the whispered words, and at each entry descend a tone as far as 'et lux perpetua', voices accompanied by bassoons, violas, and double-basses. The organ plays a prominent part in the repeat of the opening words. We already encounter here one of the most appealing things in the Requiem, the use of modal harmony within the diatonic major-minor system. This needs a word of explanation. Of the two forms of the minor scale one is called harmonic, the other melodic. It is with the melodic scale of D minor that we are here concerned. Going up it retains C sharp, the leading note that demands to be followed by D. Going down C sharp becomes C natural, B natural B flat. Out of this downward scale can be made common chords of C major, A minor and F major, all of which are impossible in the harmonic form of the D minor scale.

The beauty and modal sounding character of Fauré's harmonic writing in the Requiem arises from the availability of such chords, used with the art of one who had studied the Gregorian modes in his student days at the Niedermeyer School.

Ex. 1

Fauré's cadences are most beautiful and such a one as that above must have sounded new and strange, except to those who knew the best of the songs he had so far composed, such as *Lydia*, which makes a musical pun in its use of the Lydian mode.

Ex. 2

Fauré makes no direct quotation from the plainsong Requiem throughout his Mass but it seems to be perfumed with the chant, as for example in the psalm verse of the Introit.

The Offertory, *adagio molto*, is preceded by seven bars for orchestra alone (strings and organ) which end with one of Fauré's favourite harmonies, technically a secondary chord of the seventh, that is, one not built on the dominant. (*Ex.* 2.)

Altos and tenors then begin 'O Domine Jesu Christe' in close canon. A slight tremor comes into the strings at 'poenis inferni' up to the repeat of the words as above, adding now 'de ore leonis, ne absorbeat eas Tartarus' and then, with the basses joining in, a repeat of the canon.

Very quietly and unexpectedly, the solo baritone begins the verse 'Hostias et preces tibi'—there is a plentiful use of seventh chords all through this lovely section; there is no fugue at 'quam olim Abrahae', just the continuing serene music. The full chorus repeat the canon, to the opening words, and the Offertory ends with a lovely 'Amen' (interpolated by Fauré) to which Palestrina would have been proud to sign his name. The two harps and the muted violas softly prepare the entrance of the truly heavenly *Sanctus*, begun by the sopranos, responded to by the tenors and basses, and above the latter we hear for the first time the (first) violins, not muted, like an aureole of sound (the score gives 'violins', but the passage is usually played on a solo violin). 'Hosanna' is sung by full chorus, with horns and trumpets ringing out in the accompaniment. The burst of glory fades and the skies close at a final softly breathed 'Sanctus' and a delicate high trilling on the violin. As I have said, the *Benedictus* is omitted.

In the soprano solo 'Pie Jesu Domine', like many composers before him, Fauré adds the word 'sempiternam' which, in the liturgical text, comes only at the end of the last petition of *Agnus Dei*, and this is entirely in accord with his view of the prayer for the departed. The shape of the musical phrases requires the word to be placed before, not after, 'requiem'. This is a spiritual lullaby of child-like simplicity, needing the greatest artistry in performance.

Warmth floods into the music with the orchestral prelude to the *Agnus Dei*, for here the violins are scored in and the accompaniment, except for two brief entries of bassoons and horns, is given wholly to the strings. The first and third petitions are sung by the tenors, the second one, into which there comes a note of pain, by the full chorus. They, also, sing the Communion 'Lux aeterna luceat eis' which increases in volume to the strong and splendid lead to 'Requiem aeternam', etc. This, after an effective pause of one bar, virtually recapitulates the music of the opening section of the Introit, but Fauré ends with the genial orchestral prelude to the *Agnus Dei*.

The baritone solo with which *Libera me* begins is the most haunting melody in the work. I can never read the words without it coming into my mind. Up to 'Dies illa, dies irae' the cellos, double-basses, and organ mainly provide the accompaniment. Horns call loudly at the above words, and the violins are now used more prominently. The repetition of the baritone's melody at 'Libera me' by the choir, in octaves, is extraordinarily moving, and no less so the coda, with the soloist praying yet again, 'Libera me, Domine, de morte aeterna', and the chorus whispering the first three words. There is no fear or doubt as at the end of Verdi's Requiem, there is a solemn realization of the fate that awaits us all, but a confidence that we shall pass from death to life. And now the angels are prepared to lead the holy souls into the heavenly city of Jerusalem; the voices, so soft for the greater part of the exquisite movement, swell out in joy as they repeat the name. The mention of Lazarus in the liturgical text has always seemed to me an inspiration. Poor, afflicted with sores, he lay unregarded at the rich man's gate but it is he and not Dives who shall help to guide us when cleansed of our sins and faults—a joyful period of suffering—into unimaginable bliss. The lovely accompaniment, at first for organ and muted strings, sounds to me like sunlit waters lapping at the shores of heaven. When Lazarus is mentioned the harps too sound, till the vision fades and the body is committed to burial, and awaiting its promised resurrection.

I have been led into rhapsody, no doubt, by this beautiful work but have no need to apologize for that. Let me rather quote what a dear friend of mine, Nadia Boulanger, has written about Fauré's Requiem. 'It might be said that Fauré understood religion more after the fashion of the tender passages in the Gospel according to St John, following St Francis of Assisi rather than Bossuet. His voice seems to interpose itself between heaven and earth, unusually perceptive, quietly fervent, sometimes grave and sad, never menacing or dramatic. . . . To have given this to our unhappy hearts, to have combined charity with beauty, hope with love, is not this the most beautiful mode of participating in the work of the Church?'

Fauré's Catholicism was infused with Hellenism, no new thing in the history of the church; he would perhaps have felt at home among the members of the Florentine Academy, and especially in the company of the brilliant young Giovanni Pico della Mirandola who held that a finite sin was incapable of receiving infinite punishment. This was one of his 999 theses on a variety of theological topics, many of which were condemned as heretical in 1486 by Pope Innocent VIII. He also defended Origen's doctrine of universal salvation. That famous pre-Nicene Father of the Church, whose influence was enormous (*c.* 185–*c.* 254) was twice condemned by two Councils, in 400 and 553, and ecclesiastic authority held strictly to the doctrine of eternal torment for the wicked, based on Christ's stern words about Hell in St Matthew's Gospel, Chapter 25, and the lake of fire and brimstone (the 'profundo lacu' of the Offertory in the Requiem Mass) in Revelations 20: 14–15.

This is not perhaps the place for a discourse on a subject which offers many contradictions but I feel the need to say something about it. In the parable of Dives and Lazarus the rich man showed charity in wishing to have his five brothers spared his fate. Would not that spark of good have saved him? The gentle St Francis de Sales when tormented one day by the idea of predestination received a message. 'My name is not the one that damns. My name is Jesus.' The saying that 'Hell is a place of eternal torment, eternally unoccupied', attributed to Cardinal Manning, makes God appear as a revoltingly cruel practical joker. The modern mind revolts against what Dean Farrar called 'the abominable fancy'. Remove the tendentious Sequence from the Requiem Mass and there still remains after the Mass the Absolution, one of the sources of its origin 'Libera me, Domini, de morte aeterna, in die illa tremenda'. There is no difficulty about Purgatory, a state, gladly entered into, of being cleansed from sins, faults, failings, for those who believe in the eternal life, whatever spiritual suffering it may involve when we see the results of all our wrong actions. The difficulty is over the fate of those who, in the face of an absolute goodness and beauty which we cannot begin to conceive, can still say 'We will not serve', and so can only go where God is not. That is enough, for that is Hell. Even so, can Love, who is God, not work on them so that they too at length repent and are saved?

An undated entry in Julian Green's *Diary, 1920–1957* (Harvill-Collins, 1965), puts the matter in a way that utterly wins my allegiance.

> If I were to die to-night and were asked what moves me most in this world, I would perhaps reply: It is the way God passes through men's hearts. Everything is swallowed up by love, and although it is true that we shall be judged according to the degree of love we possess, it is beyond question that we shall be judged by love itself, which is none other than God. I believe that if lack of charity were called Evil, instead of weighing down the wretched human body under this curse, the whole of false Christianity would be turned upside down and at the same time the kingdom of God be opened to millions of souls.

Blake said, 'What the imagination seizes, that is truth', and what Green says does seize my imagination. Moral theologians will have to suffer for driving so many souls out of the Church, terrifying others, repelling many more.

I suppose all this can be written off as sentimental and wishful thinking. So be it. The Requiem Mass warns that debts must, at the end, be paid, there must be a reckoning: but not a torture-chamber, with the saved rejoicing in the spectacle of the damned.

★

It is not surprising that Maurice Duruflé, French organist and composer, born in January 1902, is so little known except among organists, outside his own country. His published compositions up to date are less than ten in number, half of them for organ, the whole crowned by the Requiem op. 9, for soloist, chorus, orchestra, and organ, composed in 1947 and dedicated to the memory of his father.

Felix Aprahamian writes of him in a note on the sleeve of the recording of Duruflé's Requiem, 'His preferred media are the organ, on which he is a highly skilled performer, and the orchestra . . .

he considers that these two seemingly inexhaustible worlds of sound still offer rich possibilities, whereas he modestly regards himself as "incapable of adding anything significant to the pianoforte repertory, views the string quartet with apprehension, and envisages with terror the idea of composing a song after the finished examples of Schubert, Fauré and Debussy".'

Duruflé was certainly an apt pupil of Paul Dukas, equally fastidious and self-critical—his published compositions amount to only one more than Duruflé's—and one recalls the handful of works by Henri Duparc, the major part consisting of fourteen songs, though it is true that the last fifty years of his life were overshadowed by a nervous disease.

Duruflé became assistant organist at Ste Clotilde—the church where César Franck officiated for so many years—to Charles Tournemire, who wrote an immense work for the organ, 255 pieces for fifty-one Offices of the liturgical year, which is practically unknown today and demands revival. Those portions of it which I possess show a striking use of the relevant plainsong themes and it is this which distinguishes Duruflé's Requiem. It was the result of a commission from his publishers to compose a suite of organ pieces based on plainsong themes from the Mass of the Dead but, on the death of his father, it became, in extended form, a Requiem. It would not be difficult to write it off, on a superficial view, as a pastiche of Fauré's Requiem. The same sections are set, two soloists are used—baritone and mezzo-soprano—and only a slightly larger orchestra. The style, however, is not so pure. There are echoes of the harmonies of Debussy, Ravel, and Dukas, but if these on paper suggest a work less integrated than that of Fauré, the result in performance puts the matter in a more favourable perspective. There is a personal quality that surpasses these influences and unifies the disparate elements. The recording of the Requiem was made in the Church of St Etienne-du-Mont, Paris, of which the composer has been organist since 1930. Duruflé pays more attention to liturgical requirements than Fauré; he separates Introit from *Kyrie, Agnus Dei* from Communion but, in spite of his extensive use of plainsong, his style is less liturgical in feeling and less concise than Fauré's, and perhaps he intended the work as a concert rather than a church Requiem. Tenors and basses, in unison, sing the plainsong melody of the Introit unchanged, and so barred as to prevent it being made metrical in rhythm, altos and sopranos vocalizing an 'oh' in harmony between the three entries with the words. This is a dangerous device. The vocalized phrases add nothing to the prayer and so must be regarded as equivalent to being scored for, say, woodwind: but the voice always makes a personal appeal. However, it is, musically, undeniably effective. The psalm verse sung by sopranos, then altos, is preceded by Debussyian (or Ravellian!) harmonies on the woodwind. A nice point is the way the composer transfers the last four notes of the plainsong cadence to the violas after 'in Jerusalem' and again, melodically extended, at the end of the altos singing of 'Exaudi orationem meam'. Another nice point is that at the repeat of the Introit 'Requiem aeternam', etc., the violins are given the plainsong melody, the sopranos and tenors a slowly moving counter melody. All the voices come in at 'et lux perpetua' to the end. When I first heard the Requiem it caught my interest at once and I was eager to see what Duruflé would do in the succeeding movements. He does not disappoint. In the *Kyrie* he follows well-trodden ways and presents the plainsong melody, with some small alteration at the end of its one phrase, on all the voices, which enter successively, basses, tenors (a fifth higher), altos, sopranos (a fifth higher). More than this, he revives the ancient habit of putting the *cantus firmus* into long notes, filling out a whole bar, and giving it to the trumpets and trombones.

Ex. 3

The composer gives soprano and altos plainsong-like phrases at 'Christe eleison'—for until the final 'Kyrie eleison' the plainsong Requiem does not vary the melody—and then with fine effect all the voices sing the last 'Kyrie' to its plainsong melody, building it up from bass to treble and with trumpets and trombones playing it in long notes as before.

After a few preliminary bars at the start of the Offertory the composer puts the plainsong melody in the bass (double-bassoon), woodwind and strings then taking it up in turn, but the altos, who begin the words, have a counter melody of plainsong-like character to fit in with the orchestral texture.

Duruflé perhaps indulges in too much verbal repetition in this movement. The writing is forceful and dramatic and makes much use of motives from the plainsong, in the vocal and orchestral parts, but there is too much of the 'pains' and the 'lion' and the rest, and it is a relief to have Michael the Archangel brought quietly on to the scene by the sopranos in the plainsong phrases that belong to him.

'Quam olim Abrahae' is disposed of, in plainsong, in six bars and then the English horn introduces the verse 'Hostias et preces tibi' and the first entry of the baritone soloist. The music becomes very quiet and still as the baritone sings 'Fac eas, Domine, de morte transire ad vitam' to a chord tremolo on the violas. The sopranos and altos repeat 'Quam olim Abrahae', sopranos alone singing 'et semini ejus'. The use of the plainsong in the movement, the expressive phrases for orchestra alone separating the vocal entries in these last quiet pages, is original, imaginative, and prayerful.

The gently radiant atmosphere of the *Sanctus* is reminiscent of Fauré's, but the actual texture is quite different. The plainsong melody is used but raised a third at the two repetitions of the words up to 'Sabaoth' and melodically slightly varied at the second one. It is resumed at 'Pleni sunt coeli et terra', etc.

The composer now begins a long build-up, in crescendo, from the altos' 'Hosanna', with the other voices gradually coming in to rise up to a big climax, *ff*, reaching its high point on the middle syllable of 'excelsis'. This is followed by a diminuendo and the brief singing, sopranos and altos, of 'Benedictus', etc., with no increase of tone at the 'Hosanna'.

'Pie Jesu', which follows, as in Fauré's Requiem, is quite different in conception. It is scored for mezzo-soprano with accompaniment for organ and solo cello, *ad lib*, violas and cello *divisi*, and begins with the phrases of the plainsong Sequence at this point. This results, as the frequent changes of time-signature show, in a much less square melody than Fauré's, indeed one very free rhythmically, and the use of the singer's lower register in the first section and the upper, in quicker time, with impassioned appeal on voice and instruments in the second, is far removed from the childlike innocence of the Fauré. This is not an appeal by an angel, but by a fallible human soul, praying for others like her.

At the quiet close the singer intones 'requiem sempiternam' on low C, while the cello most expressively plays the opening phrases of her solo.

Ex. 4

The plainsong is treated in much the same free style in the *Agnus Dei* as in the preceding movements but the syncopated accompaniment lends tension to it. At the second petition, the orchestra is given a wide-ranging counter-melody—certainly not a quotation from plainsong—which I feel holds some significance for the composer unknown to us; it recurs at the last 'dona eis requiem', which is separated from 'sempiternam' by seven bars recapitulating the start of the movement.

The composer makes a haunting use of the plainsong motif to the words 'quia pius es' in the Communion. It comes in the short orchestral prelude, after the chorus have sung 'Lux aeterna luceat eis, quia pius es', and later in the orchestral part preceding the repeat of 'quia pius es'.

Duruflé dispenses, for all practical purposes, with plainsong in the Absolution, though one might trace some of the 'Libera me' phrases in the agitated orchestral accompaniment, in which the brass, so long silent, are prominent. Plainsong comes in again with the entry of the baritone soloist singing 'Tremens factus sum ego' and, to the sound of the trumpets, the basses announcing 'dies illa, dies irae', etc., which draws in the full chorus and brass. When the 'timor et tremor' die down, the chorus, in unison, softly repeat 'Libera me, Domine, de morte aeterna', altos and tenors having the same words at the close. It is a very impressive movement, but it is hard to put Fauré's haunting melody out of mind when listening to it. The antiphon *In Paradisum* is very simply treated. The sopranos sing the plainsong melody up to 'Chorus Angelorum' where it is taken over by flutes and organ to the end, the full chorus singing the lovely words to an independent melody. The orchestration is very delicate.

*

This chapter may fittingly end with Ildebrando Pizzetti's Requiem for mixed voices, basically in five parts, but increased by division to twelve parts. To say, as I believe, that this is the finest *a cappella* Requiem Mass since the sixteenth century is faint praise, since the competition in the field of unaccompanied works is negligible. Pizzetti's intensive study of the church music of the masters of the great ages of polyphony during his six years' training at the Conservatory of Parma bore fruit in his operas, particularly in *Debora e Jaele* (1910–21) and *Fra Gherardo* at the Metropolitan Opera, New York. In fact he seems to be very little known outside Italy and even there his operas have not found a place in the repertory. He has never swerved from his ideal that 'drama must be the pivot of opera, so much so that lyrical points of repose should never interrupt the unfolding of the action, nor even bring the continuous emotional process to a standstill.' In practice this means the declamatory element is preponderant, and fine and just declamation imbued with melody.

Strong rhythmic vitality and an innate sense of drama are the outstanding characteristics of his operas, and, as we shall see, of his
Requiem. The operatic public, unfortunately, rate unmistakable,
not diffused lyricism as a prime factor in the operas they take to their
hearts and these the rather austere composer has not been able to
reach. His operatic version of T. S. Eliot's *Murder in the Cathedral*
(*L'Assassino nel Cattedrale*), first produced at the Coventry Festival of
1961, won praise chiefly for its masterly choral writing. In the
Requiem, Pizzetti is, of course, not concerned with drama in the
operatic sense. Life and death are not set in opposition. Instead 'it
constitutes a lyrical glorification of the Christian themes of eternal
life and resurrection', for this is a Requiem by a man of unquestion-
ing and profound faith. He quotes plainsong only in the Sequence but
the vocal texture throughout the work is, so to say, pervaded by
the spirit of plainsong. Pizzetti uses time-signatures and bar-lines but
the rhythmic freedom of his music will be seen if one removes the
bar-lines from the Introit.[1]

Ex. 5

There is a wonderful serenity at the reprise of 'Requiem aeternam'
brought about simply by the downward scales over the pedal note
(D) in the bass. This is a piece of classically perfect polyphony.

('Requiem aeternam')

Ex. 6

The same is true of the *Kyrie*. The simple theme, which has a
flavour of the plainsong *Kyrie*, moves up into all the parts. I wish I
could quote the whole beautiful section.

('Kyrie eleison')

Ex. 7

---

[1] *In this complex work Ex. 6–9 have to be given in short score and without text for reasons of space.*

Pizzetti begins *Dies irae* in four parts; altos and basses have the plainsong theme in octaves, second sopranos and second tenors (the first tenors and sopranos come in at the verse 'quid sum miser') a vocalized 'Oh!' also in octaves. I criticized Duruflé's use of this device as having no bearing on the text but in this case (and Pizzetti employs it frequently in the movement) a phrase beginning in as ordinary a way as Duruflé's suddenly reaches an augmented fourth (here G sharp) and again in all subsequent entries. This makes the phrase both distinctive and poignant.

('Dies irae, dies illa, solvet saeclum et favilla')

Ex. 8

In the primitive parts of Southern Italy there was, and still may be, an age-old custom of wailing at funerals as in many other countries of the East and the West. I wonder if Pizzetti had this in mind in using the vocalized 'Oh'? There is no attempt to dramatize 'Tuba mirum' or 'Mors stupebit', but in the latter verse the wail is higher and more poignant, and is increased in length in 'Liber scriptus proferetur', and the verse following.

In 'Quid sum miser' the composer omits all but the first phrase of the plainsong theme and soon increases his voices, by division, to eight for the splendid 'Rex tremendae majestatis', which imitates a fanfare of trumpets.

At 'Qui Mariam absolvisti' (still eight parts) first sopranos and first tenors carry their ululation through sixteen bars. By now one has either fully accepted this as an imaginative idea or resented it as intrusive. Each to his own! 'Lacrimosa dies illa, qua resurget ex favilla' is sung to open fifths, with great effect after so much close harmony. There is a brief pause after 'parce, Deus', which comes to a close on an astringent discord caused by the G sharp that has characterized the wail. Then the composer builds up a chord of G major through the eight parts at 'Pie Jesu Domine, dona eis requiem'. After another brief pause the words are set to a D major chord, in which mode the Sequence ends. Cold words cannot describe the exquisite effect, so simply brought about by the masterly use of these chords. It has a remote similarity to the lovely passage I described at the end of the Offertory in Berlioz's Requiem (*see Ex.* 9).

Pizzetti does not set the Offertory but proceeds straight to the *Sanctus*. For this he divides his forces into three groups (1) two

sopranos, two contraltos, (2) two tenors, two basses, (3) the same;
twelve parts in all. The first two groups respond to one another in
rapid fanfare-like phrases, while the third provides a solid slow-
moving foundation of tone. All join in 'Pleni sunt coeli et terra', and
with most splendid effect at 'Hosanna in excelsis'. The voices are
reduced for 'Benedictus'.

Agnus Dei, in four parts only, takes up only two pages of the
octavo score and has none of the usual repetition of the words: it is a
little gem of a movement, calm and sweet, and with the simplicity
of greatness.

The high point of the 'Libera me, Domine', in which the plainsong
at 'Dies illa, dies irae' is paraphrased rather than quoted, is the
exquisite rising phrase for sopranos and tenors, *calmo dolce*, at the
verse 'Requiem aeternam dona eis, Domine, et lux perpetua luceat
eis'.

('Pie Jesu Domine, dona eis requiem')

Ex. 9

It is in this case particularly unfortunate that the liturgy requires
a repeat of 'Libera me, Domine' so that the light dims and the last
words left with the listener are of the judging of the world by fire.
The urgent prayer for deliverance from eternal death on 'that awful
day' has been made, in the first person singular; the last thought
should be of the person or persons for whom the Mass has just been
offered, and whose coffin is presently to be borne down the church
on its journey to the grave as 'In Paradisum' is sung. I wish Pizzetti
had set the antiphon.

2

Holy Week Music

CHAPTER ELEVEN

STABAT MATER

There is no certainty about the authorship of the beautiful poem which so vividly and poignantly pictures the Mother of Christ sorrowing at the foot of the Cross, knowing now, as she always had known it would be, that the prophecy of Simeon had come true, in full measure, 'and thine own heart a sword shall pierce'. The ascription to Jacopone da Todi, the town in Umbria where he was born about 1230, is the earliest and still the most favoured. Jacopone, who died in 1306, was by profession a lawyer, but on the death of his wife he became a Franciscan friar.

The contemplation of Mary's sorrows is the main theme, arousing an ardent wish in the poet to share them and to feel Christ's wounds in his contrite heart. The poem is used as a sequence in the Passiontide Mass of The Seven Sorrows of the Blessed Virgin Mary (24 March), which is repeated on 15 September, and is divided into three portions, as a hymn, at Vespers, Matins, and Lauds of the March Feast. Verses 1, 2 and 4, are based on the description of the scene in St. John's Gospel (19: 25).

Widely loved as it was and used in the devotional exercise of the Stations of the Cross, *Stabat Mater* was not officially incorporated into the Roman Missal and Breviary until 1727. The Council of Trent had excised a large number of sequences, including many beautiful ones, such as *Laetabundus* for Christmas, that had invaded the liturgy, leaving only four (*Dies irae, Lauda Sion, Veni Sancta Spiritus, Victimae Paschali*), and possibly, in their reforming zeal, the very popularity of *Stabat Mater*, attached to some extravagances of Mariolatry, made them reject it for liturgical use.

There is a large number of English translations, some good, others prosaic; I have chosen an eighteenth-century one that keeps fairly close to the Latin:

Stabat mater dolorosa,   *At the Cross her station keeping,*
Juxta Crucem lacrimosa,   *Stood the mournful Mother weeping,*
Dum pendebat Filius.   *Close to Jesus at the last.*

Cujus animam gementem,	Through her heart, His sorrow sharing,
Contristatam, et dolentem,	All His bitter anguish bearing,
Per transivit gladius.	Now at length the sword has passed.
O quam tristis et afflicta,	Oh how sad and sore distress'd
Fuit illa benedicta,	Was that Mother, highly blest
Mater unigeniti!	Of the sole-begotten one!
Quae moerebat, et dolebat,	Christ above in torment hangs;
Pia Mater, dum videbat,	She beneath beholds the pangs
Nati poenas inclyti.	Of her dying glorious Son.
Quis est homo, qui non fleret,	Is there one who would not weep
Matrem Christi si videret,	Whelm'd in miseries so deep
In tanto supplicio?	Christ's dear Mother to behold?
Quis non posset contristari,	Can the human heart refrain
Christi Matrem contemplari,	From partaking in her pain,
Dolentem cum filio?	In that Mother's pain untold?
Pro peccatis suae gentis,	Bruis'd, derided, curs'd, defil'd,
Vidit Jesum in tormentis,	She beheld her tender child,
Et flagellis subditum.	All with bloody scourges rent.
Vidit suum dulcem natum,	For the sins of His own nation,
Moriendo desolatum,	Saw Him hang in desolation,
Dum emisit spiritum.	Till His spirit forth He sent.
Eja Mater, fons amoris,	O thou Mother! fount of love!
Me sentire vim doloris,	Touch my spirit from above;
Fac, ut tecum lugeam.	Make my heart with thine accord.
Fac ut ardeat cor meum,	Make me feel as thou has felt:
In amando Christum Deum,	Make my soul to glow and melt
Ut sibi complaceam.	With the love of Christ my Lord.
Sancta Mater, istud agas,	Holy Mother! pierce me through;
Crucifixi fige plagas,	In my heart each wound renew
Cordi meo valide.	Of my Saviour crucified.
Tui nati vulnerati,	Let me share with thee His pain,
Tam dignati pro me pati,	Who for all my sins was slain,
Poenas mecum divide.	Who for me in torments died.
Fac me tecum pie flere,	Let me mingle tears with thee,
Crucifixi condolere,	Mourning Him who mourned for me,
Donec ego vixero.	All the days that I may live.
Juxta Crucem tecum stare,	By the cross with thee so stay,
Et me tibi sociare,	There with thee to weep and pray,
In planctu desidero.	Is all I ask of thee to give.

Virgo virginum praeclara,	*Virgin of all virgins best*
Mihi jam non sis amara!	*Listen to my fond request:*
Fac me tecum plangere.	*Let me share thy grief divine.*
Fac ut portem Christi mortem,	*Let me, to my latest breath*
Passionis fac consortem,	*In my body bear the death*
Et plagas recolere.	*Of that dying Son of thine.*
Fac me plagis vulnerari,	*Wounded with His every wound,*
Fac me Cruce inebriari,	*Steep my soul till it hath swooned*
Et cruore Filii.	*In His very blood away.*
Flammis me urar succensus	*Be to me, O Virgin, nigh,*
Inflammatus et accensus,	*Lest in flames I burn and die,*
Per te, Virgo, sim defensus.	*In His awful Judgement day.*
In die judicii	*Christ when Thee shall call me hence,*
Christe, cum sit hinc exire,	*Be my mother, my defence,*
Da per Matrem me venire,	*Be thy Cross of victory.*
Ad palmam victoriae.	
Quando corpus morietur,	*While my body here decays,*
Fac ut animae donetur,	*May my soul Thy goodness praise,*
Paradisi gloria.	*Safe in Paradise with Thee.*
Amen.	*Amen.*

The plainsong *Stabat Mater*, as a Sequence, has one melody for each two verses, but each melody is a new one (unlike *Dies irae* which has only three melodies in succession, thereafter repeated throughout) and there is also not the marked variation in pitch which is a characteristic of many, but not all, Sequences. There are, therefore, ten strains to the twenty verses of *Stabat Mater*, but none of them of much melodic distinction. The poem with three lines to a verse as a hymn has a simple plainsong melody, evidently of late origin, and is sung by the congregation during the devotion of the Stations of the Cross, for which purpose it is eminently suitable.

Stabat Mater do-lo-ro sa jux-ta crucem lacry-mosa dum pendebat fi-li-us

Ex. 1

Liszt quotes the above melody in his remarkable choral work *Via Crucis*, but I know of no other instance, or of any quotation of the earlier plainsong.

One of the earliest extant settings of the poem, by Josquin des Prés (*c.* 1445–*c.* 1521), is very celebrated, but very rarely heard. The composer uses as a *cantus firmus*, in long notes, and throughout, in the tenor part of this setting, the melody of a secular song '*Comme femme desconfortée*' by Binchois. One cannot help regretting that Josquin has taken this course and not written his motet in the style, for example, of his exquisite 'Ave Maria virgo serena', also a Sequence. The tenor part, underlaid with the Latin text, is intolerably strung out—the two words 'Stabat Mater', for example, occupy thirteen bars—and the part could only have been intended to be played on an instrument such as a trombone, not sung. The continual procession of long notes can become exasperating, unless kept well in the background.

Gustave Reese, whose opinions I regard highly, thinks that Palestrina's more celebrated setting has been over-rated. I cannot agree. The fact is that his *Stabat Mater* is very rarely sung really well. The choir is either too large or too small, the style wrong, and the singers sometimes give the impression that they have no real idea as to what they are singing about. 'Paradisi gloria', which should glimpse Paradise, is nearly always a casualty, and sounds merely like any other descending scale. The absolutely perfect performance can only be had, perhaps, by reading the score and imagining a choir of angels singing it!

The work, written for double-chorus, is laid out so as to secure great variety of texture. Thus at the start Choir 1 goes as far as 'dolorosa', Choir 2 sings 'Juxta Crucem lacrimosa', Choir 1 adding 'Dum pendebat Filius'. Both choirs come in with poignant force at 'O quam tristis et afflicta', then separate again.

The antiphonal effects, usually obscured in performance, need the most careful judgement in the matter of dynamics. I would dearly like to hear the glorious music in such a church as St Mark's, Venice, with its two choir galleries.

Theorists of Palestrina's period, and after, failed to put the marvellous opening bars into any modal category nor can they be explained in terms of modern tonality. On paper the seven opening bars present the extraordinary spectacle of seven different chords, major and minor, in root position, in the course of which the sorrowing Virgin Mary seems to come before us. The effect of the B flat on the third vowel of 'dolorosa' is a master stroke. I can think of only one other passage in the whole range of polyphony known to me that can compare with the mystical beauty of these harmonies, and that is the start of Byrd's motet *Ave verum*.

Sta-bat Ma-ter do — lo-ro-sa   Jux–ta   cru–cem la–cri — mo — sa

Ex. 2

The death of Jesus is profoundly moving. Choir 1 sings 'Vidit suum dulcem natum', Choir 2, at a lower pitch, 'Moriendo desolatum', then both choirs 'Dum emisit spiritum', the second rising above the first, and both ending in an exquisite cadence.

There is a division of voices at 'Juxta crucem tecum stare', etc., sung by sopranos and altos of Choir 1 and Choir 2, as one combination, not antiphonally. If carefully judged, the high G of the Choir 2 sopranos echoed, together with the rest of the phrase, by Choir 1, makes a lovely effect.

The heavens begin to open for the visionary moment at 'Paradisi Gloria'. Falling and rising phrases of Choir 2, then the sopranos of Choir 1 disclose the brief and glorious vision, their high note shining radiantly above.

Pa-ra—di-si glo — — — — — — — — ri - a.

Ex. 3

Josquin's *Stabat Mater* is in two parts. Palestrina's divides by its double-bars into four. In both works there is no break in continuity, but the case is very different when we come to the majority of settings after 1650. The poem was then put into the fetters of cantata form and subjected to instrumental accompaniment, as for example in the well-known setting by Giovanni Battista Pergolesi (1710–36), one of the few works, in a huge catalogue of wrong attributions, allowed really to have been composed by him. His *Stabat Mater* was scored in its original form for solo soprano and contralto—both *castrati*—with accompaniment for two violins and continuo. There is a rather pallid charm in the long chain of melodious duets, which are always burgeoning into thirds, but there are one or two sections that do have some correspondence with the poignance of the words, such as the opening stanza, 'O quam tristis', 'Quis est homo?' and the last stanza 'Quando corpus morietur'. To avoid monotony and to make the slow sections more impressive, composers now had to use as much variety of tempo as possible. Pergolesi has 'Eja mater, fons amoris' sung *allegro*, and also 'Quae moerebat', which is quite out of accord with the sentiment of the words.

Pergolesi was writing in the spirit of his time. The *a cappella* polyphonic style, still used as a 'first practice' in church works, was felt unsuited to be wedded to the new instrumental style, wholly secular in origin, and so the vocal writing was that of the secular cantata or the opera. The little work reveals its best qualities sung, not, as it often is today, by a chorus, but by two singers able to apply, with taste, the ornamentations called for. One feels a sense of guilt in criticizing the last work of a desperately ill man who died, in his twenty-sixth year, so poor that all his possessions had to be sold to pay off a few debts and the expenses of the funeral. He was cast into the common burial pit of the poor. The Confraternity of San Luigi di Palazzo at Naples had commissioned the *Stabat Mater* from him as a substitute for a setting by Alessandro Scarlatti (1660–1725), which had up to then been sung there annually on Good Friday. Scarlatti's setting is, as one would expect from so much more gifted a composer, stronger in construction and more imaginative in conception. There are only five duets, including the fugal 'Amen'. The tempi vary from *adagio*, through *andante* and *moderato* to *allegro*, the latter direction given only for 'Virgo virginum praeclara' which can support it, and the 'Amen'. It is one of the drawbacks of sectionalized works employing soloists that there must be, or generally is, an equal distribution of material so that, as in this case, if the soprano has a display piece, so must the contralto. It may be of interest to show the contrast of styles in the vocal parts at the start of these two works, where both composers are at their best.

Ex. 4 (Scarlatti)

Ex. 5 (Pergolesi)

Scarlatti introduces two accompanied recitatives towards the end of his work, at 'Fac ut portem' and 'Fac me cruce inebriari' perhaps to throw into high relief the soprano aria 'Inflammatus et accensus' and the duet 'Quando corpus morietur'. The fugal 'Amens' in both works may be supposed to give fuller and joyful expression to the vision of 'Paradisi gloria' than the settings allow for. One thinks of

Palestrina's quiet repetition of 'gloria' at the final cadence of his setting, though as 'Amen' is a liturgical addition to the poem he should, by rights, have included it.

The *Stabat Mater* of Antonio Caldara was, for me, an exciting discovery. It is not mentioned in any of the reference books I consulted but a modern vocal score of the work, edited by Jan Meyerowitz, was published by Broude Brothers, New York, in 1954.

The music far surpasses, in beauty and interest, the settings by Pergolesi and Alessandro Scarlatti.

Caldara, who was born in Venice in 1670, studied under Giovanni Legrenzi, Master of the Music at St Mark's from 1685 up to his death in 1690. After some years of travelling about Italy and Spain, his reputation growing both as composer and cellist, he became, in 1716, assistant conductor to Johann Joseph Fux at the court of the Emperor Charles VI in Vienna and remained there until his death in 1736.

He was a prolific composer of operas, oratorios and church music and though he drew on the harmonic vocabulary and technical resources of his own time it was to the past that he went for inspiration in his religious music. The combination of the reserved Palestrinian style with the rich Venetian style lends a special fascination to the choral writing in his *Stabat Mater*, giving it clarity, dignity and conciseness.

The work is scored for four soloists, chorus and an orchestra consisting of strings, two trombones, and continuo (organ). There are eleven short movements (compared with eighteen in the Scarlatti setting), five of which are for chorus alone, one (the first) for chorus and solo quartet. The remainder, for the solo group, are a quartet, trio, duet and two arias.

The opening bars of the work in the example below will give some idea of the fine and expressive quality of the music.

Ex. 6

In the solo quartet 'Quis est homo' (No. 2) the long-drawn vocal lines in the Palestrinian style first appear at the words 'Fac, ut tecum

lugeam', and most beautifully of all in the soprano part of the chorus
'Fac me tecum pie flere' (No. 5) at the second word of 'crucifixi
condolere'.

cru — ci –fi — xo con – do – le – — — — — — — — — — — — re.

Ex. 7

The chorus 'Christe, cum sit hinc exire' (No. 10) ends with a
poignant melisma on the third syllable of 'morietur' ('Quando corpus
morietur') and the concluding chorus, into which it goes without
pause, begins with the phrase with which the work opened. The
representation of 'Paradisi gloria' is very restrained and perhaps a
little disappointing. This is a work choral societies should take up.

I had never heard the complete *Stabat Mater* by Rossini (1792–
1860) until I began this chapter. All I knew were records of tenors
belting out 'Cujus animam gementem' and sopranos, 'Inflammatus
et accensus'. At these I turned up my liturgical nose and desired to
hear no more.

Edward Dannreuther, in the 1905 volume of *The Oxford History
of Music* which is concerned with 'The Romantic Period', quotes
Heine as saying, after he had heard the work, in 1842, in Paris, 'The
ineffable martyrdom was presented and reproduced, but in the most
naïvely juvenile way—the terrible plaint of the Mater dolorosa
was intoned by little maiden voices.' Thus further warned, and thus
prejudiced, I opened the Novello Rossini score. It is one of those
hilarious affairs which gives, inescapably, the Latin text but 'with
English words adapted by'—in this case a certain William Ball, who,
in company with the egregious Dr Troutbeck, sought to deodorize
the texts of all Popish works for Protestant choirs. Mr Ball translates
the first three lines as follows

> Lord most holy! Lord most mighty,
> Righteous ever are thy judgements,
> Hear and save us, for thy mercies sake.

In this manner Ball genuflects to Luther, Calvin, Cranmer, Uncle
Tom Kensit and all. My prejudices began to wilt as I read the score
and I hastened to acquire a recording of the 'Mariolatorus piece'.
(You would have thought Mr Ball must have been aware there was
scriptural authority for Christ's Mother being present at the foot of
the Cross.)

I was amazed at the dramatic solemnity of the orchestral introduction, the cellos' rising phrase, the pungent woodwind chord as it

reaches its highest note, and impressed by the chorus and the solo quartet that follows, and the hammer-blows (a unison D) at 'dum pendebat filius'. The repetition of the words has to be accepted as an occupational disease of cantata settings, but the moving recapitulation of the opening phrases of the orchestral introduction makes a poignant coda to the movement. Then comes the tenor's showpiece 'Cujus animam gementem' to a typical pom-pom-pom accompaniment, and equipped with a cadenza at the end taking him up to a D flat above the stave. Here I paused and reflected for a while. When I was living in Rome, I went many times to Naples and, by a happy chance, got on friendly terms with one or two Neapolitan families of the poorer classes there. A home without a picture of the Virgin Mary would be unthinkable, and not only a home but also a bar or, as I heard, a brothel. Neapolitans feel that Our Lady is someone, a human being, who always understands. She is tragic, sorrowful, contemplative, but she also smiles—whoever heard of Christ smiling except as a child in her arms? And so this tenor solo speaks in intelligible operatic terms of the sword that pierced her heart, its fervour telling of the acute sympathy the words awaken. This is an absolutely inconsistent view of one who worships at the shrine of Palestrina but nothing is so dull as consistency, and my love for the Neapolitans silences aesthetic, and even spiritual, considerations.

The orchestral introductions to the numbers are all memorable, the one in the duet for the soprano and contralto, 'Quis est homo', has a Mozartian beauty—it is scored for horns responded to by violins. Rossini had a love for Mozart unusual in an Italian.

The charm of this introduction is shattered by a fortissimo run up the scale—curtain up: we are in the theatre again. The vocal parts need virtuoso singing and the demisemiquaver figure, which continues quietly almost throughout in the orchestra, never distracts the attention, but rather focuses it wholly on the soloists. I must confess to finding the bass aria 'Pro peccatis' rather dull, but the chorus and recitative 'Eja mater' is splendid. The tempo changes from *andante mosso* to *allegro moderato* and six-eight time for a ravishingly lovely section 'In amando Christum Deum' sung *sotto voce*; very brief, but fortunately heard again after another bit of 'recitative'.

Ex. 8

The contralto has her chance in a cavatina, 'Fac ut portem Christi mortem', which is given a beautiful introduction for horns and clarinets and some fine dramatic writing for voice and orchestra at 'Fac me plagis vulnerari'. Then it is the soprano's turn, the celebrated and splendid aria with chorus 'Inflammatus et accensus'. It has a well planned off-beat entry for the solo voice and towards the end takes the soloist twice up to high C's within a matter of three bars, a show-stopping conclusion.

'Quando corpus morietur', coming after this brilliant number, is scored for the chorus unaccompanied and so they, too, have a chance to show good ensemble and intonation. 'Paradisi gloria' out of tune would be disastrous.

Rossini adds to 'Amen' the words 'In sempiterna saecula gloria' which are set to a well worked out double fugue.

The composer has, however, still a trump card to play. The chorus come to an abrupt end on an unresolved discord. There is a brief silence, and then Rossini brings back the introductory orchestral phrases to the whole work for cellos and woodwind, very softly, the chorus whispering 'Amen' before the expected final outburst.

Much as I enjoyed this first experience of hearing Rossini's *Stabat Mater* it was impossible to suppress the wish that the music could all have been on the level of the orchestral introductions and the best parts elsewhere, but to ask for that is to ask him to be a different kind of composer. As it is, one is repeatedly translated from the Lady Chapel to the auditorium, as it were, of the theatre next door. But at the end one would be glad to slip into the Lady Chapel, if it were conveniently handy, and put up a candle before her statue in gratitude for this work.

The next composer—as I am writing about the settings of my choice in chronological order—is Dvořák, whose setting of *Stabat Mater*, composed in 1877, was the first oratorio of modern Czech music. It had a great success wherever it was performed and especially in England, the land of oratorio, and it is still occasionally heard: but it seems to me now, as it did not twenty-five years ago when I wrote a critical biography of the composer, that its chances of survival are rather slender, but less so than those of his Requiem Mass.

In 1891, when being invested at Cambridge with the honorary degree of Doctor of Music, Dvořák was overcome with embarrassment at not being able to understand a word of the dean's oration, except the reference to his *Stabat Mater*. But in his delightfully down-to-earth way he wrote in a letter to a friend about this occasion, 'However, when all is said and done, that *Stabat Mater* of mine is more than Latin.' That is indeed true, but also it isn't Latin enough.

It does not much matter that the declamation is sometimes faulty. 'Virgo virginum', for example: he puts the accent on the second vowel of 'virginum' because the melody at this point is syncopated, but too often he gives insipid phrases to the most telling lines. One instance must suffice, the bass solo 'Fac, ut ardeat cor meum'.

Fac, ut ar-de-at cor me-um

Ex. 9

That hardly expresses the wish that the heart may burn with the love of Christ, and one feels the movement exists for the sake of the charming section of what sounds like a melody strayed from the composer's *Slavonic Dances*.

Ex. 10

The alto solo 'Inflammatus et accensus' is also a poor effort—remember the dramatic impact of Rossini's soprano solo with these words—but the most damaging things are the prevailing slowness of tempo and incessant verbal repetition.

I have said something in writing about Pergolesi and Scarlatti of the difficulty composers had in varying tempi in their settings of the poem. This difficulty can only vanish when it is not sectionalized but through-composed (*durchkomponiert*) and with a minimum of verbal repetition. Dvořák, who evidently and understandably had the English oratorio market in mind, has filled out the necessary large canvas only by wearisome and unnecessary verbal repetition. In his first movement, twenty-five pages of slowly moving music, he is forced to repeat 'Stabat mater dolorosa' to 'dum pendebat Filius' nine times, and so this also forces him to overwork his expressive chromatic theme. In almost every number such repetitions, though never so large a number, recur. It is always fatal when one feels the words are being made to conform to the music in a forced, not a true marriage. It is a case of 'prima la musica, dopo le parole' (the theme of Strauss's last opera *Capriccio*) but the question of the primacy of one or the other lies with the changing nature of the text. There is a glaring instance in Schubert's E flat Mass where, in the Creed, the composer repeats 'Et incarnatus est—Crucifixus', so that Christ is twice made man and crucified! Beethoven's immediate repetition of 'Et vitam venturi saeculi' at length in his *Missa Solemnis* is another matter altogether. He is triumphantly asserting belief in everlasting life. I recall a French film, *Roman d'un tricheur*, in which a small boy was sent out to collect mushrooms for a family feast, but strictly forbidden to eat any. As the mushrooms were of the poisonous variety the entire assemblage, all but he, perished. I can see him now, with an expressive shrug of the shoulders, saying to the Curé, 'I could be sorry for one, but *eleven*!' Well, I can be sorry, so to say, for the Virgin Mary, many times, but not *nine* in succession.

Dvořák's *Stabat Mater* is, then, a gravely flawed work with, nevertheless, some beautiful and imaginative music in it. The widely spaced unisons in the first bars of the orchestral prelude at the start paint a poignant picture of the Mother looking up at her tortured Son on the Cross; the agonized emotion generated thereafter in a slow rise to a catastrophic climax is very moving and the broad chromatic melody that succeeds is also treasurable. All this is woven into the movement, but with the climax too often repeated.

In the final movement the same material is used but the crescendo that led to a shattering discord before now *ascends* to a radiant 'Paradisi Gloria'.

The best of the remaining movements are the first section of the solo quartet 'Quis est homo' and the choral 'Eja mater', set as a funeral march, and there are many felicities of orchestration all through.

Dvořák's operas, full of lovely music, all suffer from a lack of stage sense, and that is what is lacking here also. *Stabat Mater* is a drama just as the Requiem Mass (or any Mass) is a drama and—especially in a non-liturgical work—that is a consideration that must not be neglected. The great polyphonic composers did not think in this way, they achieve restrained drama by reason of being penetrated by the texts they were setting and the liturgical occasion, but today, with the apparatus of soloists, chorus, and orchestra and a huge harmonic vocabulary, the composer without a dramatic sense is in peril of boring us. There is sincere emotional feeling, in plenty, in Dvořák's *Stabat Mater*—the work was born of grief at the death of one of his children—but that, alas, is not enough. A perceptive critic wrote of a recent performance of the work, 'Any setting of words, to be valid, must illustrate and enhance the full range of their meaning', and it is in this, amongst other considerations, that Verdi's setting excels.

There are no soloists in Verdi's work, the writing, in four parts throughout, is predominantly harmonic and not a single line is repeated. The open fifths on the orchestra in the first three bars, the *second*-beat entry of the chorus in the next bar on the accented C sharp paint a heart-breaking picture of the lonely figure at the foot of the Cross.

Sta-bat Ma-ter do—lo—ro-sa, Juxta crucem la-cry—mo-sa.

Ex. 11

Verdi had made an intensive study of Palestrina when composing *Stabat Mater* and *Te Deum* and he employs the Roman master's technique—which is, of course, shared by all the great sixteenth-century polyphonists—of inventing motifs suggested by each line of the text and, so to say, dropping them into the flow of the rhythmic stream, where they become absorbed.

The dynamics in the work require, but do not always receive, the closest study. Thus the cry 'Per transivit gladius' for sopranos and tenors in octaves is marked *ppp*, for altos and basses *pp*, both phrases on the orchestra *pp*. How often is that balance realized?

At the shout of 'Et flagellis subditum' the horn is left sounding, diminuendo. As ever it warns, and it warns that Mary's Son is dying, forsaken, His human soul tells Him, in this darkest hour by His Father. The music is stark and, as the breath leaves the Saviour's body ('Dum emisit spiritum'), realistic.

Ex. 12

What could follow but an anguished sob (woodwind), at once checked, and an exquisitely consolatory move by the woodwind to the major key (E major) for the unaccompanied singing of 'Eja Mater, fons amoris'?

After the dramatic 'Crucifixi fige plagas, Cordi meo valide' the tension drops and the music from 'Tui nati vulnerati' to 'Fac me tecum plangere' is not distinctive, just quietly expressive of the words. This is surely deliberate, for the time quickens and at 'Fac me cruce inebriari' there is a big crescendo to 'Flammis me urar suc-census', with the first vowel of 'urar' singled out for strong emphasis and taking the sopranos up to high B flat. The dreaded flames burst

out in the orchestral part, only to die away as the poet, as the distant
trumpet sounds, prays for Mary to be with him on the Day of
Judgement that he may be victorious over death. The horn warns
again, and this time at the thought of death. The inspired last
lines of the poet, 'Quando corpus morietur', for basses alone, then
the whole chorus, *estremamente p*, as Verdi asks, sing 'Fac ut animae
donetur'. There is now the whirr of angelic wings, the sound of
harps, as the voices rise from the utter quietness of the last syllable
of 'Paradisi', with ever-increasing volume, to the radiant cry of
'gloria' (six-part chord, altos and basses divided). The fluttering
of the wings dies away, but the master dramatist has two exquisite
things for the orchestra to say. First of all, before 'Amen', the cellos
have a melodic phrase that seems to me to 'speak' and so echo, very
softly, the last words, 'Paradisi gloria'. After the 'Amen'—the
orchestra recalls the choral entry at the start: this was the price paid
in suffering, human and divine. What a master stroke that F natural
is—producing not a diatonic cadence, as a D there would have done,
but a modal cadence—and in some way giving a timeless feeling
at the close.

Ex. 13

Gounod's two settings of *Stabat Mater*, one of them to a French
text, are not worth discussion, and, as far as I can discover, the next
French composer of any repute to set the *Stabat Mater* was Francis
Poulenc (1899–1963) and memorably.

Martin Cooper says of him, in his book *French Music* (Oxford
University Press, 1961), 'He is a musical clown of the first order, a
brilliant musical mimic and an adroit craftsman, who pieces together
the most heterogeneous collection of musical styles to form an
unmistakably personal style of his own.' His was, indeed, a musical
personality without precedent in musical history. Vocal music was
always his strong suit. He wrote beautifully for the voice, as his
many songs attest. But he not only added to the gaiety of nations or,
in more serious mood, to the treasury of lovely lyrical songs. In 1936
he made a pilgrimage, moved by the tragic death of a friend in a car
accident, to the shrine of Our Lady of Rocamadour, where stands
one of the mysterious Black Virgins, of which the best known, I
suppose, is Our Lady of the Pillar in Chartres Cathedral. This
pilgrimage inspired Poulenc to compose his first religious work,
Litanies à la Vierge Noire, and led to further religious pieces and, in

1949, to the *Stabat Mater*. In the dedication of this work he commends the soul of his friend Christian Bérard, a notable figure in the theatrical world, to Our Lady of Rocamadour. He did, it is said, consider composing a Requiem Mass on the death of this friend, but felt unequal to dealing with the Day of Judgement! The work is scored for solo soprano, chorus, and a rather large orchestra, which includes three bassoons, three each of trumpets and trombones, tuba, and two harps. Poulenc makes no radical change of style. He retains his quirky, abrupt cadences at the end of the opening movement, and of 'Eja mater' and 'Fac ut ardeat', and concludes the work with a resounding dominant seventh chord. Many of his figures of accompaniment are familiar in other and sometimes frivolous connexions. Monotony of tempo, in this sectionalized work, is completely avoided. The composer ranges from very slow, as at 'O quam tristis', to very fast at 'Quis est homo'.

He is often at fault in the accentuation of the Latin text, as in 'dolōrosa' instead of 'dolorōsa', and this is the more exasperating as he sometimes gets it right. He can write, correctly, 'afflicta' and in the very next bar 'āfflicta', with a long note to underline the false quantity, but such things are not likely to bother the ordinary listener. It is interesting that he used the arpeggio accompaniment to the opening movement 'Stabat Mater dolorosa' in very much the same form in his opera *Dialogue des Carmelites* (1962), in the tragic last scene of the opera where the nuns, singing 'Salve Regina', are guillotined one by one. In the first scene of Act 3, where the assistant Prioress proposes the vow of martyrdom to the community, the orchestral introduction is a strongly rhythmic Sarabande. With Bach-like figuration, in *Stabat Mater*, the orchestral part of 'Fac ut portem Christi mortem' is marked *tempo de Sarabande* and is clearly the source for the scene mentioned. The poignant first movement, which repeats the opening words and ends with 'filius', unaccompanied, is followed by a violent setting of 'Cujus animam gementem' arising from 'per transivit gladius', and that last word is repeated, *pp*, with a sudden snarl on the trumpet in the orchestral part. 'O quam tristis et afflicta', a moving combination of unaccompanied and accompanied sections, has a pathetic phrase for brass, before the repeat of the first line, balanced by the final cadence on the strings. These two cadences are characteristic of Poulenc's harmonic inventiveness.

Ex. 14

Ex. 15

The setting of 'Quae moerebat' puzzles me. Woodwind are given amiable, conversational phrases at the start and finish and chorus and orchestra sound almost jaunty in the bulk of the movement and out of keeping with the words.

After a highly dramatic 'Quis est homo' comes a lovely setting of 'Vidit suum dulcem natum' begun by the solo soprano in most expressive phrases.

Vi — — — dit — su·um— dul — —cem na — — tum

Ex. 16

Shrill woodwind cries break out as the chorus end 'Dum emisit spiritum' as if earth felt the wound. The composer, imaginatively, brings in the arpeggio figures of the orchestral accompaniment in the first movement at the close, the chorus then murmuring 'spiritum' unaccompanied.

It is said that there is a Massenet lurking in every French composer of his time. If that is so he comes to the surface in the luscious tune, on the violins, that we hear as the chorus begin 'Virgo, virginum praeclara', and for once I am glad the words are repeated so that we get the tune and its emotional accompaniment again.

Ex. 17

'Fac ut portem', as I have mentioned above, is a Bach-like Sara-bande (exit Massenet): it is the strongest movement in the work and the marked rhythm is maintained throughout.

'Quando corpus morietur', the last movement, begins impres-sively, unaccompanied, but the 'Paradisi gloria' phrases, adequate to the occasion, are spoilt, to my mind, by blatant smothering orchestral chords which have a very material effect. Poulenc, how-ever, repeats the words six times and for the last three brings back once more the 'très calme' string arpeggios of the first movement, which just about save the situation. Such is the offering of this very sophisticated *Jongleur de Notre Dame* and one can be sure it was graciously accepted by Our Lady of Rocamadour.

We come now to an English work, Lennox Berkeley's *Stabat*

Mater for six solo voices and chamber orchestra (strings, single woodwind, horn, harp, cymbals, and timpani) composed for The English Opera Group in 1940 and dedicated to Benjamin Britten. The composer studied with Nadia Boulanger in Paris and that wonderful and forceful teacher has left her mark on his style, and Stravinsky, perhaps, his on Berkeley's orchestration. This is a subtle, intimate work without the surface appeal of the Poulenc. Its ten movements are the equivalent, as far as the analogy will go, of the illuminations in one of the Prymers of mediaeval times that contained the *Stabat Mater*, together with the Little Office of the B.V.M. and the Office of the Dead.

The delicacy of the writing is at once apparent in the orchestral introduction before the voices enter *a cappella*. Against a background of gently pulsating notes on the harp and soft, spaced-out clashes on the cymbals, there are stressed chords on first violins and the violas

Ex. 18

over a pedal note on the cellos. The flute mourns in phrases the two sopranos will presently sing, and all the rest thereafter in octaves at 'per transivit gladius', their F sharps clashing against the G of the strings at this climactic moment.

Ex. 19

Berkeley's vocal lines are beautifully moulded and respect proper accentuation, as in the phrases for the lovely 'O quam tristis et afflicta'. Harp chords and a tremolo here and there on second violin and viola quietly intensify the compassion the composer puts into 'Quis est homo, qui non fleret' for solo baritone. 'Pro peccatis', *allegro*, is the first quick and dramatic movement, the tempo slowing for 'Vidit suum dulcem natum' with 'dum emisit spiritum' mono-toned in octaves by the vocal quartet. This is unexpectedly followed by an anguished outburst on the full orchestra. The solo tenor is given 'Eja mater, fons amoris'. His beautifully designed vocal line ends with the very expressive phrase below.

Ex. 20

The composer weaves the sorrowful figure from the introduction to the work into the accompaniment of 'Fac me tecum' for contralto solo, the first of the two longest movements in the work, with the orchestral part dividing the single lines with interludes.

After the lovely 'Virgo, virginum praeclara' Berkeley summons up all his forces for a dramatic setting of 'Fac me plagis vulnerari', etc., for solo soprano. Wailing phrases on clarinet and bassoon at first accompany the voice, the tension and volume of tone grow, a drum rolls, the flute and clarinet rush one up the other down, and at last the soprano declaims 'Flammis', the woodwind vividly illustrating that word. The soprano then sings the whole line with a great swirl of a phrase on the first word, and so reaches the peak climax 'Per te' in three short utterances, the last rising to high B flat 'Per te, Virgo, sim defensus'.

The orchestral introduction to the last movement is exquisite and must be examined in the score to see the fine choice of instrumental colour and the perfect placing of each part.

The flute—which was in classical Greece an instrument of mourning—murmurs a melody of consoling beauty, with bass clarinet and horn joining in. Long notes in each bar for harp, woodwind, horn, and then strings, sound like tolling bells as the voices sing 'Christe cum sit hinc exire', continuing the melody at 'Quando corpus morietur', but there is no crescendo, simply a *forte* mark at 'Fac ut animae donetur' succeeded by *p*, then *pp*, at 'Paradisi gloria', which is sung by all six voices, unaccompanied, up to the final vowel of 'gloria'. Here the opening bars of the orchestral introduction quietly return. This time the flute (and harp) still mourns, but in the background; it is the rising phrases on the strings, reaching the heights, that take us with them and hold us till the beatific vision fades.

After the great success of Karol Szymanowski's setting of *Stabat*

Mater at its first performance in 1928, in Poznan, the Polish composer wrote, 'Each man must go back to the earth from which he derives. Today I have developed into a national composer, not only sub-consciously but with a thorough conviction, using the melodic treasures of the Polish folk.' He had long since exorcized the spell cast over him by the music of Richard Strauss, he had taken stock of, without becoming enslaved by, polytonality or atonality, but he remained faithful (as his Mazurkas of 1924–26 for piano alone show) to the fruitful influences of Chopin, of Debussy and of Stravinsky, and out of these forged a truly personal style. In his *Stabat Mater*—scored for solo soprano, alto and baritone, chorus and an orchestra of medium size—strings, double woodwind, two trumpets, horn, percussion, and organ—Szymanowski laid aside the intense sensuous-ness of his settings of Oriental poets, such as Hafiz and Tagore, of earlier years, in which the pages are black with notes, fascinating, but sometimes rather enervating music, and wrote with appealing simplicity. I am not at all familiar with primitive Polish folk song but Szymanowski's melodic lines sometimes suggest the spirit of that, and sometimes are clearly of immediate origin. Flute and English horn in duet create at once an atmosphere of desolation in the short orchestral introduction. The stressed notes are the prime motif of the work, which I shall call 'motto'.

Ex. 21

The first words are sung by the soprano soloist, the chorus sopranos and altos echoing 'dolorosa' in the whole tones we associate with Debussy.

Ex. 22

The composer uses a Polish version of the text which intensifies the impression of his people at prayer in these Litany-like utterances, with their typical repetition of phrases, which form the middle section of the movement.

'Quis est homo, qui non fleret' for baritone solo and chorus has an

obsessive orchestral part for most of its length, one of the kind called
ostinato, always moving quietly, except for a brief crescendo at 'tanto
supplicio'. In the second section the motto is prominent in solo,
chorus, and orchestral parts, bursting out with full force at 'Pro
peccatis suae gentis, Vidit Jesum in tormentis', in the baritone part,
with stressed chords for chorus and orchestra, and so continuing,
as the orchestra return to the *ostinato*, up to the close of this powerful
movement. It brings to mind a pilgrimage in Holy Week to the
famous Shrine of Our Lady at Czestochowa. 'Dum emisit spiritum'
is marked *ff*. It was a hard death.

In 'Eja mater', for alto solo and chorus, the soloist is in two-part
counterpoint with the English horn, and there is a lovely movement
when she sings 'Sancta Mater istud agas' to the vocalized 'ah' of the
chorus, accompanied by full parallel chords in the orchestra. In this
movement, too, the motto is prominent.

'Fac me tecum pie flere' is an exquisite *a cappella* chorus which,
paradoxical as it may seem, recalls Palestrina's *Stabat Mater*. He could
never have disposed his parts in this way, but the inner fervour is
here and the same clarity of texture. There is a most beautiful
cadence at 'Donec ego vixero'. Almost everything in this work is
unexpected.

Ex. 23

'Virgo virginum praeclara', marked *allegro moderato*, a vigorous
baritone solo, gives again the impression of a crowd of pilgrims
murmuring in response. Now comes the most powerful and
dramatic section of the work, a long crescendo from 'Fac me plagis
vulnerari' to 'Flammis me urar succensus'. The basses in the orchestra
reiterate a rhythmic figure up to the great climax when the organ
brings in a deep pedal note below the tempestuous upper parts, vocal
and instrumental. Here the motto is constantly declaimed by the
singers. This is indeed the 'die judicii'. The tempo changes from
allegro moderato to *andante tranquillissimo* as, to the accompaniment of
two flutes, the solo soprano sings 'Christe, cum sit hinc exire' with a
lovely version of the motto in the orchestral part, echoed by the
chorus.

The composer makes 'Paradisi gloria' a quiet prayer for the granting of the Beatific Vision. At the close the soloist and chorus, un-accompanied, sing 'Fac ut animae donetur, Paradisi' to very full harmonies, there is a rest of one beat, then they end with 'gloria' to a spacious chord, with orchestra, of C sharp major.

This superb setting should be far better known than it is.

CHAPTER TWELVE

LISZT'S *VIA CRUCIS*

In his huge oratorio *Christus*, composed between 1855 and 1867, Liszt combined texts from 'the Holy Scripture and the Catholic Liturgy'; the latter included settings of *Stabat Mater* and the Christmas poem, also by Jacopone da Todi, *Stabat Mater speciosa*, a picture of the Virgin Mary watching beside the cradle of Our Lord at Bethlehem, and by far the better music of the two settings.

In 1878 he began to compose *Via Crucis* on a libretto arranged from biblical quotations, Latin hymns, and German chorales for soloists, representing Jesus, Pilate and the mourning women, and chorus with organ accompaniment, completing the work in the following year. It failed to find a publisher in his lifetime and was not published or performed till more than forty years after his death. The first public performance took place in London in 1952 and was recognized as being a noteworthy example of Liszt's desire to renew sacred music by 'uniting the means of the Church and the theatre' —no new idea!—which he had expressed in an essay 'On the Church music of the future' written in 1834, when he was only twenty-three years old. In the last seven years of his life Liszt seemed to be composing for himself, not for the public. His harmonies are experimental—the use of whole tones and acute dissonance—and a number of the songs and piano pieces of this period have no conclusive end. His glittering career seems to have become as dust and ashes to him and he has expressed in these works a profound sense of disillusion.

The Stations of the Cross are a series of fourteen pictures, or carvings, which depict incidents in the last hours of Christ's life, his condemnation to death by Pilate, after being mocked, beaten, and spat upon, His carrying of the Cross to Calvary along the *Via dolorosa*. Only two of the incidents in this tragic journey are related by the Evangelists: Simon of Cyrene being made to help in bearing the Cross, and Christ's words to the Daughters of Jerusalem, 'Weep not over me, weep for yourselves and for your children.' Arrived at Calvary, the incidents of the tenth to the fourteenth stations are those of the Passion, the stripping of Christ's clothes, the proffered gall, the nailing to the Cross, His death, and the Deposition. The origin of this devotion goes back to the practice of the early Christian pilgrims in following the traditional route from Pilate's house to Calvary in loving companionship with the Saviour. The devotion was popularized by the Franciscans in the later Middle Ages, but the sequence of incidents now included was not settled until the eighteenth to the nineteenth centuries.

The Prelude to Liszt's *Via Crucis* is a setting of the great Passiontide hymn by Venantius Fortunatus (*c.* 535?–*c.* 600) 'Vexilla regis prodeunt' ('The royal banners forward go'), written for the reception of a relic of the Cross at Poitiers on 19 November 569, and once used as a processional hymn on Good Friday. In the now reformed liturgy it is sung only at Vespers during Passiontide, and on the Feasts of the Cross on 3 May and 14 September. Liszt sets the first and the fourth verses in unison, following this after 'Amen', with the ninth verse 'O Crux ave spes unica' ('Hail, Cross, our only hope') in four-part polyphony, concluding with a double 'Amen'. The harmonic treatment is neo-modal.

The First Station, 'Jesus is condemned to death', is depicted in a turbulent organ solo, after which Pilate (solo baritone) cries, 'I am innocent of the blood of this just man.' The pattern is much the same for the Second Station, an organ solo with stressed chords as the heavy Cross is laid on Christ's shoulders and, after a silent bar, the baritone sorrowfully chanting, 'Hail, hail, Cross.' The organ concludes the movement with an *ostinato* bass section—the dolorous march has begun—and over this bass a mournful theme rises, formed out of the bass notes at the start of the movement.

Ex. 1

At the Third Station the tenors and basses, in octaves, cry 'Jesus falls', to violently dissonant chords on the organ; as these cease, there is a reference to 'O Crux ave' in single notes.

Ex. 2

Liszt now brings in the first verse of *Stabat Mater* sung by the sopranos, in thirds, to the plainsong hymn melody. The chromatic nature of his writing comes to the fore in the Fourth Station, 'Jesus meets his Mother', a most moving organ solo which, as He rises from the ground and sees His Mother kneeling before Him, ends with a poignant and very simply accompanied melody (directed to be played on the choir manual).

Ex. 3

The Fifth Station, 'Simon of Cyrene helps Jesus to carry the Cross', is again an organ solo with some deeply compassionate phrases derived from the 'Crux ave spes unica' verse of 'Vexilla regis'. The march section of the Second Station is then recapitulated. For the Sixth Station, 'Jesus meets Veronica', Princess Wittgenstein chose the Lutheran Passiontide hymn by Paul Gerhardt *O Haupt voll Blut und Wunden* (1656), best known to us in Bach's settings to the melody of Hans Leo Hassler's *Herzlich thut mich verlangen* (1601) and one of three settings of the melody in the St Matthew Passion. I think it possible that the Princess, or perhaps Liszt, remembered the beautiful use of the chorale melody in Bach's Church Cantata (No. 159) for Quinquagesima, *Sehet, wir gehen hinauf nach Jerusalem* ('See now, we go up to Jerusalem'), which is based on the Gospel for the Sunday, Luke 18: 31–43, and which ends with the chorale 'Jesu, deine Passion' ('Jesu, all thy bitter pain was for my salvation'). In the Cantata, after Jesus's words and a long recitative for alto commenting on the prophecy of his Passion, the latter has an aria, 'I follow Thee now through shame and through woe', during which the Passion chorale melody is sung by the solo sopranos to the words, 'I stand here, Lord, beside Thee, O bid me not depart', one of Bach's beautiful weavings together of complementary thoughts, and separate melodic strands. Liszt reproduces Bach's own harmonies but prefaces the chorale with sorrowful phrases, in single notes on the organ. The Seventh and Ninth Stations have the same words and music as the Third ('Jesus falls'), but raised a semitone and a minor third respectively. And in each case the first verse of *Stabat Mater* is sung as before but raised a semitone for the Seventh (B flat) and put in B flat minor for the Ninth.

In the Eighth Station, 'Jesus speaks to the women of Jerusalem', the music, a great deal more chromatic and dissonant than in the Fourth, where Jesus sees His Mother, generates tremendous emotional tension: it breaks off on a harsh chord.

Ex. 4

There is a short silence, then Liszt repeats the single-note phrases that preceded 'O Sacred Head, sore wounded', after which Jesus speaks, unaccompanied, 'Weep not for me but for yourselves and for your children'. The women burst out again in lamentation. Suddenly trumpets ring out in a brief section marked *allegro marziale*.

Liszt's fanfare calls to mind the callous brutality of the Roman soldiers who will not let their victim linger on the way and continually urge Him on. And so, utterly spent, He falls a third time (Ninth Station).

At the Tenth Station the procession has arrived at Calvary: Jesus is stripped and offered gall to drink. The music, for organ alone, has an obsessive chromatic phrase in almost every bar, underlining the humiliation of the Son of Man, with a counter-melody expressive of his refusal to accept any alleviation of the dire pain to come (Eleventh Station) when He is nailed to the Cross and the crowd (tenors and basses) shout out 'Crucify' to violently dissonant chords on the organ.

The Twelfth Station begins with Christ's great cry from the Cross, 'Eli, Eli, lama Sabacthani?' (bass solo unaccompanied) ('My God, My God, why hast Thou forsaken me?'), left untranslated, followed by poignant, despairing chords on the organ, and these by His prayer 'In manus tuas commendo Spiritum meum' ('Into Thy Hands I commend my Spirit'). The recitative, which ends on a note of absolute peace, is succeeded by a very beautiful section for the organ based on the melody of 'O Crux ave spes unica' which gradually rises in triumph as the Saviour dies, conquering Death for good and all. He utters His final word 'Consummatum est' ('It is finished') and this is very softly repeated by the altos, then, in two parts, by the sopranos, as if murmured by the sorrowing women at the foot of the Cross.

The chorus now sing the chorale 'O Traurigkeit, O Herzeleid', harmonized by Liszt.

The Thirteenth Station, 'The body of Jesus is taken down from the Cross', for organ, beautifully recapitulates the *Stabat Mater* melody and the music of the Fourth Station ('Jesus meeting His Mother'), thus depicting her receiving the body of her Son into her arms. At the Fourteenth Station, as 'The body of Jesus is laid in the tomb', the chorus sing 'O Crux ave spes unica' ('Hail Holy Cross, our only hope. In this season of Passiontide give us an increase of holiness to the good and pardon to sinners. Amen'). The opening words 'Ave Crux', after the 'Amen', are repeated five times, the last time unaccompanied.

So ends this profoundly moving work. It is, in effect, a private meditation for those who can enter fully into the spirit of it. To others it may perhaps seem fragmentary, its slow tempi monotonous, and may seem to throw too great a burden on the organ. We are fortunate to have a fine performance and recording of it.

CHAPTER THIRTEEN

THE HOLY WEEK OFFICE OF *TENEBRAE*

Reforms, however necessary, are apt to remove desirable as well as undesirable accretions and put nothing so valuable in their place. To my mind such was the case when the reformed rites were put into force on 16 November 1955, by the general decree of Pius XII (*Maxima Redemptionis Nostrae Mysteria*) and carried out the next year during Passiontide. Up to that time, ever since the later Middle Ages, the beautiful service of *Tenebrae* was sung on the evenings of Wednesday, Maundy Thursday, and Good Friday; but as this was not a primitive practice, and because of the restoration of rites that had their origin in the seventh and eighth centuries to their proper place, displacing later accretions, *Tenebrae* can now only be sung, if at all, in the mornings. *Tenebrae* (Darkness) is simply another name for the Night Offices of Mattins and Lauds and symbolizes the darkness that covered the whole earth from the sixth to the ninth hour when Christ died, illustrated by the practice of extinguishing one by one the lights in the church as the service proceeded. It was a long-established custom for the secular clergy bound to the recitation of the Divine Office to anticipate Mattins and Lauds of the day following on the previous evening, but in monastic houses these two Offices are sung or more usually said, any time from after midnight up to five-thirty—the stricter the order, the earlier the hour! The reform, however, ruled out the possibility of anticipating Mattins and Lauds on the evenings of Wednesday to Friday in Holy Week and the Office is now said or, more rarely, sung in the mornings of the correct days. The result has been the virtual disappearance of some of the most beautiful music in the Church's great treasury, and so it is left to the radio and the gramophone record to give us what they can of it, but of course divorced from the symbolic setting now to be described.

A tall triangular frame on a stand, made to hold fifteen candles, was set on the Epistle side (that is on the right hand as seen from the nave) of the Sanctuary. Each side of the triangle held seven candles, the fifteenth one being placed at the top. Mattins of the three great days of Holy Week, Maundy Thursday (the traditional English name for the day and derived from the practice of the symbolic washing of the feet, carried out by Our Lord at the Last Supper (John 13 : 24)), Good Friday, and Holy Saturday consists, musically, of the chanting of psalms and antiphons, and the singing of lessons and responsories, divided into three 'Nocturns'. Each of these Nocturns contains three psalms, with their antiphons sung before and after each psalm, three lessons, taken, in the first Nocturn, from the Lamentations of the prophet Jeremiah, in the second Nocturn from a Tract by St Augustine on the psalms, and in the third Nocturn from the First Epistle of St Paul to the Corinthians, and on Good Friday and Holy Saturday from St Paul's Epistle to the Hebrews. The 'lessons' are all followed by responsories. These latter take their material wholly or partly from Scripture (figurative and prophetic passages from the Old Testament, narrative from the New Testament, and original material of unknown authorship dating from about the fourth century). They follow an invariable pattern: Opening and Conclusion, Versicle, Conclusion repeated, but at the end of the third responsory both Opening and Conclusion are repeated. These patterns form the sequence, A, B, C, B and A, B, C, B, A, B. George Malcolm, in a note on the sleeve of the fine recording with the Westminster Cathedral Choir, of Victoria's Responses for *Tenebrae*, says, 'The Lessons unfold the doctrine of the Redemption, whilst the choral Responsories provide, in dramatic and often highly imaginative form, a series of vivid glimpses into the events, and the human emotions, of Christ's last days on earth.'

During Matins one of the candles on the triangular stand is extinguished at the close of each psalm, first on one side then on the other, so that by the end of the Office, nine candles will have been put out. The same practice is followed in Lauds, which comes immediately after and consists of five psalms, the first of which, on each of the three days, is Psalm 50, 'Miserere mei Deus' ('Have mercy on me, O Lord, according to Thy mercy'), so that fourteen candles will now have been extinguished, leaving only the fifteenth candle at the top of the stand. During the singing of the Canticle of Zachariah, 'Benedictus Dominus Deus, Israel' ('Blessed be the Lord, God of Israel'), the acolyte goes up to the High Altar and after each verse puts out the six great candles burning there, moving rhythmically as he does so, in alternation, from the Gospel to the Epistle side. While the antiphon is repeated the acolyte takes the fifteenth candle from the stand and places it, leaving it lit, behind the High Altar on the Epistle side. All the lights in the church are put out: it is left in darkness.

After the *Benedictus*, the antiphon 'Christus factus est', which has a beautiful plainsong setting, is extended on Good Friday and Holy

Saturday in the following manner. The example below shows the splendid rise of the melody at the close.

Christus factus est pro nobis obediens usque ad mortem— mortem autem crucis—propter quod et Deus exaltavit illum et dedit illi nomen, quod est super omne nomen.	*Christ became obedient for us unto death—even the death of the Cross —wherefore God hath also exalted him, and hath given him a name which is above every name.*

Propter quod et De-us ex-al-ta-vit il——lum———

Ex. 1

In the darkness the odd verses of the psalm 'Miserere mei, Deus' are sung by the choir, the even ones are said by the clergy and people. After this the presiding priest quietly recites the following prayer:

'Look down, we beseech thee, O Lord, upon this thy family, for the sake of which Our Lord Jesus Christ hesitated not to be betrayed into the hands of wicked men, and to undergo the torment of the cross. Who with thee—' The rest of the little doxology is said silently. After a short pause a small noise is made with the choir books on the desks to signify that the service is concluded. The lit candle is brought from behind the altar, and the church is illuminated as all rise and depart.

The entire service, clothed in plainsong, was sung in monasteries of strict observance, but in the great age of polyphony it naturally attracted many fine settings of the Lamentations, the Responsories, the 'Benedictus' and the psalm 'Miserere mei, Deus'. The best known of settings of the Lamentations are by Palestrina, Victoria, Lassus, Tallis and Byrd.

The Lamentations mourn the desolation of Judah after the destruction of Jerusalem in 580 B.C. Each of the five chapters which comprise the book contains twenty-two divisions, which is the number of consonants in the Hebrew alphabet, and each strophe begins with its respective letter, Aleph, Teth, Jod, and so on. The form is that of an acrostic.

Mendelssohn was greatly impressed with Palestrina's *Lamentations* when he heard them sung in the Sistine Chapel in Holy Week of 1831, but he was disturbed by the copious ornamentation the Pontifical Choir applied to the composer's vocal lines—a bad tradition that had arisen towards the end of the sixteenth century. With a singular lack of imagination he took Palestrina to task for wasting beautiful music over the announcement 'Incipit Lamentatio Jeremiae Prophetae' and the Hebrew letters that I have mentioned above, not perceiving that these sections were of the nature of instrumental preludes to what followed.

The plainsong melodic formula or 'tone' for the Lamentations is very ancient and Jewish in origin.

In ci-pit Lamenta-ti-o Je-re-miae Prophet-ae. AL-eph———

Ex. 2

This formula is used in part in all the settings by the composers I have mentioned above, and most notably, I think, by William Byrd at the end of his setting, the only one he composed, of the first *Lamentation* of Maundy Thursday. He quotes the first phrase only.

Composers could set the Hebrew letters with far more contra-puntal freedom than was possible in the texts. The latter demanded to be declaimed and this entailed a great deal of chordal writing, but with frequent use of points of imitation and contrasted note values in one or more of the parts. The result, for those who take the trouble to follow the splendid texts as they listen to the music, is extremely impressive. The vocalizations on the vowels of the letters, Aleph, Beth, Lamed, etc., reflect the sorrowful emotions of the texts they precede and sometimes, also, anticipate their musical material. In the first of the Lamentations for Maundy Thursday in his Second Book Palestrina announces 'Beth' briefly and simply, but how poignant is the first tenor's cry arising above the top part!

Ex. 3

Those downward going notes become the chief motive of the moving verse that follows ('Weeping, she weepeth in the night, and her tears are upon her cheeks' Ex. 3(b)).

Palestrina composed four complete sets of Lamentations. In this set, as in the other, he varies the scoring from three to eight parts, and also the distribution of the voices. Tallis, on the other hand, scores for five voices throughout his setting of the two of Maundy Thursday's Lamentations, the only ones he composed. His setting of 'Beth', more elaborate in texture than Palestrina's, is most beautiful. The A flat the sopranos hold throughout the four bars, and the first sound heard is an inverted 'pedal point' to the lamenting parts below.

Ex. 4

The top part, in all these settings, is made to stand out with unusual prominence.

Each Lamentation ends with the words, 'Jerusalem, Jerusalem, convertere ad Dominum Deum tuum' ('Jerusalem, Jerusalem, turn again to the Lord thy God').

When I heard the Lamentations sung in the plainsong tone by a magnificent solo tenor in the basilica of St John Lateran, this simple refrain sounded as if the prophet was addressing mankind not only in the past, but all down the ages to this very day. Tallis, at the end of the first section of his work, has given the words the most imaginative polyphonic setting of any that I know. There is a heart-breaking urgency in the repeated notes, a warning that cries to be heeded.

Ex. 5

I come now to the Responsories with which each Lamentation and Lesson conclude in the three Nocturns of *Tenebrae*. The whole twenty-seven were set by Marc Antonio Ingegneri (*c.* 1545–1592) and for long passed as a work by Palestrina. Beautiful as they are, the eighteen settings in Victoria's masterpiece *Officium Hebdomedae Sanctae* ('The Office of Holy Week') published in Rome in 1583, surpass them, and all others. This great collection includes settings of the Passions of St Matthew (Palm Sunday) and St John (Good Friday), the Lamentations, the canticle Benedictus, and Psalm 50, 'Miserere mei, Deus' in Lauds.

Victoria's dedications of his works are to Popes and Prelates, Princes and Kings, but the *Officium* is dedicated to the Holy Trinity. Into the Responsories, this 'priest who happened to be a composer' put the whole of his deeply religious being. He is living through the tragic and dramatic events of Holy Week in every bar of his music. One can only regret that he did not set also the Responsories of the first Nocturns but probably he felt that his settings of the *Lamentations* precluded this on account of their length. I can here only select some of the most outstanding numbers.

GOOD FRIDAY. SECOND NOCTURN, SECOND RESPONSORY. MATTHEW 27: 35, 45–6

Tenebrae factae sunt dum crucifigerent Jesum Judaei: et circa horam nonam exclamavit Jesus voce magna: Deus meus, tu quid reliquisti? Et inclinato capite emisit spiritum. *V.* Exclamans Jesus voce magna, ait: Pater, in manus tuas commendo spiritum meum. Et inclinato. etc.	*There was darkness when the Jews crucified Jesus: and about the ninth hour Jesus cried with a loud voice My God, why hast thou forsaken me? And He bowed His Head, and gave up the ghost. V. When Jesus had cried with a loud voice, he said: Father, into Thy hands I commend my spirit. And He bowed His Head, etc.*

These words inspired one of the finest pieces of plainsong and one which gives the lie to those who deny the word-painting in this generally reserved art. The contrast between the last low-pitched phrase of 'voce magna' and the high-pitched 'Deus meus' leaps to the eye.

Vo - ce —— ma — gna De —— us me —— us.

Ex. 6

This plainsong was well known to Victoria. By tradition his setting of the responsory, as that of the second responsory of Holy

Saturday 'Aestimatus sum', was sung by men's voices only. Jesus's great cries take the first tenor above the stave in the first part of the responsory.

ex–cla ma–vit Je–sus vo ce ma – – – gna:

Ex. 7

'Emisit Spiritum', sung in detached notes, makes an unforgettable effect.

GOOD FRIDAY. THIRD NOCTURN, THIRD RESPONSORY (LAM. I: 12)
A hard-bitten choirmaster, eminent in his profession, confessed to me that he could never conduct this responsory without weeping, nor can I hear it dry-eyed.

Caligaverunt oculi mei a fletu meo quia elongatus a me, qui consolabitur me. Videte, omnes populi, si est dolor similis sicut dolor meus. *V*. O vos omnes qui transitis per viam, attendite et videte. Si est etc.

Mine eyes are dim with weeping, there because the Comforter who should console me is far from me. Behold, all ye nations, if there be any sorrow like unto my sorrow. V. O all ye who pass by, behold and see. If there be, etc.

The words, 'Si est dolor' are thrown into high relief with piercing beauty, and poignancy, at the treble entry.

Si est do-lor si – – – – mi–lis sic– –ut do-lor me – – – us

Ex. 8

The verse 'O vos omnes' is scored for alto, tenor, and bass at a low pitch so that on the return to 'Si est dolor' the high treble entry wrings the heart again.

HOLY SATURDAY. SECOND NOCTURN, SECOND RESPONSORY.
The words of this responsory begin with those of the verse in 'Caligaverunt', 'O vos omnes', and then add those of the conclusion, 'Si est dolor'. Victoria set this responsory twice, and in the earlier version used the falling fifth that is one of his most expressive fingerprints. The cadence in the 1585 *Officium* is less moving but 'Si est dolor' is even more grief-stricken than in 'Caligaverunt'. The remainder of the text, 'Similis sicut dolor meus', has a top part very

similar to that in 'Caligaverunt', but with the added pathos of a repeat of 'sicut dolor meus'.

The high tide of emotion flows through the verse 'Attendite universi populi, et videte dolorem meum' ('O all ye nations behold and see my sorrow') for two trebles and alto, in which the first treble is kept at the top of the stave at the start and finish. His last phrase is identical with the one at 'Si est dolor', now to be repeated, which intensifies the imagined cry of the lonely, stricken Christ. Victoria's art, in such aspects as these, has been compared, sometimes in extravagant terms, to that of his great contemporary El Greco. In the course of making this comparison Cecil Gray writes in his *History of Music* (Kegan Paul, 1928), 'In no other music, in hardly any other art whatsoever do we find such intense religious exaltation, such unearthly ecstasy, such white-hot incandescence of spirituality, such burning aspiration towards the infinite. . . . Victoria's frenzied, exultant rhythms and soaring melodic lines frequently generate an emotional intensity which is apt to be slightly disturbing, and is certainly less conducive to the cultivation of a devotional mood than the calm self-possessed movement and suave concord of his Roman rival—that is Palestrina.'

Mr Gray is altogether too rhapsodic and, in any case, there is an equal ecstasy, etc., in the Lydian slow movement of Beethoven's String Quartet in A minor op. 132 which almost goes 'through' the string tone; but if, as is probable, he had heard the Responsories sung by a Spanish choir, I can understand how he was carried away. The Roman Church in this country has inherited the Anglican tradition of reserved choral singing, if not its voice production, but the hearing of 'Caligaverunt' and 'O vos omnes' in Westminster Cathedral in the great days of Richard Terry, when *Tenebrae* was one of the outstanding musical events of the year and drew, as they say, 'all London', certainly justified the substance if not the expression, of what Gray says.

At his most dramatic Victoria is never 'frenzied' nor, for that matter, is Palestrina always 'calm and suave'.

To come to Lauds, the *Benedictus* is sung in alternate plainsong and polyphony, with the polyphonic sections ornamenting and elaborating the plainsong psalm tone, and Victoria sets Psalm 50, 'Miserere mei, Deus' to a simple harmonized psalm tone throughout. It is much more effective to confine polyphony to the odd verses and leave the even ones to be spoken, as I have described above.

A word should be said about two famous settings of Psalm 50.

The nine-voice setting by Gregorio Allegri (1582–1652) was so jealously guarded by the Sistine Choir that to copy it was a crime punishable by excommunication. In spite of this the Emperor

Leopold I, King of Portugal, prevailed on the Pope to grant him copies. Mozart took it down from a performance in 1770, while in 1790 Burney published it in a book, *La Musica della Settimana Santa*, having got his copy from one of the Papal singers.

It is difficult to understand, today, why such a fuss should be made about what is fundamentally a simple and expressive piece of polyphony, but the answer lies in Leopold's dissatisfaction when, having secured a copy from the Pope, he had it performed in the Imperial Chapel in Vienna. The magic had vanished: he thought the Pope had palmed off some inferior composition on him. The fact is that the magic was largely imparted by the wonderful setting of the Sistine Chapel, and by the ornamentation of the embellished cadences. How sensational the treble's ascent to the high C at 'munda me' sounds can be heard in the King's College Chapel, Cambridge, recording of the piece.

The Allegri *Miserere* was sung in the anticipated *Tenebrae* of Maundy Thursday and Good Friday. The Popes did not always attend *Tenebrae* because of its lengthy music, particularly that of the 'Misereres'—the psalm has twenty verses. Pius VIII ordered that only six verses should be sung in 'figured music' and the rest, quickly, in plainsong. He was obviously a prototype of Mozart's Archbishop Colloredo of Salzburg.

The other setting, certainly also too long for liturgical purposes, is by Josquin des Prés. It is for five voices. At the eighteenth bar the tenors sing 'Miserere mei, Deus' to the first half of a plainsong psalm tone starting on D, and repeat the phrase at irregular intervals down six degrees of the scale, C, B, A, G, F, E. In the second part of the motet the procedure is reversed, the tenors moving upwards, each time, from E, and in a new rhythm, to their original starting point. The effect of this plea for mercy, rising to a climax, then humbly falling, is deeply moving.

3

Lutheran Funeral
Music

CHAPTER FOURTEEN

GERMAN REQUIEMS

Schütz and Brahms

Prayers for the dead, that they may rest in peace, are absent from both the official Lutheran and Anglican service books, although the initials R.I.P. are to be found on innumerable gravestones in English churchyards, which seems to show some confusion of thought! The Lutheran Reformers taught that souls are freed from sin by faith in Christ alone, without any works; and therefore, if so saved, go straight to heaven. The famous ninety-five theses which Luther nailed to the door of the Schlosskirche at Wittenberg in 1517 were directed against the doctrine of Indulgences, or pardons, which had been the subject of gross abuses in the late Middle Ages, and still was. Together with this doctrine Luther and his disciples rejected Purgatory, Masses for the dead, and many other Catholic practices. I am not writing a theological treatise but it is necessary to allude briefly to this radical break with the ancient practice, dealt with in the first three chapters of this book, of prayers for the dead and the resultant *Missa pro defunctis*.

The concept of 'rest' was retained—'rest in the Lord'—but free from its Catholic associations. At the funeral service in the church a hymn was sung, a sermon preached, and a concluding *Trauerlied* (funeral cantata) performed. It is such a work that I am here concerned with, the *Musikalisches Exequien* by Heinrich Schütz. A very interesting account of the origin and nature of his work is translated in the score, admirably edited by Arthur Mendel and published by Schirmer of New York, from which, with their kind permission, I shall quote extensively.

The title page is as follows:

MUSICAL EXEQUIES
As they were Observed at the Grand Funeral Ceremonies
in Christian memory
of the late Honoured
PRINCE HEINRICH
the Younger and Eldest Reuss (Lord of Plassen)

Member of the Council of His Imperial Roman Majesty
in Gretz (Cranichfeldt) Gera/Schleitz/Lobenstein/etc.
on the Fourth Day of February last in Gera/before and after the Funeral
Sermon/ and in Accordance with the Wishes often Expressed by his late
Highness during his life-time.
Sung to a Soft and Concealed Organ
for 6, 8 or more voices
and
with accompanying *Basso Continuo* in two copies, the one for the Organ,
the other for the Conductor, or the Violone
Together with a Detailed List of the Musical Contents of this Little
Work
and Instruction for the Necessary Arrangements, Addressed to the
Gracious Reader.
Humbly set to Music, by Command, in final Commemoration and
published in print by
Heinrich Schütz—Electoral Saxon Capell-Meister
Printed in Dresden by Wolf Seyffert in the year
1636

Schütz was born exactly a hundred years before Bach and in a
later chapter (p. 233) I have given some account of his life before he
finally settled in Dresden and of his profoundly religious nature.
He pays a warm-hearted tribute to Prince Heinrich, who was
sixty-four when he died, in some dedicatory verses in the preface
of the above publication, which, from the absence of formal
compliments, prove clearly that the Prince was his good friend as
well as his patron. He was not only an enthusiastic patron of the
arts but, 'Like David sang and played with true art'. In some of the
verses Schütz reveals, as Bach so wonderfully was to do in his music,
his attitude to death. He pictures his friend joyfully singing in the
heavenly choirs and assures him that when he (Schütz) is lifted
out of this vale of tears, he will join his friend with all the Cherubim
and Seraphim in singing round the throne of the Lamb of God.

The verses are followed by a description of three parts of the
'little work', which is in fact so long that part of it was sung after
as well as before the sermon.

1. All these sayings from Holy Writ and those verses of the Christian
hymns (chorales) which His late Highness during his life time secretly
had inscribed on the cover and on both sides and at the head and foot
of his sarcophagus, gathered together in a Concerto[1] and arranged in
the form of a German Mass, like the Latin *Kyrie, Christe, Kyrie eleison,
Gloria in Excelsis: Et in terra pax:* etc.

---

[1] *A title Bach often gave to his church cantatas.*

2. The words which His late Highness had chosen as the text for his funeral sermon 'Lord, if I but thee may have', etc.

3. The Song of Simeon 'Lord, now lettest thou thy Servant depart in peace', etc. which His late Highness had chosen for his burial. In the course of which a separate choir is introduced, singing different words 'Blessed are the dead', etc. There follow the Instructions for the Necessary Arrangements for each concerto.

These arrangements, except for the third part of the work where they are of special interest, need not be quoted.

The 'Concerto in the form of a German Requiem' is scored for six voices: two sopranos, one alto, two tenors, and one bass, these being used as solo voices or as an ensemble. At certain points the composer writes *cappella* in the sense that the sections so marked are to be sung by the chorus. Luther's holocaust did not extend to Gregorian chant. He adapted many plainsong hymns and had a great admiration for the church music of Josquin des Prés of whom he said, 'Others do what they can with notes, he does what he likes.' It is not surprising, therefore, that Schütz begins his concerto with the first tenor intoning the first half of one of the plainsong psalm tones. The male voices complete the tone and then move freely.

Ex. 1

Schütz's reference to the *Kyrie* becomes relevant at the choral section 'Lord God, Father in Heaven, have mercy on us all'. The two sopranos respond with 'Christ is my life, death is my gain' (corresponding to *Christe eleison*), the chorus continue 'Jesus Christ, God's son, have mercy on us all.' This is followed by the final *Kyrie* for alto and bass solos, 'Living, we live unto the Lord God, dying, we die but unto the Lord God. . . . Holy Spirit have mercy on us all.'

The next movement begins, as the first did, with a psalm tone for tenor to the words, 'For God so loved the world that He gave His only begotten Son', with the solo voices concluding the sentence, 'That whoever in Him believeth should not ever perish, but should have life everlasting.' I do not find any correspondence to the *Gloria* of the Mass in this section. It also introduces the first of the chorales the Prince had inscribed on his tomb, 'Nun freut euch, liebe Christen mein'.

The music is beautifully varied in texture and scoring and though simple in its appeal shows a masterly use of counterpoint and, as a study of the German text reveals, a great respect for correct declamation. The influence of 'the sagacious Monteverdi' whom Schütz had studied with in Venice some years before, is charmingly apparent in the several canonic duets.

A little farther on come the words 'but they are at peace' and each of the many times 'peace' is repeated in one or another voice it is always given notes of longer value than those preceding it. There is a descriptive section beginning 'Lo, our life doth reach but seventy years, or if higher only eighty' and in the same literal way that Bach, for example, set high ('priest') to a high note, Schütz, in like manner, puts (if) 'higher' on a high note, and when the note is twice repeated raises the note in pitch each time. There is a pathetically halting phrase after 'and tho' some sweetness it doth contain 'tis but toil—and trouble'.

After this burdened music comes a beautiful setting of 'I know that my Redeemer liveth' which, in point of a vocal line 'framed to the life of the words', is not surpassed by Handel.

Ex. 2

The movement ends in happy mood with the Redeemer's promise fulfilled.

> I die that I may set thee free and sin no more pursue thee.
> My life hath choked the serpent death,
> Rise up to heav'n with Me He saith,
> Where God will ever bless thee.

The motet, for two equal choirs, has the words of the text the Prince chose for his funeral sermon. 'Lord, and whom but Thee have I? Naught else do I ask in heaven or on earth. And tho' my flesh and spirit faint, yet Thou art my God, even my strength and heart's desire.' This is a most eloquent and finely constructed piece with a very effective stroke introduced in the penultimate bar, the rise of the first sopranos to their highest note.

And so we come to the third and best-known part of this grand
work, often sung by itself, the setting of the Song of Simeon, and
here I must quote Schütz' description of what he intends.

It must be known that this Concerto has two choirs, each choir with
its own words. The First Choir has three voices and recites the words of
Simeon, 'Lord, now lettest thou thy servant . . .' The Second Choir
has three voices, two sopranos and a baritone or high bass, and sings
the following words 'Blessed are the dead that die in the Lord'. By
means of this invention, that is by means of the Second Choir, the
author has wished to suggest to some degree the joy of the disembodied
souls of the blessed in heaven, in the company of the heavenly spirits
and holy angels. The First Choir should be close to the organ, while the
Second is in the distance—or however it seems best to arrange them.

Did Schütz, I wonder, take a hint here from Monteverdi's 'De
profundis', part of his lost funeral music for the Duke of Tuscany,
of which I spoke in Chapter 6? That, as described by a contemporary, was a dialogue between the souls in purgatory and the
angels visiting them. Schütz labels his solo sopranos Seraphim 1 and
2, and his bass solo 'Beata anima cum Seraphinis'.

The tenor sings the plainsong intonation of the canticle.

Ex. 3

The chorus continue 'in peace depart' and as they repeat these
words, very softly, the first soprano of the Second Choir, at a higher
pitch than the one singing the Canticle begins 'Selig sind die Todten
die in den Herrn sterben', the other two voices entering successively
thereafter. How well Schütz's sense of the dramatic serves him! The
music is exquisite and exquisitely devotional. A joyful 'Light to
lighten the Nations and to be the glory of Thy people Israel'
concludes this inspired work.

*

An incautious friend once questioned Brahms as to the nature of
his religious beliefs and received an abrupt answer which precluded
any further conversation on the topic. 'I have my faith', he said.
We know from Max Kalbeck, one of Brahms's greatest champions,
and the author of a four-volume biography of the composer (1904–
1914), that 'Nothing made him angrier than to be taken for an
orthodox church composer on account of his sacred compositions'.

The reference is to the motets with German words, and to the *Three Sacred Choruses* to Latin words familiar in the liturgy of the Roman Catholic Church. Brahms composed these, and many others, all for unaccompanied voices, for his Hamburg Ladies Choir (disbanded in 1858 when he moved to Vienna) and for the Vienna Philharmonic Society's Chorus, not for church use.

Brahms presumably chose to call his greatest choral work A German Requiem to disassociate it from the Latin Requiem Mass and make it clear that the text came from the Lutheran Bible. Schütz's title *Musikalisches Exequien* associates his work with an actual burial service but Brahms's came to be associated with, and in part inspired by, the deaths of Schumann in 1856 and of his own mother in 1861. The second number, 'Behold all flesh is but as grass', had its origin in a slow movement for an abortive symphony begun at the time of the Schumann tragedy, of which material from the first movement was used up in the corresponding movement of the D minor Piano Concerto, and in 1861 he had already arranged the text of four movements of what was turning out to be a cantata. By 1866 he had added two more movements, and last of all—and surely with special thought of his mother—came the lovely soprano solo, with chorus, 'Now hath man sorrow but yet I shall again behold you and fill your heart with rejoicing', to which the chorus respond 'Yea, I will give you comfort as one whom his mother comforts'.

Brahms was a life-long student of Luther's Bible and Florence May, his friend, pupil, and first English biographer, tells us 'the texts culled from various books of the Old and New Testaments and the Apocrypha have been chosen . . . as parts of the people's book of Luther's Bible, the accepted representative to Protestant Nations of the highest aspirations of man, and have been arranged so as to present the ascending ideas of sorrow consoled, doubt overcome, death vanquished'. Brahms does not pray once, let alone twice, for the dead. He expressed his point of view about his work—it is one of his rare confessional utterances—in a correspondence with Dr Karl Reinhalter, organist and choirmaster of Bremen Cathedral, where the six movements were performed under the latter's baton on Good Friday of 1868. In a letter dated 5 October of the previous year, Reinhalter wrote about the Requiem:

It occupies not only religious but purely Christian ground. The second number deals with the prediction of the return of the Lord, and in the last number but one there is express reference to the mystery of the resurrection of the dead 'We shall not all sleep'. For the Christian mind, however, there is lacking the point on which everything turns, namely the redeeming death of Jesus. . . . Moreover you say in the last movement 'Blessed are the dead which die in the Lord *from henceforth*', that is to say, after Christ has finished the work of redemption.

Brahms was not to be trapped into the logical argument. He explained that he had humanity as a whole in mind, that he had deliberately omitted verses such as those of John 3: 16, and selected others, 'Because I am a musician, because I needed them, because I cannot dispute the "from henceforth" of my revered poets, or strike it out'. There is, therefore, no commitment to Christianity in the Requiem, as Brahms saw it; though as he said it was for all humanity, it might have crossed his mind that it was for all mankind, past, present, and future, that Christ died, and in so doing conquered death. There is no knowing what he thought of Christianity, but there is ample evidence of his intense preoccupation, or, as some say, his obsession with death, as shown in his catalogue of works. In 1858, when he was in his twenty-fifth year, he composed a *Funeral Hymn*, for mixed voices and wind band (without flutes or trumpets, but with trombones), the theme of which foreshadows that of the first number of the *Vier Ernste Gesänge* (*Four Serious Songs*).

There are phrases in 'Feldeinsamkeit' and 'Mit vierzig Jahren' which remarkably foreshadow the frightening one in the second of the *Four Serious Songs*. The summer peace of the singer, lying in the grass gazing up at the blue sky flecked with white clouds, is faintly disturbed by the thought of death, and though the dark angel is not mentioned in 'Mit vierzig Jahren' the implication is that a man of forty is well on the way to the grave!

A chilling wind blows through 'Auf dem Kirchhof' ('At the Churchyard') tempered by a hush (where the music modulates into a consolatory C major) at the thought of the peacefully sleeping dead, at which point Brahms, as he himself admitted, introduces a reminiscence of the last chorale in Bach's *St Matthew Passion* 'Wenn ich einmal soll scheiden' ('If I should e'er forsake Thee, forsake me not, O Lord'). The majority of the *Eleven Chorale Preludes*, composed at various periods of his life and completed in the year before his death, are also concerned with death. The final one is a most moving setting of the melody with the words 'O Welt, ich muss dich lassen' ('O world, I must now leave you').

Brahms's point of view, in part, could be that of one who looks back from death to life, and there finds consolation. This is the spirit of the great funeral speech upon those who have fallen in war which Thucydides puts into the mouth of Pericles.

'I do not now commiserate the parents of the dead who stand here; I would rather comfort them. You know that your life has been passed amid manifold vicissitudes; and that they may be deemed fortunate who have gained most honour, whether an honourable death like theirs, or an honourable sorrow like yours, and whose days have been so ordered that the term of their happiness is likewise the term of their life . . . remember that your life of sorrow will not last long, and be comforted by the Glory of those who are gone.'

As G. Lowes-Dickenson says in his little gem of a book *The Greek View of Life* (Methuen, 1896), 'This represents perhaps what we call the typical attitude of the Greek. To seek consolation for death, if anywhere, then in life, and in life not as it might be imagined beyond the grave, but as it had been and would be lived on earth. . . . It is the spirit', Mr Dickenson adds, 'that Goethe noted as inspiring the sepulchral monuments of Athens.'

The choice of texts for the Requiem, however, seems to contradict this looking back from death to life lived and lost, and it is here again that Brahms may have made some equation between the Christian and Greek expressions of religion in their purest form. Michael Hamburger is very interesting in discussing this. 'As far as the ideological issues are concerned it would be nearer the truth to say that Hölderlin converted Christianity to himself, that is to say, he reconciled the principles with his previous (Greek inspired) system of thought and belief, very much in the same way as Leconte de Lisle did in his later years.'

Brahms set Hölderlin's *Hyperion's Song of Destiny* in 1868, two years after the completion of the Requiem. The first stanza of the poem speaks of the felicity of the immortals in their abode of beauty and light, the second of the hard and irremediable lot of man on earth.

> . . . Suffering men
> Dwindle and fall
> Blindly from one
> Hour to the next,
> Hurled like water
> From rock to rock,
> Downwards for years to uncertainty.[1]

This third and last stanza Brahms repeats twice to music harsh and bleak all through. Then he returns to the lovely melody of the E flat orchestral Prelude, put here into C, and a major sixth higher in pitch, and virtually with the same orchestration, flute and muted strings. Is this to be taken to mean, contrary to what Hölderlin expresses in his first two stanzas, that the uncertainty is resolved, or

---

[1] Poems of Hölderlin, *trs. Michael Hamburger (Nicholson & Watson, 1943).*

that the gods care nothing for man's fate and even, in some sense like the revolting, unchristian, and one hopes, now discarded doctrine of St Thomas, that the happiness of the blessed is increased by observing the torments of the damned or, finally, is it simply that musical considerations impelled Brahms to end his work in this way and not in an ineffective darkness?

The Requiem is not an oratorio, it is a choral symphony. Brahms had only once before, and not altogether successfully, in the D minor Piano Concerto, scored for full orchestra and now he used even larger forces, adding three trombones and tuba to the brass section, a third drum and a harp to the percussion, and paying far greater attention to tone colour. This is immediately apparent in the opening movement from which clarinets, all bright tones—trumpets and violins—are excluded, for the music is in mourning.

Brahms quotes the words of Christ twice, 'Blessed are they that mourn: for they shall be comforted' (Matthew 5: 4, the third of the Beatitudes, in the first movement in the work) and 'Now hath man sorrow, but yet I shall again behold you and fill your heart with such rejoicing as no man taketh from you' (John 16: 22) at the start of the fifth and last composed movement.

Comfort breathes in every measure of the lovely tranquil melody (cellos, violas) of the orchestral introduction to the first movement, which the chorus do not sing till the second of the two last verses of Psalm 126, and so is an anticipation of the 'coming again with joy' after the 'weeping' of that verse. The gently rising phrase the oboe plays and the chorus echoes, a beautiful moment, meditates on the comfort of which the words speak. The music is infused with the spirit of the German *Lied* whose treasury Brahms had already liberally enriched and which makes this work so grateful to sing. The use of the harp at the close, woodwind gently pulsating above, is a beautifully calculated touch of tone-colour.

It would be interesting to know how many listeners to the Requiem have noticed the reference Brahms makes in the second movement, 'Behold all flesh is but as grass', to the chorale *Wer nur den lieben Gott lässt walten* ('If thou but suffer God to guide thee'), the words and melody by Georg Neumark (1621–81). Bach uses it in eight of his church cantatas, the best known of which is No. 21, *Ich hatte viel Bekümmerniss* (My spirit was in heaviness), and he wrote four chorale preludes for organ on it. It can be found most easily in *The Little Organ Book* (No. 24) (Novello edn.).[1]

---

[1] *In an interesting article on this subject in* The Musical Times, *December 1952, John Gardner finds all the material in Brahms's Requiem derived from this Bach chorale.*

Wer nur den lie-ben Gott lässt wal ——— ten,

Ex. 4

This is not fortuitous: further evidence is supplied by the first
two notes of the chorale on the string basses in the first two bars
of this movement. The heavily burdened measures of the funeral
march in the dark key of B flat minor (muted strings and wind,
horns, trumpet and harp stressing the second beats) in the orchestral
introduction form a counter-melody to the chorale melody sung
by the chorus, 'Behold all flesh is but as grass', etc. (Peter I. 1: 24–5).

A German audience might be expected to recognize Brahms's
gloss on the chorale and hear in it an allusion to the words of the
trio, in the major key, of this funeral march, 'Be patient therefore
dearly beloved, unto the coming of the Lord' (James 5: 7–8), which
accords with the trust in God's guidance expressed in the first verse
of the chorale. Inevitably the sombre march returns, scored as before,
to be followed by a new section (not another trio) based on Isaiah
30: 10 'And the ransomed of the Lord shall return again', preceded
by a 'head-line', 'But the word of the Lord endureth for ever', with
trombones and trumpets prominent, that leads straight into the
allegro non troppo. This makes a feint at being a fugue, but fortunately
does not succeed. It is a rather conventional section but has an
imaginative coda, 'Joy everlasting shall be upon their heads' where
the clarinet, oboe, and flute in succession quietly recall the vigorous
theme at the start, the trombones more loudly a little later on, and
joy bubbles out in the rising scale passage on the strings.

The quiet end prepares us for the austere start of the third movement for solo baritone and chorus, 'Lord, let me know mine end
and the number of my days' (Psalm 39: 5–8). Brahms is so well read
in sixteenth-century polyphony and in Bach that one is continually
being reminded of things done before and repeated here, not copied
but thought out anew. Such is the fine declamation for the baritone,
accompanied only by horn, string basses and drums at the words,
'See now Thou hast made my days as but a span long before Thee,
and my lifetime is as nought to Thee'. What character the semi-
quavers give to the phrase! But the point I want to note here is the
raised pitch of the phrase, which begins at 'and my lifetime', and
the way it is approached. I have mentioned this matter of pitch
alteration in Chapter 9, but here the closer reference is to Bach's
Church Cantata No. 60 *O Ewigkeit, du Donnerwort* ('Eternity, thou
word of thunder') dealt with in the next chapter. The reader with
a score will notice the way the little semiquaver figure in (a) and (b)

below is woven into the instrumental texture throughout the movement.

Ex. 5

There is a wonderful moment when the chorus cries, 'Lord, what have I to hope for?' to agitated wind chords. On one of these chords the voices cease and the orchestra dies away. Then, as the music goes into D major, comes hope and trust in the great aspiring phrases in all the vocal parts. This is unforgettable. This time, to words from Wisdom 3: 1, 'But the righteous souls are in the hand of God and they shall rest ever more', we do get a fugue, and one constructed on a pedal point low D which is maintained in every one of the thirty-six bars. It was this D that a drummer played *forte* throughout at the first performance of three of the movements at Vienna in 1867, drowning the chorus and exasperating the nerves of the more susceptible members of the audience. Brahms, however, found that, beaten soft, it did not come through as he wished and so he cued in the organ as well. The effect conveyed is of unshakeable confidence. 'Rest' has its first mention here and will have one more in the last movement. The Wisdom text, it may be of interest to mention, in its Latin form 'Justorum animae in manu Dei sunt' is used as the text in the Gradual, Alleluia (verse), Offertory and Communion for Feasts of Martyrs, and has been set most beautifully by Byrd, but finely also by Palestrina, Lassus, and others.

The mellifluous, gently flowing fourth movement, 'We love the place where thine honour dwells, O Lord of hosts' (Psalm 84: 1–5), for chorus only, is well placed to relieve the tensions of the previous movement: but Brahms's carefully devised scheme is disturbed by the interpolated fifth movement, the famous and beautiful soprano solo, with chorus, 'Now hath man sorrow, but yet I shall again behold you and fill your heart with rejoicing', which takes us back to the sorrow and comfort and joy of the opening movement. The last words of the fourth movement, 'We love the place where thine honour dwells', speaking before of the soul longing and fainting for the courts of the Lord, lead naturally to the sixth movement, with its reminder that here we have no abiding city. This movement is keyless—in spite of the E flat key signature—up to the end of the baritone entry 'Behold I show you a mystery'. The cadence, one of common currency for years, is just what is needed to resolve the shifting tonalities firmly into F sharp minor. Then the trumpet sounds (in fact trombones), death is vanquished, the dead arise incorruptible and are changed, and the great C major fugue, 'Worthy art thou, Lord, to receive honour and glory', bursts out.

There can, of course, be no question of omitting the fifth movement in performance, though it is so often sung by itself as an anthem with organ that it would not be neglected. Moreover, it sounds at its best with a good boy soprano. The words are from John 16: 22, Isaiah 62: 13, and Ecclesiasticus 51: 27.

The crushing of the sting of death, in this movement, the victory over the grave, are celebrated in some of the most dramatic music ever written and one is thrilled by it, but yet made uneasy by the void it creates. Conquest by whom for what? Chapter 15 of the First Epistle to the Corinthians concerning the resurrection of the dead, is one of the best known in the New Testament, 'If Christ be not risen then your faith is vain. . . . Since by man came death, by man also came resurrection from the dead and as all die in Adam so also shall all be made alive in Christ.' Brahms, as we saw, told Rheinhalter that he couldn't 'dispute the from henceforth' of his revered poets, but he could dispute the essential message of St Paul. He may have decided that those of his hearers who were Christians could be left to fill in mentally what he had left out. One could hardly charge him with intellectual dishonesty.

The final movement, 'Blessed are the dead which die in the Lord' (Revelations 14: 13) with its reference back to the first movement, now has violins included in the scoring for 'for the former things have passed away'. The figuration in the orchestral part seems to have been inspired by almost identical passages in Bach's 34th Church Cantata *O ewiges Feuer* ('O light everlasting') in which comes the exquisite alto aria, 'Wohl euch, ihr auserwählten Seelen die Gott zur Wohnung ausersehn' ('Blessed ye hearts whom God has chosen to be his dwelling place').

The Requiem must be for some of us a flawed work because of the composer's inability to identify himself fully with his texts and because one is left asking questions that cannot be answered. Who to him were 'Lord' and 'God'? In any case his greatest spiritual work is the *Serious Songs*. In that work, 'a struggle between the words of the Bible and his own life experience' as Max Friedlander says in his *Brahms's Lieder* (O.U.P., 1928), he can make every word his own. 'I have my faith,' he said; he had surely some hope, and, as the last song, based on St Paul's words about faith, hope and charity shows, most assuredly he had love, the greatest of these.

CHAPTER FIFTEEN

SIX BACH CHURCH CANTATAS

A group of musicologists has been engaged for a number of years in doing research work, at present chiefly textual, into Bach's works which, they hope, will result in presenting a more faithful picture of Bach, as man and musician, than the romantic view of him as 'supremely the church musician, with the ascendency of the churchman over the musician', handed down by Spitta, in his great life of Bach, and left fundamentally unchanged, though with valuable retouchings contributed by such writers as Schweitzer, Pirro, and Sanford Terry. In a lecture delivered at the Bach Festival of the International Bach Society in Mainz on 1 June 1962 (and subsequently printed in an English translation by Stanley Godman in *Music and Letters*, July 1962), Friedrich Blume, one of the group mentioned above, suggested that Bach had no special liking for church work, that it was not a spiritual necessity for him, and continued, 'Bach the supreme cantor, the creative Servant of the Word of God, the staunch Lutheran, is a legend. It will have to be buried along with other traditions and hallowed romantic illusions.' Now it is common knowledge to those who have studied the available evidence that Bach was anything but 'a supreme cantor' in the sense that he had discovered his true vocation in the Leipzig cantorate. His quarters were in a wing of the noisy and insanitary St Thomas's School, only seventeen of his fifty-four scholars were competent musicians, he was no disciplinarian, and his quarrels with the authorities were frequent; and he had the sorrow of the loss of seven of his thirteen children. It is revealing that one of his grandsons, who sang in his choir, remembered only that 'he cuffed us a lot and they [the cantatas] sounded awful'.

I do not know exactly what Blume means by 'a staunch Lutheran'. The list of books in Bach's library, which included seven volumes of Luther's works, shows his deep interest in theology: his choice of librettos for the cantatas reveal the devotionalism which, we cannot but believe, he professed and practised. As Sanford Terry puts it in his *Bach: the Historical Approach* (O.U.P., 1930):

It can be defined in a word as Pietistic or Mystic. The Cradle at Bethlehem and the Cross at Calvary were its most vivid visions. They inspired in him an intense, almost feminine, devotion to the personality of Jesus, whose sacred name in his texts never failed to draw from him a gesture of adoring affection. . . . But while Pietism touched Bach with its spirit . . . and though his music and friendships reveal his affinity with its outlook, he was repelled by its Puritan opposition to what he deemed an essential of public worship. For it opposed the intrusion of music in the domain of the spiritual, and only admitted the Hymn-book to its approval. Hence the artist in Bach rejected Pietism as a system, though his nature yearned for a warmer religion than official Lutheranism afforded. He was, in fact, neither wholly Pietist nor wholly Orthodox, but a mystic, like Luther himself.

Thus, apart from their musicianship, the Cantatas reveal Bach as a man singularly pondering, emotional, and, above all, controlled by a religious sense as profound as it was simple.

This, with a reservation about Bach as a mystic, seems to me as true a picture of Bach's religion as one could hope to have. He was happiest in the service of Leopold of Anhalt-Cöthen, who was devoted to music and liberal minded—and there the composition of secular music was his chief activity, which he would have regarded as doing as much for the glory of God as his sacred music.

The goodwill of an employer has no sure foundation and when the bachelor prince married a Princess of Anhalt-Bemburg, whom Bach called an 'amusa', or person with no love for music or art, his court conductor realized that a move was inevitable. 1 June 1723 found him being formally installed as Cantor of St Thomas's, Leipzig.

The need to provide a continuous series of church cantatas—not called for at Weimar, or needed at Cöthen—for each Sunday and major feast-day in the ecclesiastical year did indeed release in Bach in the three cycles that have come down to us—from the First Sunday after Trinity, 1723 to Whitsunday, 1726—a torrent of creative activity. There were, of course, times when, under pressure of other activities or when confronted by a prosaic libretto, Bach adapted pre-existing material with texts of different significance. Too much fuss, by far, has been made over this. Notes, after all, are indifferent material in themselves; the purpose to which they are disposed is what matters. Sometimes, certainly, Bach was careless over his adaptations, but at others he went to enormous trouble in refashioning the old material, with superb results.

Blume dismisses the claim that Bach was 'the creative servant of the Word of God, the great biblical interpreter'. This is to fly in the face of the overwhelming evidence to the contrary provided by the great majority of the church cantatas, the Passions, the B minor Mass. I leave it to the unprejudiced reader to listen to and study the cantatas dealt with in this chapter and then decide if he can imagine Bach as anything but a deeply religious man.

The Bishop of Hanover well said in a sermon at the time of the bi-centenary of Bach 'he creates from a single centre of faith in Christ': and where is there to be found, in the whole realm of music, so beautiful a portrait of Christ as Bach has painted in the Cantatas and Passions?

Bach needs no defenders but I cannot resist ending this dis-quisition with a quotation from a scholar who did not share his Christian faith, and so speaks all the more convincingly to the unconverted.

'The art of the Bach cantata is an exposition of the foundations and principles of the Christian faith, and none more searching or more inexorable, deeper or more precise has ever been. The temporal life and the eternal, works and faith, mortality and death, sin and repentance, suffering and salvation—all the emotions and inspirations of the Christian soul exalted this, the greatest of preachers since Luther, not to theological abstractions but to a passionate presenta-tion by symbolic means of an incomparably vivid musical imagination.' (Alfred Einstein, *A Short History of Music*—Cassell, 7th ed., 1965.)

The cantatas were performed in the principal Lutheran service on Sundays and Feastdays before the sermon or, if in two parts, one before it and one after. The Gospel, and more rarely also the Epistle, from which the preacher took his text, and on which the liturgy centred, was also the matter on which Bach's librettists based their material. It is vital to the spiritual as opposed to the merely aesthetic understanding of the cantatas that the listener should be aware of the scriptural references in them. Until fairly recently both German and English vocal scores gave few, if any, clues about these—some-times not even a reference to the Sunday, or Feastday, for which the cantata was composed. Later reprints of the standard edition (Breitkopf) add this information, and there are miniature full scores of a number of the cantatas now available which contain an inset with the libretto in German and English and the sources of all the relevant scriptural quotations.[1]

In view of the limited space available I have had to limit myself to a discussion of seven only of the twenty extant cantatas in which Bach deals directly with death.

We have to ask ourselves, in considering this marvellous series of

---

[1] *Most of these are in the Eulenberg edition.*

works with death as their central motif, how can it be that this vital man, with his feet on the ground, even if his head was often in the stars, who united, uniquely, the temporal with the spiritual, was so possessed with the longing for death he so sublimely expresses? Did he, indeed, wish, in St Paul's words, 'to be dissolved and to be with Christ', or was it, as has been suggested, that he gladly used such imagery as a means of releasing that higher form of life he felt already in his composer's noisy room at Leipzig? We can never know, but for the Christian there is infinite strength and consolation in these cantatas.

Julian Green wrote beautifully in his diary on 26 May 1953 (Collins, 1965):

'Listening to Bach's Cantata No. 32,[1] I realized how very near the invisible world is to us, if we do not drive it away. When I heard his cantata for the first time, around 1926, it stirred me so deeply that I foresaw it would be necessary for me to change my whole life, but that I should remain in the world. Impossible to express how great a part Bach has played in my life; it is he, more than any other, who has reconciled one to the idea of dying.'

Green's experience is not unique. In such words, and such experience, shared by many, the doubting scholars are confounded. But they will never understand this.

No doubt it is in tune with Lutheran moralizing that in 'Edifying thoughts of a tobacco smoker', some verses which appear in Anna Magdalena's *Second Little Clavier Book* (1725) and are thought to be by Bach, the author draws such analogies as this after poking his finger in the bowl and burning it:

> If in the pipe such pain doth dwell,
> How hot must be the pains of Hell.

It is to be hoped that Bach was joking, but anyhow he becomes cheerful in the last verse:

> On land, on sea, at home, abroad,
> I smoke my pipe and worship God.

In the *First Little Clavier Book* (1722) devised for his wife's instruction, Bach included a dedicatory song expressive of his love for her, the melody of which is based on the chorale 'Fret not, my soul: on God rely'. This is the well known 'Bist du bei mir'. It ends:

---

[1] Liebster Jesu, mein Verlangen ('*A dialogue between Jesus and the Soul*').

If thou be near, I go rejoicing
To peace and rest beyond the skies.
Nor will I fear what may befall me,
For I will hear thy sweet voice call me,
Thy gentle hand will close my eyes.

I like to think that, blind and paralysed as Bach was as he lay dying, the memory of her singing of the exquisite little song was allowed to penetrate his unconsciousness and comfort him.

Bach composed twenty-four of the sixty-nine sacred arias in the hymn-book published in 1736 by Georg Christian Schemelli, and one of these, the aria *Komm, süsser Tod* ('Come, sweet death'), the words by an unknown poet, sums up in twenty-one bars of utterly simple music Bach's deepest thoughts on death.

Komm, süsser Tod, komm,	*Come sweet death, come happy rest!*
sel'ge Ruh!	*Come, lead me into peace,*
Komm, führe mich in Friede,	*For I am weary of the world;*
Weil ich der Welt bin müde;	*Ah! come, I wait for you,*
Ach komm, ich wart auf dich,	*Come soon and lead me,*
Komm bald und führe mich,	*Close my eyes,*
Drück mir die Augen zu	*Come, happy rest.*
Komm, sel'ge Ruh.	

(there are two more verses)

The opening and closing bars will give some idea of the exquisite beauty of the little aria and especially of its last aspiring phrase and its falling to the longed-for rest.

Ex. 1

Two of the three cantatas[1] we know Bach to have composed during his one year as organist of St Blasius, Mühlhausen in 1707, interesting though they are, do not prepare one for the masterpiece he produced there at the age of twenty-two in *Gottes Zeit ist die allerbeste Zeit* (106) ('God's time is best') sub-titled *Actus tragicus*, one of the most perfect, and best-loved, of all his cantatas.

The music is scored throughout for two recorders (*not* flutes), two

---

[1] *By cantatas I mean always those composed for church use.*

violas da gamba and continuo (bass gamba and organ). These are the tone-colours Bach wanted, and to use flutes and violas, while not disastrous, does not convey his intention.

The lovely *Sonatina* with which the cantata begins paints a touching picture of the restrained sorrow felt by the mourners. There are two motifs, the falling fifths and sixth (a) at the start, the gentle clash of seconds (b)—as of tolling bells—that follows—both played by recorders.

Ex. 2

These two little motifs recur constantly, as we shall see, in the course of the work. The music obviously speaks of personal mourning and the use of Luther's version of *Nunc dimittis* in the penultimate number suggests that the deceased person was an old man. His identity is not known for certain but the available evidence seems to point to Bach's uncle, Tobias Lämmerhirt, who died in September of this year, leaving his nephew a small legacy. This came in very useful for the latter's wedding to his cousin Maria Barbara on 17 October 1707 in Dornheim, a village near Arnstadt.

The libretto, a mosaic of texts contrasting the two different concepts of death in the Old and New Testaments, shows the hand of one, perhaps Bach himself, deeply read in Scripture. The chorus, after the *Sonatina* ends, sing cheerfully that God's time is always best and then words of St Paul from the Acts of the Apostles, 'In Him we live and are as long as He wills'.

W. G. Whittaker, in *The Cantatas of J. S. Bach* (Oxford University Press, 1959) refers to 'Bach's faultless scanning bringing every word on important notes, defining musically idea after idea, detaching single words, besides making the music a fitting mate to the thought of the author.' All these qualities are evident in this youthful cantata.

At 'lange' in 'so lange er will' ('as long as He wills') Bach, typically, gives the sopranos alone a note sustained for three bars, the rest of the chorus coming in again after.

The mood becomes grave when the music goes into the minor key at 'In ihm sterben wir zu rechter Zeit' ('In Him we die at the appointed time, when He wills'). In this brief and poignant section

Bach dwells continually on the words 'in Him we die'. The two motifs of Ex. 2 are woven into the vocal and viola da gamba parts of the sombre tenor arioso that follows. 'Ach, Herr! Herr, lehre uns bedenken . . . dass wir sterben müssen' ('Ah, Lord, teach us to remember that we must die').

ach, Herr! Herr, leh-re uns be–den — ken,Herr, leh-re uns be-den-ken,

Ex. 3

daß wir ster-ben, müs-sen, daß wir ster-ben müssen,

Ex. 4

The tempo changes from slow to fast for the bass arioso 'Bestelle dein Haus, denn du wirst sterben und nicht lebendig bleiben' ('Set thy house in order for thou shalt die and not remain among the living' (Isaiah 38: 1) which has a flickering recorder part suggestive of sudden haste. In the wonderful fugal chorus that ends this section the lower voices declaim the stern pronouncement 'Es ist der alte Bund: Mensch, du musst sterben' ('It is the old decree: man, thou must die') (Ecclesiasticus 14: 17) to continuo accompaniment only, the string basses moving with an inexorable tread (one of Bach's 'walking basses'). Then suddenly there comes the trustful voice of the New Testament, words from Revelations 22:20 'Ja komm, Herr Jesu, komm' ('Yea, come, Lord Jesus, come') sung by the solo soprano. To this Bach adds the melody of the chorale 'I have cast my cares upon God', which he puts in the *lower* register of the recorders, bringing in the violas da gamba at the same moment. The reference, made purely instrumentally, would not have been lost on the congregation. The lower chorus voices continue with their stern words, but cannot now prevail. The end of the movement is one of Bach's most wonderful inspirations. The recorders and gambas conclude the chorale and at once begin a slow trill ((b) of Ex. 2); the organ ceases, leaving the bass gamba playing; the chorus sing 'sterben' in a despairing crescendo, abruptly cut off as the soprano's radiant 'Ja komm, Herr Jesu' rings out above, this time to the lovely long drawn phrase below. As she reaches 'Jesu' at the end, the throbbing bass gamba ceases and the Holy Name is left in the sounding air.

Ja komm, Herr Je - - - - - - - - - - su, Herr Je-su!

Ex. 5

About 1700 the secco recitative and *da capo* aria of the opera had
invaded the church cantata and it is difficult to see how Bach could
long have held out against it, but it is entirely absent in the Mühlhausen cantatas. The music flows along, in this cantata, with a
natural response to the varying emotions portrayed and so without
artificial divisions. What I have been discussing is really one movement, and there are now two more to come. The first of these is an
alto solo with continuo accompaniment only in which the bass
gamba has the melodic part. It is a ground bass which ends its phrases
with the slow trill of motif (b) of *Ex.* 2.

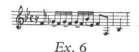

Ex. 6

The words are those spoken by Christ on the Cross. 'In deine
Hände befehl' ich meinen Geist' ('Into Thy hands I commend my
spirit'). As this moving prayer ends the bass soloist, still to continuo
accompaniment only, sings the words of Christ to the penitent thief.
'Heute, wirst du mit mir in Paradies' ('Today thou shalt be with me
in Paradise'). If the bass is a sensitive singer the effect is beautiful, but
one rarely hears the words sung softly enough; and when the
chorus altos begin the chorale 'Mit Fried' und Freud' ich fahr'
dahin' (technically a counter-melody) it is crucial that the tempo
should not be too fast. It should in fact be determined by the pace
of the quickest notes in the bass part. The violas da gamba enter
with the altos, who, as the bass ends the constant repetitions of his
words, conclude the chorale.

At 'der Tod ist mein Schlaf worden' ('Death has become my
sleep'), the violas da gamba have a lulling motif related to *Ex.* 2(a).

The final movement, in two parts, has the same inevitability as
everything else in this splendidly integrated work. Recorders, of
course, now join the violas da gamba and in the introductory bars to
the chorus quote and extend the first melody line of the chorale 'In
Dich hab' ich gehoffet, Herr' ('In Thee have I hoped, Lord') and then
the chorus sing joyfully and mostly in block harmony the whole
chorale, with the recorders adding decorative phrases between the
lines. Bach uses the last line for a fine fugal conclusion 'Durch Jesum
Christum, Amen' ('Through Jesus Christ, Amen').

There is no terror in the face of death in *Gottes Zeit*, no horror at
the thought of the corruption of the body in the grave; these concepts are found in the two settings of *O Ewigkeit, du Donnerwort*
(Nos. 20 and 60). In the earlier setting, for the first Sunday after
Trinity, a long work in two parts, the librettist uses a paraphrase of
all but four of the sixteen verses of Johann Rist's hymn, whereas in

the second setting only the second verse is used. The theme of Death and Judgement, represented in such grim terms in No. 20, derives from the Gospel for the 1st Sunday after Trinity, St Luke 16: 19–31—the parable of Dives and Lazarus. The two other cantatas for this Sunday, No. 75, *Die Elenden sollen essen* ('The wretched shall eat') and No. 39 *Brich dem Hungrigen dein Brot* ('Give the hungry man thy bread')—a particularly lovely work—dwell on the sufferings of Lazarus, not the fate of Dives; and so in these two works there is no hint of hell fire or eternity of torture as depicted in No. 20. The Gospel for the twenty-fourth Sunday after Trinity, for which Bach composed the second setting of *O Ewigkeit, du Donnerwort*, is concerned with the raising of the daughter of Jairus (St Matthew 9: 14–27). The Epistle is a prayer for the increase of Grace, the motet 'In te Domine speravi' ('In Thee, O Lord, have I hoped'). All of this leaves no occasion for the use of Rist's hymn. Yet Bach's librettist does, in fact, use the first verse in the first number of this astonishing cantata and takes from the Sunday Biblical texts only the idea of hope. The cantata is cast in the form of a dialogue between Hope (tenor) and Fear (alto). Bach seldom used the term 'cantata', more usually 'piece' (*Stück*) or 'concerto', and occasionally —which would be a just description of No. 60—'dramma per musica'. There are two duets separated by one of the three recitatives passing into ariosos. The scoring is for horn, two oboes d'amore, two violins, and continuo. Of the two themes in the orchestral prelude to the first duet one (strings) depicts Fear's horror of death, the other (oboes) Hope's utter trust in God, underlined by a long sustained bass pedal note in the continuo part, marked *tasto solo*— that is, for string bass only. The solo alto sings the first verse of the chorale 'Eternity thou word of thunder', with the horn doubling the vocal line, and just before the fourth line, 'Eternity thou timeless tide', the solo tenor comes in with a verse from Psalm 119, 'Lord, I have longed for thy salvation and done thy commandments', repeating the words over and over again in confident and, musically, florid phrases, while the alto continues with the chorale. Then, with their contrasted characters established, the dialogue begins. Fear, in this recitative, is full of despair and pain ('the fear of death tortures these limbs'). Hope responds, urging trust in God and resignation to His will. Each section of the recitative ends with a florid arioso: the alto has a realistic one on the word 'martert (diese glieder)' (tortures these limbs), the tenor on the words 'tragen' (Jesus endures with me). The duet that follows is scored for one oboe or violin solo and continuo. Hope continually tries to calm Fear: the grave, he says, will be a 'house of peace' ('Friedenhaus') but Fear can only express terror of sickness and death, of having a faith that falters and no hope of peace in the grave. Bach could not set these opposed sentiments convincingly to music and so compromises by making for contrast the tenor and violin solo parts more ornate than the alto.

Hope has done all he can: he departs. Now, in the third recitative-arioso, comes the high point of the drama. Fear cries out that all men dread death, the thought of it shatters hope and robs us of our courage. Then, with extraordinary beauty, a voice (solo bass) comes from Heaven 'Selig sind die Todten' ('Blessed are the dead') (Revelations 14: 13). But Fear is still not comforted. She feels death

Ex. 7

near, the jaws of Hell, perchance, opening to receive her, the doom of eternal damnation. The heavenly voice speaks again, completing the consoling words (the lovely phrase here raised a tone, as was Fear's last cry) 'Blessed are the dead, which die in the Lord'. But Fear is not yet reassured. If she dies confessing faith in Christ can she be sure to receive His blessing, and albeit must worms feed on her and dust return to dust? Is that perhaps all? She is the prototype of the over-scrupulous, self-regarding penitent. The voice repeats the consoling words in an extended lyrical passage of great beauty, and at last Fear recovers her senses and passes into joyful acceptance of her destiny.

The concluding chorale begins with a phrase of three whole tones —repeated at the third line. No one has ever explained how such an astonishing thing came to be.

Ex. 8

Bach's bass follows suit, and his harmonization of the last two lines has a descending chromatic bass we meet with again in the last section of Chopin's C minor Prelude. It was this chorale that Alban Berg used so poignantly in the last movement of his Violin Concerto, in the manner of a requiem for a beloved friend.

Ex. 9

It should be said that Lutherans, in Bach's time, no longer felt the fears and terrors expressed in this libretto, and even theologians did not stress them so strongly as here.

The group of four cantatas Bach composed for the 16th Sunday after Trinity, of a very different character, are all on the theme of death, inspired by the Gospel for the day, the bringing back to life of the son of the widow of Nain. The motet, 'Media vita in morte sumus' (Notker's celebrated antiphon, see p. 207), directed to be sung on this day, sounds a warning note, and the inevitability of death, coming perhaps like a thief in the night, is stressed, but the tone of the librettos never approaches the extravagances of the two cantatas above.

From this group, all masterpieces, I have chosen Cantata 161, '*Komm', du süsse Todesstunde*' ('Come, thou lovely hour of death'). The other two cantatas are No. 8, *Liebster Gott, wann werd' ich sterben?* ('Gracious Lord, when wilt thou call me?') with its exquisite orchestral introduction depicting the departing soul and the tolling funeral bells, and No. 27, *Wer weiss, wie nahe mir mein Ende?*' ('O teach me, Lord, my days to number'), almost equally fine.

Komm', du süsse Todesstunde is scored for solo alto and tenor, chorus, two recorders, two violins, and continuo. The libretto, by Salomo Franck, has only a very superficial connexion with the gospel story of the bringing back to life of the widow's son, but it does represent a view of death radically different from that of Cantata No. 60. The world-despising soul here longs to see its Saviour in Heaven, and this gave Bach the chance to write some of his most beautiful music. There is no dialogue; alto and tenor soloists deliver two individual meditations on death.

In the alto aria the two flutes and the voice form a trio, sharing all through the beautiful melody the flutes introduce. Tempo, as so often in the Cantatas, is a problem here. If taken too slowly the aria becomes a dirge, if too fast it loses all its serenity. The right tempo, in my opinion, in reflective music of this kind, is one in which the notes of smallest value never sound hurried. The almost constant thirds and sixths give a mellifluous, lulling feel to the vocal line.

> Come, sweet death, thou blessed healer
> When my spirit eats honey out of the lion's mouth
> [A poetic conceit based on a famous incident in Samson's life]
> Make my departure sweet, delay not, last light, that I may
>   kiss my Saviour.

Ex. 10

Just after the reference to the lion, the organ begins to play the hymn melody by Hassler best known to us as the Passion chorale, but in the context the Lutheran congregation would hear it as associated with Christoph Knoll's words, 'Herzlich thut mich verlangen' ('Heartfelt is my longing').

The tenor's recitative, before his aria, is extraordinarily expressive, anything but 'secco' in sound. The words are a rather tiresome denunciation of the world's joys, but Bach's music manages to make the soul sound, for a moment, regretful in departing. Then the voice sinks down in contemplation of death's last hour and ends with a beautiful arioso, with string bass accompaniment only, 'I long with Christ to pasture, I long from this world to depart'. The string bass slowly, in two-note steps, moves down the scale to a low C.

The aria is, so to say, the masculine side of the composite soul represented by alto and tenor. The words continue the desire of the soul 'to be dissolved and to be with Christ' and to shine with the pure beauty of the angels.

The alto recitative is fully accompanied, and here is yet another instance of Bach's realistic symbolism. The soul prays to die in the arms of Jesus 'Er ist mein sanfter Schlaf' ('He is my soft sleep'). Voice, continuo, flutes all gently descend, violins sustaining chords in the middle of the score. One *sees* the soul sinking to its soft sleep in the Saviour's arms.

Ex. 11

Every image of the text is illustrated, the anticipated awakening, to a little burst on the orchestra, but most notably the bells—for the soul is ready now for them to toll. How they do so is shown below.

Ex. 12

The cantata ends with a chorus and a chorale. The melody of the simply written chorus has an obvious affinity, at its start, to that of the alto aria. A charming feature is the sudden rushes of joy on the flutes (demisemiquavers) which remind me of Ernest Newman's saying that the word 'Freude' (here, 'Himmelsfreude'—'Heavenly joy') always sets Bach carolling like a lark. At the words 'Jesus, come and take me away' the swinging bell octaves of *Ex.* 12 appear again in the continuo.

The recorders sing a heavenly counter-melody above the voices in the concluding chorale. Bach does not search for images only in the first line of a chorale, and in this case the recorders perhaps suggest the coming 'beautiful transfiguration' of the mortal body. I should add, however, that André Pirro considered Bach was illustrating the natural action of the worms! He would not have shrunk from that.

> The body is indeed destroyed by worms in the earth
> But awakened shall be through Christ beautifully transfigured.
> It shall shine as the sun, and live without distress.

The structure of the opening movement of No. 95, *Christus, der ist mein Leben* ('O Christ, my all in living'), the last cantata of the four for the 16th Sunday after Trinity, is unique in that Bach uses two independent chorale choruses linked by a tenor arioso, another chorale for soprano only in the next number, and yet another at the close of the cantata. These four chorales all express a joyful loving welcome to death, as also does the one aria for tenor. The cantata is scored for horn, two oboes d'amore, two violins, and continuo. There is no gloom in this beautiful work: the syncopated figure in the orchestral accompaniment to the first chorale, homophonically treated, gives a feeling of pulsating spiritual life, its contrasted scale passages of resurrection.

> Christus, der ist mein Leben,   *Christ, who is my life,*
> Sterben ist mein Gewinn: *To die is all my gain,*
> Dem tu ich, mich ergeben,   *Thereto I yield myself*
> Mit Freud' fahr' ich dahin.   *With joy journey I thither.*

The lines are separated in the familiar way by the continuing orchestral part but the even flow of the chorale melody is laid aside at the second line for a realistic painting of 'sterben' (to die), marked *piano* [*sic*] by Bach, but the concluding words 'ist mein Gewinn' ('is my gain') *forte*. The dissonant chord, built downward voice by voice, vividly expresses the momentary pains of death.

Ex. 13

Bach maintains the accompaniment during the tenor's arioso-recitative which begins with one of the 'carollings' on the word 'Freude' I have mentioned above.

Mit Freuden, ja mit Herzenslust
Will ich von hinnen scheiden.

With joy, o yea, with joyful heart shall I
My dwelling on earth abandon.

In the recitative the orchestra comes in at varying moments, leaving the continuo at others to fill in with chords, but itself leading into the second chorale. The alternation of time-signatures is remarkable, $\frac{4}{4}$, $\frac{3}{4}$, $\frac{2}{4}$, $\frac{3}{4}$, etc. We have met with the second chorale before, Luther's 'Mit Fried' und Freud' ich fahr' dahin' ('With peace and joy I journey thither'). Ordinary oboes replace those 'd'amore' and the continuo has a running quaver figure suggesting a steady march to the desired goal. Bach marks *piano* at the words 'soft and calm', which receive a most expressive cadence. In the recitative, for soprano, before the third chorale, 'Valet will ich dir geben, du arge, falsche Welt' ('Farewell will I give to thee, thou wicked false world'), the words are world-despising, and end: 'No! No! now I can with composed spirit speak'. The succeeding chorale for soprano is truly angelic. There are three motifs in the accompaniment: (1) an arpeggio, (2) quietly joyful detached phrases for oboes d'amore with (3) an aspiring phrase attached to it. It is, quite simply, one of the most beautiful movements Bach ever composed.[1]

Ex. 14

The tenor's recitative expresses the prevailing longing for death, and Bach fills the accompaniment to his tenor aria 'Ach, schlage doch bald' ('Ah, toll for me soon') with the sound of bells (the strings are pizzicato throughout, basses tolling the larger ones, violas the smaller ones, mainly in octave leaps). There is an unwonted number of dynamic directions in this beautiful D major aria, not only *piano*, for echoed notes, and *forte*, but *più piano* and even *pianissimo*. This last direction comes when the orchestra, after momentarily ceasing and giving place to the continuo, resumes with a poignant chord (a diminished seventh) underlining the anxious words 'only call soon (thou most beloved of holy bells)' and taking

---

[1] *The melody of this seventeenth-century funeral hymn by G. M. Teschner will be familiar to many as that of 'All glory, laud and honour', a hymn for Palm Sunday, No. 622 in* The English Hymnal.

the music into the related key of A major. The middle part of the aria is arioso style with again some striking harmonizations.

One can only suppose that Bach had a tenor capable of coping with the continually high-pitched writing of his part in this aria. The bass is given a recitative accompanied, like the other two in the cantata, with detached chords on the continuo, but blossoming into a little arioso at the close in 'Mein selig Aufersteh'n auf mein Heiland gründen' ('My blessed resurrection on my Saviour I establish'). High above the closing chorale, 'Weil du vom Tod erstanden bist, werd' ich im Grab nicht bleiben' ('Because Thou from death arisen art, shall I in the grave not remain'), the first violin plays a melody, moving sometimes with the chorale tune, that suggests that the soul, freed from the body, is about to begin its ascension.

The Gospel for the Third Sunday after Epiphany is St Matthew's account of Christ's cleansing of the leper. The Epistle (Romans 11: 1, 17, 21) speaks of overcoming evil with good but for Cantata No. 73, *Herr, wie du willt, so schick's mit mir* ('Lord, as thou will so deal with me, in living and in dying') the librettist chose a theme based on the first stanza of Caspar Bienemann's hymn with the above title, which forms, with interpolated recitatives, the material for the opening choral fantasia, with a melody taken from another chorale. The same stanza is used as the concluding chorale of Cantata No. 156 for solo bass, also for this Sunday, *Ich steh' mit einem Fuss im Grabe,* ('I stand with one foot in the grave'), with the melody associated with it. This is the cantata with the lovely little *Sinfonia* for oboe and strings adapted from the *Largo* of the Clavier Concerto in F minor, which itself is thought to be an adaptation from a lost violin concerto.

It is more than possible that the librettist's choice of the chorale was suggested by the leper's words to Christ, 'Lord, if thou wilt, thou canst make me clean'. The theme of submission to God's Will in the hour of death inspired Bach to write, in Cantata No. 73, one of the finest of his arias for bass. It is an outstanding example of the way his whole being could become penetrated with the words he set.

The aria, which has accompaniment for strings and continuo, is in rondo form, with three episodes.

(a) Herr, so du willt,	*Lord, if Thou wilt,*
(b) So presst, ihr Todesschmerzen, die Seufzer aus dem Herzen, wenn mein Gebet nur vor dir gilt.	*so draw, ye death pains, the sighs from the heart, if my prayer only before Thee prevails.*

(a) Herr, so du willt,
(c) so lege meine Glieder in Staub und Asche nieder, dies höchst verderbte Sündenbild.

Lord, if thou wilt,
So lay my limbs in dust and ashes low, this most corrupt sins' picture.

(a) Herr, so du willt,
(d) So schlagt, ihr Leichenglocken, ich folge unerschrocken, mein Jammer ist nunmehr gestillt.

Lord, if thou wilt,
So strike, ye tolling bells, I follow, unaffrighted, my lamentation is henceforth stilled.

(a) Herr, so du willt.

Lord, if thou wilt.

The four-note motif that clothes the words the bass sings at the start of the aria 'Herr, so du willt' is subject to both melodic and rhythmic variation throughout the aria. Bach repeats the words three times, then after the first and second episodes three times, but after the third episode (in which the bells toll) no less than five times, the last four of them without pauses between, as heretofore, filled up by the orchestra. In this way Bach reflects lovingly on every aspect of God's will. I give below the two-bar motif and three of its ten variations.

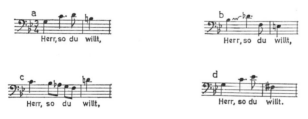

Ex. 15

The orchestra responds at once to the singer's first phrase with a legato theme, also one bar only, played by second violins, and a fourth higher, by first violins (a); to this violas add a little rhythmic figure (b).

These themes always accompany the key words. Bach often, but not consistently, marks (a) *piano*. After the third episode, however, he marks (a) *forte*, but at the fourth repetition of 'Herr, so du willt', where the voice reaches a sustained note, he puts *piano*, and when the voice ceases, *forte* again for the orchestra's final playing of (a) and (b).

The episodes reflect the emotions of the soul, broken phrases in the first, the heartfelt sighs of dread it expects to feel when death is nigh, in the second a moving highlighting of '*Sündenbild*' (sins' picture), followed by phrases of passionate pleading leading to

'Herr, so du willt'. Then, the third episode, with another representation of tolling bells as in Ex. 12, depicted both in the voice and, pizzicato, on the strings.

Cantata No. 82, *Ich habe genug* ('It is enough'), is the best known of the five Bach composed for the Feast of the Purification of the Blessed Virgin Mary. The Epistle comes from the prophesy of Malachi (3: 1–4) which foretells the future coming of the Messiah and his work of salvation: the Gospel is St Luke's account (2: 22–32) of the visit of Joseph and Mary to Jerusalem for the ritual purification prescribed by the Mosaic law. There, led to the Temple by the spirit, they were greeted by the 'good and upright old man Simeon' who had long been waiting 'for comfort to be brought to Israel'. The Holy Spirit had revealed to him that he would not die until he had seen the Lord Messiah and now, the promise gloriously fulfilled, he takes the Holy Child into his arms and says his 'Nunc dimittis'. It is Simeon's overwhelming joy at beholding the Saviour of the World that Bach's librettist stresses and the composer's music so beautifully illustrates this, and the weary old man's farewell to the world and glad departure to his heavenly rest. The cantata is scored for solo bass, oboe, violins, and continuo; there is no chorale.

In the long orchestral introduction to the first aria, the violins have a murmuring accompaniment in thirds, as of deep content, while above the oboe plays the motto phrase of the aria. It has reminded commentators of the start of the well-known aria 'Erbarme dich' ('Have mercy, Lord') in the *St Matthew Passion* and it is indeed identical with that, and also with the duet for soprano and bass, 'Wann kommst du, mein Heil?' ('When comest Thou, my salvation?') in Cantata No. 140, 'Wachet auf' ('Sleepers wake'), and there are many other variants of the phrase.

Ex. 16

The oboe breaks out into arabesques of joy as, in the middle section of the aria, the voice also does on the word 'Freuden'. The twofold repetition of 'Ich habe genug' at the start of the aria and near the end of the middle section is infinitely touching. It is as if the old man hardly dare believe his eyes that he does indeed hold the Saviour in his longing arms.

In the recitative that follows it is the poet, meditating on the scene, who speaks, quoting Simeon's words, 'It is enough', and alluding to the joy of everlasting life he hopes to share with him, trusting in Christ's promise. So he, too, will depart in peace—there is a little *arioso* to those last words. His next passage of recitative ends with another brief *arioso* of great beauty, 'With joy I bid the world farewell. It is enough', and, need I say, there is a little spray of notes on the word 'joy'.

Now begins the sublime aria of heavenly homesickness which combines the emotions of Simeon, detached from the things of this world, with those of the aspiring believer. As in the first aria of *Komm', du süsse Todesstunde*, the choice of tempo is of prime importance. It must be neither too slow nor too fast, but *just*. The long aria is in rondo form, the accompaniment for strings only.

Never were words more exquisitely fitted to music than in this aria, where every bar is precious. The closing bars of the first stanza, the pause on D flat at 'rest', and the falling phrase after 'softly and blissfully take thy rest' have an unparalleled spiritual beauty.

fal — — — let   sanft,   und se-lig   zu.

Ex. 17

The concluding aria, which comes after a short recitative praying for life's journey to be ended and a 'good night' (arioso) to the world, is filled with exuberant joy in the gladness of departure, as signified by the flying scale passages of the oboe and violin accompaniment.

How can it be doubted, in view of only the few cantatas I have been able to include, that Bach's whole thought was transfigured by 'a wonderful, serene longing for death? Again and again, whenever the text affords the least pretext for it, he gives voice to this longing in his music; and nowhere else is his musical speech so moving as in the cantatas in which he discourses on the release of the body from death.' The quotation comes from Schweitzer's great book on Bach, which has been labelled 'dangerous' because of his attempt, certainly misguided, to systematize Bach's tonal language. The danger is illusory; the insights in the book have opened windows for countless souls who will be for ever grateful to this great man. I speak of what I know.

4

Anglican Funeral
Music

ANGLICAN FUNERAL MUSIC

Purcell, Croft, Davies

Obituary notices in the daily papers concerned with deceased members of the Anglican Church refer to burial or funeral, memorial or requiem services, even, in the case of the higher reaches of Anglo-Catholicism, Requiem Mass. I believe that in the latter case the service is substantially that of the Roman Missal. The Tractarians put forward the idea of an intermediate state for the departed in place of the direct and immediate access to heaven procured by faith alone taught, as we have seen, in the Lutheran Church and—in view of what is said in the Thirty-nine Articles about Purgatory and prayers for the dead—presumably also by the Reformers in the Anglican Church. But today, according to the *Oxford Dictionary of the Christian Church*, 'there is no generally accepted teaching on the subject. The most widely received opinion would seem to be that this state (Purgatory) is not so much a process of purification from sin, as in Roman Catholic theology, as one of growth and development.' It seems reasonable to suppose that the soul, realizing its imperfections—to say the least—will gladly suffer the pains of that growth when vouchsafed a vision of beauty and goodness entirely beyond our feeble comprehension here. In the beautiful Order of the Visitation of the Sick in *The Prayer Book of Queen Elizabeth*, 1559, provision is made for the sick person to make confession if 'troubled with any weighty matter' and to receive absolution and Holy Communion: but if he does not recover there is then, officially, only The Order of Burial for him as set out in the Book of Common Prayer. This Order is derived from the *Dirge*, the traditional name for the Office for the Dead which dates from the Middle Ages, and takes its name from the antiphon to the first of the psalms of Mattins which with Lauds forms the great Night Office: 'Dirige, Domine Deus meus in conspectu tuo viam meam' —a conflation of the words of Psalm 5, verse 9. The Reformers retained the traditional name but took over only three passages from the Roman Office, the verse and response from Vespers, 'I heard a voice from heaven', the first responsory in the first Nocturn of Mattins, 'I know that my redeemer liveth', and the antiphon to the canticle 'Benedictus' of Lauds, 'I am the resurrection and the life'.

Edmund Fellowes describes Thomas Morley's setting of the Burial Service, the earliest of such works and sung at the funeral of George II, as the most complete one extant, but in fact the better-known setting by William Croft (1678–1727), which has superseded Morley, is equally complete.

Croft included in his work Purcell's second setting of the anthem, 'Thou knowest, Lord, the secrets of our hearts', composed for the funeral of Queen Mary, who died of smallpox on 28 December 1694, feeling, with a humility that does him credit, that this exquisite music could not be equalled.

Before coming to Croft we must look at Purcell's music for the Queen's Funeral. He had composed six Birthday Odes for this gentle, unassuming queen, whose piety and goodness of heart had won the affection of her people whereas her detestable husband, William of Orange, had done everything to alienate them. The finest of these Odes, 'Come ye sons of Art', was composed in the year of her death and to commemorate that, which must have deeply affected him, he used a funeral march composed three years before as part of the incidental music to Thomas Shadwell's play *The Libertine*, a striking instance of music too good for its original purpose and now found worthy of the solemnity of the occasion. It is scored for four trombones, oddly called 'four flatt trumpetts', and timpani. Purcell also used an early anthem 'Man that is born of a woman'—one of the funeral sentences directed to be sung—which he had composed *c.* 1680–82. The other piece newly composed was a *canzona* for four trombones. The funeral did not take place until 5 March. It was a bitterly cold day when the funeral procession passed through the streets, draped in black, packed with silent mourning crowds, to Westminster Abbey. Thomas Tudway (*c.* 1650–1726) never forgot the impression Purcell's anthem, 'Thou knowest, Lord, the secrets of our hearts', made upon him on this occasion, and when transcribing this work for his great collection of church music for Lord Harley, some thirty years later, he recalled the emotion he had experienced in hearing it.

'I appeal to all that were present, as well as such as understand music, as those that did not, whether they ever heard anything so rapturously fine and solemn and so Heavenly in the operation, which drew tears from all, and yet a plain Naturall Composition, which shows the pow'r of Music, when 'tis rightly fitted and Adapted to devotional purposes.'

The anthem was accompanied by four trombones, and it is a pity that in the recording of Purcell's music for the funeral it is sung unaccompanied, as also in the recording of the Croft Burial Service.

The music has a most moving simplicity but each part, in the mainly chordal treatment, has its own individuality and the music is beautifully 'framed to the life of the words'. The closing measures may well have drawn tears from the congregation.

Ex. 1

Purcell, it may be said here, also set, in his twenty-third year, the English translation of Notker's[1] superb antiphon, 'Media vita in morte sumus' ('In the midst of life we are in death'). It is one of his earliest anthems—and the first setting in English of the words—and vividly illustrates, in chromatic phrases, the words '[deliver us not] into the bitter pains of eternal death'.

Ex. 2

Eight months after the funeral of Queen Mary, Purcell died untimely in his thirty-sixth year, and at his funeral, on 26 November 1695, in Westminster Abbey was mourned to the strains of his own anthem, 'Thou knowest, Lord'.

---

[1] *Notker Babulus (so called from his slight stuttering) was born in Switzerland c. 840, entered the school of the famous Benedictine Abbey of St Gall at an early age and spent the rest of his life there. He died in 912. Notker was famed as a writer and collector of Sequences, and is best known today by the antiphon named above.*

In a preface to a collection of his church music published in 1724, Croft wrote:

At the End of this Volume is printed an *Entire Burial Service*, which it is hoped will not be unacceptable, there being scarce any thing of that kind that is correct in any *Cathedral in England*: for Want whereof great Confusion and Perplexity in that Kind of Performance generally ensues, to the great Detriment and Disadvantage of those solemn Rites. In that *Service* there is one Verse composed by my Predecessor, the Famous Mr. Henry Purcell, to which, in Justice to his Memory, his Name is applied: the Reason why I did not compose that Verse anew (so as to render the whole Service entirely of my own Composition) is obvious to every Artist: in the rest of That Service composed by me, I have endeavoured, as near as I possibly could, to imitate that great *Master* and celebrated *Composer*, whose name will for ever stand high in the Rank of those who have laboured to improve the English style, in his so happily adapting his Compositions to *English* words in that elegant and judicious Manner, as was unknown to many of his Predecessors, but in this Respect both His and My worthy and honoured *Master, Dr. Blow*, was known likewise to excell.

Croft, it should be said, succeeded Blow as organist of Westminster Abbey in 1708.

Croft works well within his limitations in his Burial Service and his 'imitations' of Purcell's style are few and far between. The order of the pieces, up to the lesson, is:

1. 'I am the Resurrection and the Life saith the Lord' (John 11: 25–6)
2. 'I know that my Redeemer liveth' (John 30: 25–7)
3. 'We brought nothing into this world, and it is certain we can carry nothing out' (Timothy 6: 7; Job 1: 21)
   'The Lord gave and the Lord hath taken away, blessed be the name of the Lord.'
4. 'I said I will take heed unto my ways' (Psalm 39)
   'Lord thou hast been our refuge' (Psalm 90)

Croft prints a choice of five chants for the psalms, including one by Purcell and one of his own. In the recording of his Service neither of the above psalms is sung but Psalm 130, 'Out of the depths have I cried to thee, O Lord, Lord, hear my voice' to Croft's chant.

After the lesson, taken from the fifteenth chapter of the Epistle of St Paul to the Corinthians ('Now is Christ risen from the dead and become the first fruits of them that slept', etc.) the anthem, 'Man that is born of a woman hath but a short time to live', is sung, together with, 'In the midst of life we are in death'.

Croft felt able to compose these words as Purcell's settings were of such an early date. Purcell's 'Thou knowest, Lord' comes next and finally Croft's 'I heard a voice from heav'n saying unto me, Write. From henceforth blessed are the dead which die in the Lord: ev'n so saith the Spirit.'

The Service ends with a chanted *Kyrie*, the monotoned Lord's Prayer, a prayer, a collect, and the blessing.

The singing of four 'sentences' (without any intervening readings) in which the clear enunciation of the words is of the first importance, fetters a composer. Croft's choral writing is given great dignity and solemnity by the words themselves but his music makes a worthy contribution, and the rests are effectively placed so as to let the words of one sentence sink in before the next begins. One senses the composer's pleasure in being able, in his setting of 'In the midst of life we are in death' to introduce a natural point of imitation at 'deliver us not' (into the bitter pains of eternal death) and even more in the 'Amen' at the end of 'I heard a voice from heav'n', where Croft becomes quite expansive. Both from the spiritual and the aesthetic points of view the Anglican Burial Service suffers greatly from comparison with the Requiem Mass. It has an amorphous form and though the words of the superb translation of the Vulgate are most beautiful the ultimate effect does not measure up to the realities of death and judgement.

It is, however, open to Anglican church musicians to devise a form of memorial service without reference to the Book of Common Prayer and this can be given a more satisfactory design. In 1915, for example, Walford Davies composed a short Requiem 'in sacred memory of all those who have fallen in the war', which perhaps has ceased to be used but could well be revived for any funeral service. The service begins with a setting of 'O Saviour of the World' ('Salvator Mundi') and continues with Psalm 130 'Out of the deep have I called unto thee, O Lord' to an Anglican chant by Davies, with 'Requiem aeternam', etc. (in Latin) in place of the *Gloria Patri*.

In similar manner the chanted Psalm 121, 'I will lift up mine eyes unto the hills: from whence cometh my help' is followed by a second and more elaborate setting of 'Requiem aeternam' and this by a sentence from the Book of Common Prayer Burial Service, 'I heard a voice from Heaven, saying unto me, Write, From henceforth blessed are the dead which die in the Lord.' The Service is concluded by responses, a prayer, a hymn, 'No more to sigh, no more to weep, the faithful dead in Jesus sleep' and a joyful *Gloria* 'in which all available voices and instruments should join'. Finally, there is a setting of a poem by John Lydgate entitled, inaccurately, 'Vox ultima crucis'. 'Tarry no longer toward thine heritage, Haste on thy way and be of right cheer.' It ends, 'Come on, my friend, my brother most dear, For thee I offered my blood in sacrifice'. A solo voice then sings, unaccompanied, 'Tarry no longer'.

This is not great music, but it is the work of a sensitive and deeply spiritual composer who never betrayed his high ideals.

5

Memorial Music
and Laments

CHAPTER SEVENTEEN

MEMORIAL MUSIC AND LAMENTS

A custom arose in the fifteenth century of writing laments for recently dead musicians in which they were named and in which the plainsong Requiem Mass was briefly quoted. Thus in Ockeghem's lament *a4* on the death of Gilles Binchois (*c.* 1400–1460) the top part has a French ballade text beginning with the words 'Mort tu es navré' ('Your death has wounded us') while at the close the tenor sings the last line of *Dies irae*, changing 'eis' into the singular, 'Pie Jesu, Domine, dona ei requiem', with a slight modification of the melody. The best known of these laments is Josquin des Prés' *La Déploration de Jehan Ockeghem, a5*. The poem is by Jean Molinet, who also wrote an epitaph in Latin verse on the dead composer. This poem pictures Ockeghem being greeted in heaven by a host of musicians including Dufay, Dunstable, and Binchois. Another poet, Guillaume Crétin, who spoke of Ockeghem's Requiem Mass as 'perfect and exquisite', exhorts other composers besides Josquin to

> . . . lament our master and good father
> The loss is great and should be chronicled.

Josquin's motet-chanson is in two parts, in the first of which the tenor sings the plainsong 'Requiem aeternam dona eis, Domine, et lux perpetua luceat eis', with a rhythm conformable to the movement of the other voice parts, which have the French poem.

> Nymphes des bois, Déesses des fontaines,
> Chantres expers de toutes nations,
> Changez vos voix fort claires et haultaines
> En cris tranchants et lamentations:
> Car d'Atropos les molestations
> Vostre Ockeghem par sa rigeur attrape,
> Le vrai trésoir de musique et chef d'oeuvre,
> Qui de trépas désormais plus n'eschappe
> Dont grand doumage est que la terre coeuvre.

All voices, except the tenor, sing the 'que la terre coeuvre' twice as the tenor sings (luceat) 'eis'.

In Part 2, the tenor is silent while the others call on surviving composers to put on mourning garments for their 'good father' and then, at the close, all sing 'Requiescat in pace. Amen'.

> Accoustrez-vous d'habits de deuil,
> Josquin, Brumel, Pierchon, Compère.
> Et plorez grosses larmes d'oeuil.
> Perdu avec vostre bon père.
> Requiescat in pace. Amen.

This very moving piece is symbolically written in black notes and is an early example, Gustave Reese tells us, of 'eye-music'; a device that could not of course be heard but only seen. The style of Part 1 is in that of Ockeghem. Part 2 is chordal to bring out the names cited the more clearly. (The modern edition uses ordinary notation.) The example below gives the beautifully devised roll-call of the mourning musicians' names and the concluding 'Requiescat in pace'.

Ex. 1

Ex. 2

The custom of writing laments for musicians or friends or public persons was taken up by the madrigalists. One of the earliest of these is by Jacob Arcadelt (*c.* 1510–97), known to us chiefly by his madrigal 'Il bianco e dolce cigno' ('The sweet white swan') and an *Ave Maria* which is, in fact, an arrangement of a secular part song. Arcadelt, born at Liége, was an Italian composer by adoption and one of the masters of the early madrigal. In his *Fifth Book of Madrigals* (1539) there is a lament for a deceased Florentine nobleman, thought to have been Alessandro dei Medici, who was brutally murdered by his cousin Lorenzino in 1537. Alessandro is said to have been a tyrant (that is, a dictator), but the words of the Lament, presumably by Arcadelt, calling on Florentines to mourn their 'best-loved and most cherished son', do not suggest that they regretted his reign. Madrigal Laments never quote the Requiem Mass, but the closing words are a touching prayer that the poet may join his master in peace eternal ('Rendermi col mio deo lusata pace').

Ex. 3

Italian madrigals were sung in England at least as early as 1564 and Dr Fellowes mentions in his book *English Madrigal Composers* (O.U.P., 1925) a set of part books of this date, bound in red leather in good condition, and each part book bearing the royal arms of Queen Elizabeth. Arcadelt is among the composers represented. If England—as in so many affairs—came late into the picture, her composers provided the brief madrigal period with a glorious last act and in Thomas Weelkes (*c.* 1575–1623), Chichester Cathedral's most famous organist, a composer of remarkable imagination and harmonic daring. The last number of his *Airs or Fantastic Spirits for Three Voices* is curiously placed at the end of a volume, published in 1608, consisting of short light-hearted pieces. It is for six, not three voices, and was composed 'as a remembrance for my friend Mr. Thomas Morley', who had died in 1603. The poem begins:

> Death hath deprived me of my dearest friend,
> My dearest friend is dead and laid in grave.

The solemn music, which underlines 'death' with an E flat major chord after one in G major, comes to rest on a low and long-held D major chord bringing to a close what has gone before, but having a codetta with the words 'in grave he rests'. A silent bar follows. Then, beginning with the lowest voice and taken up in rapid succession by the other five come the words 'until the world shall end', to music suggestive of a 'tuba mirum'; the words are repeated to emphatic chords.

Ex. 4

After half a bar of silence the words 'all things must have an end that nature wrought, must unto dust be brought' are solemnly declaimed up to the peaceful final bar.

Both Morley and Weelkes composed elegies on the death of Henry Noel, an amateur musician, devoted to madrigals and a favourite at the Court of Queen Elizabeth. She is said to have made the following rebus, or picture puzzle, on his name:

> The word of negation, and letter of fifty
> Make that gentleman's name who will never be thrifty.

Morley's elegy *a*6 begins with the visionary words 'Hark! Alleluia cheerly with angels he singeth that here loved music dearly' and has a phrase that 'ringeth' in all the voices with great splendour to the words 'whose echo heaven ringeth'.

Ex. 5

Weelkes's lengthy elegy, also *a*6, 'Noel, adieu thou Court's delight, upon whose locks the graces sweetly played' paints a delightful picture of his friend: the 'adieu' at its repetition passes from voice to voice.

Ex. 6

After one of Weelkes's half-bar pauses the mood becomes more grave at 'Now thou art dead', and on the last word Weelkes writes one of his striking harmonies, the first tenor's A clashing with the second soprano's B flat, with poignant effect.

Ex. 7

In the second half of the section beginning 'Bedew, my notes, his death-bed with your tears', the composer writes C sharp against C natural no less than three times in the course of nine bars. This device, favoured notably by the madrigalists but also, in later years, by Purcell and his contemporaries, is by no means harsh to our ears, but truly expressive of the sorrow of the words.

Ex. 8

William Byrd, who gloriously enriched every field of music known to him, composed two 'Funeral songs of the honourable gent, Sir Philip Sydney, Knight', several of whose poems he had set. 'Come to me grief for ever' *a5* is the first, and best, of these songs (Nos. 34–35 of *Songs of Sadness and Piety* published in 1588).

A lovely point is the eliding of the vowel sound in 'day' in the line 'Come to me tears, day and night'. It comes again on 'ah' in the next line 'Come to me plaint, ah, helpless'.

Ex. 9

This lament has the simplicity of genius. It is a joy to read each part and see, before hearing, how finely each phrase is planned.[1]

Byrd's grief at the death of Philip Sidney, on the evidence of these 'funeral songs', must have been real, not official, though of

[1] *Byrd sets only the first verse of the six in the poem.*

course a composer may respond to grief in itself and forget about its object. There could have been no question of that in another of the *Songs of Piety* (No. 33). 'Why do I use my paper, ink, and pen?' *a5*, the words of which were written by Henry Walpole as 'An Epitaph on the life and death of the most famous Clerk and virtuous Priest Edmund Campion'. Campion, a member of the Society of Jesus, was arrested in 1581, charged with conspiracy against the Crown, put on the rack, and executed at Tyburn on 11 December of the same year. The Queen did not believe the charge and would have spared Campion if he had been willing to apostatize. This he refused to do, but his last words were, 'I do pray for Elizabeth, your Queen and my Queen'. This event must have made a deep and lasting impression on Byrd, who all his life had perforce to earn his living and practise his art, at least openly, in the service of the Anglican Church. Elizabeth knew him to be a stiff Papist but also a loyal subject. I wonder if she ever saw and heard this moving and noble monument to Campion and the English Martyrs. The music rings out magnificently in the lines, 'I speak of Saints whose names cannot decay, an Angel's trump were fitter for to sound their glorious death, if such on earth were found.'[1]

'Ye sacred Muses', for voice and strings, is an elegy on the death of Thomas Tallis, Byrd's master and friend, and has a beautiful close at the words 'Tallis is dead and music dies'; the rise of an octave in the penultimate bar is most affecting.

Ex. 10

Byrd's 'Carol of the Holy Child', *a5*, from the *Songs of Piety*, begins with the refrain 'Lulla, lullaby my sweet little Baby'. Edmund Fellowes has pointed out that this refrain, with which the carol also ends, has been so frequently dissociated from the verse of the song that it is not generally recognized that it forms part of a poem whose subject is the Massacre of the Holy Innocents. In the penultimate bar of the refrain there is the clash of C natural with C sharp that I alluded to in Weelkes's *Noel, thou Court's Delight*.

Ex. 11

---

[1] *Byrd sets only the first of the three stanzas of the poem.*

The poem continues:

Be still, my blessed Babe, though cause hast thou to mourn,
Whose blood most innocent to shed the cruel king hath sworn:
And lo, alas!, behold what slaughter he doth make,
Shedding the blood of infants all, sweet Saviour, for Thy sake.
A King, a King is born they say, which King the king would kill,
O woe and woeful heavy day when wretches have their will.

In the first line of this verse Byrd again makes the C natural, C sharp clash, this time between alto and bass, and yet again, alto and tenor, in the penultimate bar. These clashes are indeed needed.

Ex. 12

The man who composed one of the most beautiful of all death songs, Dido's lament in Purcell's *Dido and Aeneas*, found no one to mourn fittingly the grievous loss, at the age of thirty-five, of one of the greatest glories of our music. There was, in fact, no one great enough to fulfil the task, and to say that is not to ignore the merits of Jeremiah Clarke's *Music on Henry Purcell's Death*. Clarke (1670–1707) is known to most people as the composer of the *Trumpet Voluntary*, attributed in the nineteenth century to Purcell, but now certainly proved to be by his young contemporary. (It is one of a number of marches he called after various celebrities of his time, in this case the Prince of Denmark's March.)

His *Music on Henry Purcell's Death* is in the form of a pastoral cantata, the dead composer figuring under the name of Strephon. An overture in the French style—slow—fast—slow, is followed by an alto solo 'with trumpet, kettledrums and continuo', 'Come along for a dance and a song', and this by a recitative for bass contrasting Monarchs 'sweating beneath their heavy diadems' with Pan's peaceful and happy reign in the woods. The shepherds assemble and dance (an instrumental number for trumpet and strings). Then enter the bearers of bad tidings (a soprano solo and chorus). 'Hold back, shepherds hold, break off your joy, for lo! We came to croak the dreadful voice of doom', to which the chorus add 'Alas, we bring the doleful sounds of fate and death'. 'Strephon is dead', and the shepherds (bass solo and chorus) break their pipes. The alto aria, with recorders, that follows, is really moving.

Ex. 13

A short soprano solo 'And see Apollo has unstrung his lyre' is followed by a poignant instrumental piece called 'Mr Purcell's Farewell' for trumpet and strings with the string basses and drums reiterating a note like the tolling of a bell. The cantata ends with a valedictory chorus picturing the composer in Elysium.

> All's untuned, but yond diviner sphere,
> Strephon's soft airs are all translated there.

The music, if of no great originality, is expressive and by no means lacking in pathos, and one is grateful for this one tribute to Purcell.

The two mid-twentieth-century laments with which I end this section were also for close friends, one a poet, the other a musician. In May 1953, Dylan Thomas visited Stravinsky in Boston to discuss a commission proposed by Boston University for the two to collaborate on an opera. It was the first time they had met and Stravinsky, in one of his conversations with Robert Craft (*Conversations with Igor Stravinsky* by Igor Stravinsky and Robert Craft: Faber, 1958) talks with great compassion about the poet, by then a confirmed alcoholic. 'As soon as I saw him I knew that the only thing to do was to love him', a remark that warms the heart. Thomas's idea for the opera 'was to be about the rediscovery of our planet following an atomic misadventure'. There would be a re-creation of language, only the new one would have no abstractions; there would be only people, objects and words. He promised to avoid poetic indulgences. 'No conceits, I'll knock them all on the head.' The two were to meet at the composer's home in Hollywood, but on the 9th of the month a telegram from New York which Stravinsky expected would announce the date of his arrival, gave instead the tragic news of his death. 'All I could do was cry.'

During the following months he thought over composing something to Dylan Thomas's memory and chose the beautiful poem 'Do not go gentle into that good night' which the poet had written to the memory of his father. Stravinsky scored the song for tenor voice and string quartet and later decided 'to add a purely instrumental prelude and postlude (called Dirge-Canons) which are antiphonal canons between a quartet of trombones and the string quartet'. The title of the work, completed in the spring of 1959, is *In Memoriam Dylan Thomas: Dirge-Canons and Song*. It is one of Stravinsky's most appealing and accessible works. The basis of the music is a five-note serial theme, or tone-row, treated through-out with various devices such as inversion of the note sequence and so forth. Some of these the ordinary listener may readily recognize, others may well escape him. The fact is that these devices are really 'eye' music needing to be followed with the score, at least until they become familiar.

Instead of bothering, therefore, about how the wheels go round it is best to concentrate on the symmetry of the design and the emotion generated by the music. Cadences all of the same pattern divide the first dirge-canon (Prelude) into two sections A and B. The five-note theme is in the top part.

Ex. 14

The second dirge-canon (Postlude) begins with the cadence above, now in the bass, and the coda ends with it. The two instrumental groups, trombones and strings, are never combined, but always heard alternately. The canons, of course, derive their 'tone row' from the song. The five notes are present in all parts of its two opening bars.

Ex. 15

Do not go gentle into that good night,
Old age should burn and rave at close of day;
Rage, rage against the dying of the light.

Though wise men at their end know dark is right,
Because their words had forked no lightning they
Do not go gentle into that good night.

Good men, the last wave by, crying how bright
Their frail deeds might have danced in a green bay,
Rage, rage against the dying of the light.

Wild men who caught and sang the sun in flight,
And learn, too late, they grieved it on its way,
Do not go gentle into that good night.

Grave men, near death, who see with blinding sight
Blind eyes could blaze like meteors and be gay,
Rage, rage, against the dying of the light.

And you my father, there on the sad height,
Curse, bless me now with your fierce tears, I pray.
Do not go gentle into that good night.
Rage, rage against the dying of the light.

The whole work, song and canons, is given a fine unity by the various uses of the serial theme which, in the song, can readily be heard at the recurring refrains 'Do not go gentle into that good night' and 'Rage, rage against the dying of the light'. At the words 'And you my father' the five notes are the same as those in the bass part of Ex. 15, an octave higher, and have a specially poignant effect. Stravinsky has never written anything more moving.

Less than a month after Dylan Thomas's death the young Australian pianist, Noel Mewton-Wood, then only thirty-one years old, took his life on 9 December 1953. He was stricken by remorse at not realizing how seriously ill a most beloved friend was and so had not called in the doctor who later diagnosed a perforated appendix. His friend was equally unaware of his condition. Mewton-Wood had made his London debut in the First Beethoven Concerto in 1940 at a Queen's Hall concert conducted by Sir Thomas Beecham and was at once hailed as a pianist of great distinction. He played the same work during the Jubilee of the Promenade Concerts when Sir Henry Wood wrote 'His *pianissimo* is as beautiful as his *fortissimo*, and he reminds me of all the greatest pianists of the past, including Rubinstein, Liszt, and Busoni.' He was as successful in the modern as in the classical repertoire and played to admiration Stravinsky, Bliss, Britten, and Tippett. He was, indeed, always an ardent supporter of the modern school of British composers. And this enormously talented man threw away his life, but threw it away for sorrow born of great love.

Britten, a close friend, composed the third of his Canticles in his memory, taking one of the finest of Edith Sitwell's poems for the purpose. 'Still falls the rain' has the sub-title 'The Raids, 1940,

Night and Dawn', and no one who lived through that terrible time
in London could fail to be moved to the depths by the poem. The
music is laid out for tenor solo, horn, and piano, in the form of a
theme with six variations. These latter come after each verse of the
poem in free recitative. The theme is marked 'slow and distant'. The
piano's accompanying chords are heavy and menacing, and the
theme has the upward and downward scale passages we encounter
again so often in the War Requiem.

Edith Sitwell's poem relates the raids, destroying the innocent,
to the Crucifixion.

> Still falls the Rain—
> Dark as the world of man, black as our loss—
> Blind as the nineteen hundred and forty nails
> Upon the Cross.

In Variation 1, marked 'gently moving', the detached chords
(without pedal) on the piano hold menace. The horn moves downwards and upwards in intervals derived from the theme.

> Still falls the Rain
> With a sound like the pulse of the heart that is changed to
>   the hammer-beat
> In the Potter's Field, and the sound of the impious feet.
> On the Tomb.

The piano continues with the detached chords, but here put only
in the treble. The last line of the poem 'On the tomb' coincides
with the start of Variation 2, scale-wise phrases for horn over the
pulsating piano part.

In Variation 3, marked 'lively', both horn and piano have detached
notes, the music is still *pianissimo*, but there is a whirr of sound in the
sky, and always, at the close, the catastrophic fall from a high treble
to a low bass note.

The fourth verse is impassioned, with a wide flung phrase on
'mercy'.

> Still falls the Rain
> At the feet of the Starved Man hung upon the Cross.
> Christ that each day, each night, nails there, have mercy on us—
> On Dives and on Lazarus:
> Under the Rain the sore and the gold are as one.

Variation 4, marked 'quick and agitated'; it is near now, very
near, the anti-aircraft guns belch forth, the bombs rain down.

Still falls the Rain—
Still falls the Blood from the Starved Man's wounded Side:
He bears in His Heart all wounds—those of the light that died,
The last faint spark
In the self-murdered heart, the wounds of the sad
    uncomprehending dark,
The wounds of the baited bear—
The blind and weeping bear whom the keepers beat
On his helpless flesh . . . the tears of the hunted hare.

Variation 5 sounds like a march of doom with its heavy emphasis on the falling intervals of the theme.

Still falls the Rain—
Then—'O Ile leape up to my God: who pulls me doune—
See, see where Christ's blood streames in the firmament':
It flows from the Brow we nailed upon the tree.
Deep to the dying, to the thirsting heart
That holds the fires of the world, dark smirched with pain
As Caesar's laurel crown.

The quotation is the despairing cry for mercy from Faust's last speech in Marlowe's play *Dr Faustus*. Britten marks it to be declaimed in 'speech-song', that is on the intervals notated. This has always seemed to me to fail in performance and to be inherently less dramatic than a simple vocal line would be united to such powerful words, but this criticism arises out of a detestation of *Sprechgesang*. It is soon forgotten, however, in the poignant use of the falling intervals to the words 'Deep' (to the dying), (to the) 'Thirsting heart', 'dark smirched' (with pain). A long pause at the end of the verse precedes the final variation which unites with the last three lines of the poem.

Then sounds the voice of One who like the heart of man
Was once a child who among beasts has lain—
'Still do I love, still shed my innocent light, my Blood, for
    thee.'

The inspired words of the poet draw equally inspired music, of the same exquisite simplicity, from the composer. The variant of the theme is heard as a duet between voice and horn, the two melody lines in contrary motion, the tempo slow, as at the start, the piano, coming in later, with chords of the same character as before. The tragedy is not mitigated, but death is robbed of its victory.

Ex. 16

*

Many years ago now I made a pilgrimage to the graves of Beethoven, Schubert, Brahms, and Wolf, who are all buried in a musicians' corner of the vast Central Cemetery, Vienna. It was Schubert's song *An die Musik* that especially came into my mind then, his tribute of loving thanks to his art, which he enables us to make ours also. But now I think of the songs about death these composers wrote that could be described under the heading of 'Requiem' without theological overtones. Beethoven's has nothing here to contribute except the stern song 'Vom Tode' ('To Death'), the second of the six of the Gellert cycle, the best known of which are 'Die Ehre Gottes aus der Natur' (Nature's praise of God—'The heavens are telling the glory of the Lord') and 'Busslied' ('Penitence'). 'Vom Tode' warns that death may come like a thief in the night, therefore meditate on the thought with chastened spirit, neglect it at your peril. The song is only one page long but a powerful page, and one that possibly came into Schubert's mind when he was composing Death's utterance in one of his masterpieces of song, 'Death and the Maiden'. The resemblance is technical rather than spiritual for in Schubert's song Death comes as a friend, but in Beethoven's as a grim spectre waiting in the wings.

Of Schubert's 'Litanei auf das Fest aller Seelen' ('Litany for the Feast of All Souls') Richard Capell well said, 'There never was a truer or more touching expression of simple devotion and of grief consoled and yet still near weeping.' This is his paraphrase of the poem by J. G. Jacobi.

Surely they rest well, the souls of the departed,
There where all wounds are stanched and
The mourner is comforted. They have passed
From the world's mercilessness to the everlasting mercy.

Schubert was not at all orthodox in his religious views but even if he had ceased to be a Catholic in more than name before his twenty-first year, when he composed this song, the thought of All Souls' Day, a remembrance of the candles, as night fell, lit by sorrowing hands and flickering on the graves of the departed in the vast cemetery, thousands of points of light like prayers for the 'lux aeterna', all this may have inspired the heart-easing melody of his song. Were ever words so perfectly mated with tones as in the refrain with which the vocal line begins and ends, 'Alle Seelen ruhn in Frieden' ('May all souls rest in peace'), with the tender dwelling on 'ruhn'? The voice, it may be remembered, ends each verse with the refrain but the piano carries on the melody to its lovely conclusion. A skilled accompanist would not fail to mark the extra touch of beauty given by the chord 'out of the key', but not alien to it, in the last bar.

The earliest of a group of songs by Wolf with words by four different poets, and dedicated to the memory of his father, is 'Zur Ruh, zur Ruh!' ('To rest, to rest!'), the poem by Justinius Kerner. This song, composed when he was twenty-three, was one of the first to show Wolf's individuality and to foreshadow the splendid Mörike collection. It is impossible to listen to this noble song without thinking of the rest denied Wolf in the agonizing last years of his life, when he lay stricken with general paralysis in a mental hospital, waiting for a long-delayed death. One of his last utterances was 'loathsome music', addressed to the art he had so passionately loved and to which his whole life had been dedicated. And so, remembering this tragic clouding of his mind, one cannot hear the song without a deeper emotion than it already generates.

> To rest, to rest, the toil is over
> May slumber blest mine eyelids cover
> I am alone, earth's sorrows vanish.
> Night's sombre zone my gloom can banish.

Between the words 'I am' and 'alone' Wolf places a quaver rest which underlines the poignance of the latter word. The remainder of the song is a prayer, in quicker time, rising with ever-increasing fervour to a great climax in the last line, and then leaving the piano to recapitulate the quiet opening measures, which sink down to absolute peace.

> Lead me to night, ye powers immortal
> Into the light, through midnight's portal.
> In dreams apart from cares that grieve me,
> The Mother heart will there receive me.

Wolf, throughout his professional life, never ceased to abuse Brahms, sometimes in terms which went far beyond legitimate criticism. This arose partly from envy at the older man's success and resentment at his anti-Wagnerism. Brahms treated Wolf's often vitriolic remarks with great charity, recognizing the nature of their origin. His own last publication was the *Four Serious Songs* composed in 1896, a year before his death. He told his publisher with the ponderous humour that he often affected in speaking of his works, 'I have amused myself on my birthday by writing a few little songs'. He feared that the public performance of 'these altogether godless songs, whose words, thank Heaven, are in the Bible', might be prohibited on religious grounds, though, of course, nothing of the sort happened. A young lawyer friend, Dr Ophüls, whom he consulted over this matter, has left a very touching description of how Brahms sang and played his new work, at the house of some friends, on returning from the funeral of Clara Schumann at Easter 1896.

> He was so deeply moved during the rendering of the third song 'O Tod, wie bitter bist du' ('O Death, how bitter art thou') that great tears rolled down his cheeks, and the pathetic end 'O Tod, wie wohl bist du' ('O death how welcome art thou') he almost murmured to himself in a voice choked with emotion. I shall never forget the tremendous effect of this song. It was characteristic of Brahms, who disguised a very tender heart with an armour of outer roughness, that after the last note had died away, obviously seeking to hide his emotion, he turned to me, sitting on his left, and with a heavy slap on my leg, said, 'Young man, this is not for you: you must not think of these things at all'.

This was a view of Brahms never vouchsafed to Wolf.

Max Friedlander, in his book *Brahms's Lieder*, tells us that in the years 1897–98, when special items were introduced in memory of Brahms, the *Serious Songs* were sung in almost all the towns of Germany, Austria, Switzerland, and Holland as a sort of requiem for the master.

> O death, how bitter is the remembrance of thee to a man that liveth at rest in his possessions, unto the man that hath nothing to vex him, and that hath prosperity in all things: yea, unto him that is yet able to receive meat.

The song, to words from Ecclesiasticus 41, is a combination of accompanied recitative and arioso rather in the manner of so many movements in Bach's Church Cantatas, very familiar to Brahms.

The entry of the voice alone on 'O', the piano at 'Death' at once brings Death, a dreaded visitor to the well nourished with his accumulation of riches, who bids himself eat, drink, and be merry, the man who has chosen pleasure as his god, but whose soul is now required of him. The repeated phrases at 'bitter' are like a despairing but futile cry. The bell tolls for him in the repeated notes at 'und noch wohl essen mag'! Eating his meat he had no thought of Lazarus at the gate. Brahms repeats the opening words and music but this time meditatively, as if with some compassion for what the fool has said in his heart. Then, with a beautiful change into the major key, come the prophet's thoughts about the poor man.

> O death, acceptable is thy sentence unto the needy, and unto him whose strength faileth, that is now in the last age, and is vexed with all things, and to him that despaireth, and hath lost patience.

No recitative at the start here, but a consoling lyrical melody with a moving emphasis on 'needy' and a different kind of bitterness coming into the music as the poor man falls into despair at his lot in life, a deep sigh, the despair of one who has nothing to hope for, as he cries out in the extended phrase at 'Erwarten'. Brahms does not end with those words of the preacher. Once more the music moves into the major as, with slowly descending notes in the treble of the piano, like a benediction, the poor man, who now has a friend, murmurs, 'O Death, how welcome art thou'. Here at last is rest.

Ex. 17

This is undoubtedly one of the greatest songs ever written. Richard Strauss's *Vier Letzte Lieder* ('Four Last Songs'), composed a year before his death in 1949, are not on the same level as Brahms's *Four Serious Songs* but they are both beautiful and a most moving testimony to his life-long love of the soprano voice, and of his love for his wife, Pauline de Ahna, who, in her day, was a distinguished soprano. This remarkable woman used to explain to anyone willing, or unwilling, to listen, as Lotte Lehmann tells us in her enchanting book *Singing with Richard Strauss*, that 'she had married beneath her and regarded her husband as essentially nothing but a peasant, a country yokel', and that his music was in no way comparable to that of Massenet. She took pleasure, when singing his songs at a recital, in drawing attention exclusively to herself in various ways, and if (as in the song 'Schlechtes Wetter') the pianist had a postlude on his own she 'would contrive to make a deep bow, thus forcing the audience to applaud and interrupt the music'. Yet Strauss loved this sadistic, caustic-tongued woman truly and profoundly and seems to have enjoyed her quirks and rages. His one-act opera *Intermezzo*, which has a libretto by himself, based on their domestic life, contains a curtain line, 'Ours is a truly happy marriage'. And that is what he believed it to be. She kept him, he said, in order!

For the last of the songs 'Im Abendroth' ('At Sunset') he chose a poem by Joseph von Eichendorff, many of whose poems were set by Schumann and Wolf, to portray his wife and himself in the sunset of their old age, and near to death.

> Through troubles and joys
> We have gone, hand in hand:
> Now we both rest from our wanderings
> High over the still countryside.
>
> The valleys descend round about us;
> The skies are already growing dark.
> Only two larks, remembering a dream,
> Are rising into the haze.
>
> Come, let them fly—
> Soon it is time to sleep.
> We must not go astray
> In this loneliness.
>
> O wide still peace!
> So deep in the sunset glow,
> How weary we are with wandering—
> Can this be death?

The strings, in the orchestral prelude, have a quietly rhythmic figure expressive of the halting footsteps of old age, the voice part dwells tenderly on the words 'hand in hand', and soon two flutes trill upwards as the larks rise into the evening air. A phrase of great beauty enfolds the words 'O wide still peace' and then at 'Can this —be—Death'—the words separated by rests—there rises up from the orchestra the theme of transfiguration from the composer's tone-poem *Tod und Verklärung*, which is repeated as the voice ceases on the word 'Tod'. The larks sing faintly in the closing bars.

Ex. 18

The song is a very moving testimony to a love that never failed in spite of all provocation and I should like to think that Strauss's wife was touched to tears by it—and thought it better than Massenet!

*

The great Laments of David for Saul and Jonathan, and for Absalom have inspired music worthy of them. The earliest setting of the first of these laments is the plainsong antiphon for the Magnificat on the Saturday before the Fifth Sunday after Pentecost. It uses only the latter portion of the long Lament.

Montes Gelboe, nec ros, nec pluvia veniat super vos, quia in te abjectus est clypeus fortium, clypeus Saul, quasi non esset unctus oleo. Quomodo ceciderunt fortes in praelio? Jonathas in excelsis tuis interfectus est: Saul et Jonathas, amabiles et decori valde in vita sua, in morte quoque non sunt separati.

Ye mountains of Gilboa let there be no dew, neither let there be rain upon you: for there the shield of the mighty is vilely cast away, the shield of Saul, as though he had not been anointed with oil. How are the mighty fallen in the midst of battle? Jonathan is slain upon the high places: Saul and Jonathan were lovely and pleasant in their lives, and in their death they were not divided.

On the Fifth Sunday after Pentecost, the lessons read at the night-office of Mattins are taken from Samuel 2: 1, which recounts the slaughter of Saul and his son Jonathan so that David's Lament is anticipated in the Saturday antiphon. Plainsong is emotionally a very retrained art but it indulges in tone-painting more than is usually supposed. How could the unknown monk who composed this antiphon not be moved by the words and shape some at least of his phrases accordingly? I can only quote two instances. 'How are the mighty fallen in the midst of battle.' As so often in plainsong the emotional phrase comes on a word of secondary importance, 'quomodo' ('How'), which colours the whole passage that follows.

Ex. 19

The peak emotional climax comes in the last words 'Saul and Jonathan were lovely and pleasant in their lives, and in their death they were not divided.'

Sa—ul   et   Jo-na-thas

Ex. 20

The Lament was also set by Josquin des Prés under the title of *Planxit David*, a fine motet *a*4, in three sections, which makes a poignant use, in all parts, of the plainsong tone for the Lamentations of the Prophet Jeremiah in Holy Week.[1]

But the most moving setting and the one in which 'the very soul of passionate grief is transmuted into sound' comes in Handel's oratorio *Saul*, one of his finest works and shamefully neglected today. The bodies of the king and his son are borne to their graves in the greatest of all funeral marches, the only one not marred by the intrusion of personal emotion, nor by a trio. The mourning of the chorus for 'thy choicest youth on Gilboa slain' is followed, one must admit, by two indifferent short solos for David in which Handel may well have been handicapped by the banality of the words of the libretto provided by Charles Jennens; but all this is forgotten as the orchestra, in terms of that divine simplicity of which Handel alone had the secret, begins the prelude to David's lament over Saul and Jonathan, 'In sweetest harmony they lived.' The great solo and chorus 'O fatal day, how low the mighty lie' follows on without a break. The music goes abruptly into the minor key as David sings 'O Jonathan! O Jonathan! How nobly didst thou die'.

In sweetest har—mony   they liv'd,   Nor death,   nor death   their u—nion could di-vide,

O — — — —Jo-na-than! O – –Jo-na than! how no bly didst thou die, for thy king & coun-try slain!

Ex. 21

[1] *See page* 162.

The chorus repeat these words and then David, alone, continues to pour out his grief, his love for his friend 'passing the love of women'.

If only the words had been as fine as Peter Abelard's magnificent lament which ends, in Helen Waddell's inspired translation:

> Peace, O my stricken lute!
> Thy strings are sleeping.
> Would that my heart could still
> Its bitter weeping.[1]

David's lament for his son Absalom drew fine music from Josquin, Weelkes, Schütz, and Tomkins. Josquin and Schütz set only the actual lament, the former adding the words, 'I live no more, I go down weeping into hell.' Tomkins paraphrases the introductory words in Samuel 2: 18, 33.

> The King was deeply moved. He wept as he went up to the chamber above the gateway, and as he wept he cried 'O my son Absalom! my son, my son, Absalom! Oh that I had died instead of you, O Absalom, my son, my son.'

Josquin's motet, *Absalon, fili mi* for alto, two tenors, and bass, begins with the always effective convention of the four voices entering one after the other, from alto to bass, with the same phrase.

The emotional situation, the anguished repetitions of 'my son Absalom' could not fail, even with less fine music, to move the listener, but skilled moulding of the phrases, every one full of grief in the context, make this wonderful motet almost unbearably poignant. The range of the top part, in one phrase, spans a ninth within the same number of bars and as it ends the first tenor part rises to a high-pitched cry.

Ab-sa-lon, Ab —— sa-lon

Ex. 22

At the close of the motet, 'Non vivam ultra, sed descendam in infernam plorans', Josquin illustrates 'descendam' by a series of falling thirds in all the voices.

Schütz' setting is the thirteenth number of his *Symphoniae Sacrae* Part 1, 1624. Heinrich Schütz (1585–1672), the greatest Lutheran composer before J. S. Bach, was fortunate enough to have a generous employer in the Landgrave Maurice of Hesse-Cassel. He

---

[1] *Helen Waddell*, Mediaeval Latin Lyrics (*Penguin Books, 1952*).

perceived a special talent for music in the young law student then at Marburg University, and made it possible for him to go to Venice in 1609 to study with Giovanni Gabrielli. From this great composer Schütz learnt the secrets of the sumptuous and dramatic polychoral style and the colourful use of instruments which he applied to his settings of the Psalms for two, three, and four choirs of voices and instruments.

In 1628, twelve years after the death of Giovanni Gabrielli, Schütz made a second visit to Venice to study the technique of 'the sagacious Monteverdi' who had, since Schütz' first visit, become famous and from his music learnt new developments of the *concertato* style, particularly the idiomatic handling of instruments, the fashioning of orchestral accompaniments more ambitious than those of Gabrielli, and the greater possibilities in the expressive use and range of the solo voice. One of the best-known of the pieces in the *Symphoniae Sacrae*—it comes in Part 3, 1650—is 'Saul, Saul, warum verfolgst du mir?' ('Saul, Saul, why persecutest thou me?'), the story of the conversion of Saul on the road to Damascus. It is scored for soloists, double choir, and orchestra. It is delightful to read that the Lutheran composer could go to school, so to say, with his Catholic masters on terms of friendship, could absorb all that they, and colourful Venice, had to teach him and from what he learnt make such a wonderful fusion of Italian and German music, of Catholic emotionalism and Lutheran fervour, tempered by a natural restraint. It was from Giovanni Gabrielli that he had learnt how to use brass instruments as an ensemble, or with voices. Both these uses are found in his *scena Fili mi, Absalon* scored for solo bass, four trombones, and harpsichord (or organ). David's lament is preceded by a *Sinfonia* which anticipates the singer's entry, his voice rising from the depths of woe, in its use of thirds.

Fi—li mi, fi–li mi, fi–li mi, fi–li mi, Ab-sa-lon, fi–li mi, fi–li mi, fi–li mi, Absa—lon.

Ex. 23

The trombones are silent until David's piteous cries of 'Absalon, fili mi' begin, when their dark solemn tones enclose the vocal lines. Schütz uses major and minor thirds, fourths, and fifths, in the repeated cries of 'Absalon', to express the bitterness and anguish of David's loss. The second part of the lament is preceded by another *Sinfonia* with a new theme.

The trombones fall silent as David pleads how willingly he would have died for his son and re-enter as his cries of 'Absalon' break out again and continue to the end, where the voice of the broken-hearted father drops down a despairing octave.

Towards the end of his life Schütz became deaf and withdrew into isolation. He had long since lost his beloved wife—perhaps he mourned for her in this lament—and he found consolation in reading his Bible, the Psalms above all. He was a much more deeply religious man than Monteverdi and his music has none of his Italian contemporary's sensuousness. Much of it is functional, but whenever it is performed with understanding, even the austere settings of the four Passions, it makes a profound impression. To him, as indeed to Monteverdi, the word was master of the music. He was a master of declamation.

Thomas Tomkins (1572–1656) is the fourth and most notable of a family of twelve musicians listed in *Grove*. He was one of Byrd's pupils, and organist of Worcester Cathedral from 1596 to 1646, when the services were suspended after the second siege of the city. His anthem 'When David heard that Absalom was dead' dates from 1600 and like all his music is composed in the great English polyphonic choral tradition. The text sets the tragic scene.

> When David heard that Absalom was slain, he went up to his chamber over the gate and wept, and thus he said 'my son, my son, Absalom, would God I had died for thee, O Absalom my son'.

It is impossible to convey the harmonic subtleties in this anthem without extensive quotation but there are one or two outstanding points. The impact of the minor chord at the start, its use after the sudden breaking off of the treble part at 'his chamber', when the alto part has the minor third, all parts then completing the sentence. The drop from treble E natural to alto E flat seems to depict the shocked state of David's mind at the terrible news.

Ex. 24

Like the other two composers Tomkins continually varies David's sorrowful cries, as the illustration below shows. Simple analysis of such passages, which the eye can do, tells more than any verbal description.

The composer also varies the accented word, sometimes emphasizing 'Absalom my *son*', up to the cry, 'would God I had died for thee', but at the repetition 'Absalom *my* son' with a passion of fatherhood.

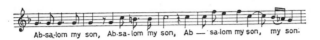

Ab-sa-lom my son, Ab-sa-lom my son, Ab — sa-lom my son, my son.

Ex. 25

In the four closing bars the top voice reiterates the note C with a sound like the tolling of a funeral bell (*see* page 195).

6

Modern Elegiac
Works

CHAPTER EIGHTEEN

ELGAR'S *THE DREAM OF GERONTIUS*

On 8 May 1889 the marriage of Edward William Elgar to Caroline Alice Roberts took place at Brompton Oratory, London. Elgar, then thirty-two and little known outside Worcester, his home town, was struggling for recognition as a composer. His wife, the daughter of a general, had been left an orphan two years earlier and had to face the disapproval of her relations at what they considered to be a misalliance with a poor, unknown musician in a different social class. It turned out to be, as all the world came to know, an ideal marriage. Elgar's military bearing concealed a hyper-sensitive nature and Alice Elgar, musically minded and with some literary talent, knew just how to calm and encourage him. She had intuitively perceived his genius from the first, but without her help the course of his career might have been very different. When she died, in 1920, a large part of him died too.

Elgar's parish priest at Worcester, Father Knight, gave him a copy of Cardinal Newman's poem, *The Dream of Gerontius*, first published in 1865, as a wedding present. Elgar, as will be seen, already possessed a copy, but this was something special. General Gordon, in the course of a talk on religion, had told a friend he had a presentiment he was going to die at Khartoum and, with this in mind, the friend sent him a copy of *The Dream*. The General marked in it passages that especially appealed to him, and on the very day he entered the doomed city gave his copy to Frank Power, who sent it to his sister in Dublin and she forwarded it on to Newman. He wrote to her, 'Your letter and its contents took my breath away. I was deeply moved to find that a book of mine had been in General Gordon's hands, and that a description of a soul preparing for death.' Father Knight copied General Gordon's markings into the copy he gave Elgar. It was, presumably, as a result of this that Elgar was moved to consider at this time composing a symphony on the subject of Gordon, a project subsequently abandoned.

In 1885 Dvořák, then in England for the Birmingham Festival, had visited Cardinal Newman at the Oratory and been given a copy of *The Dream*, in a German version, by one of the Fathers. The subject appealed to him as a work for the 1888 Festival, but objections were raised mainly on religious grounds, and the composer lost interest. For that we should be thankful. Dvořák could never have penetrated to the very heart of the poem as Elgar did, but if he had tried the latter might never have given us his greatest work. It used to annoy Elgar if people said that *Gerontius* was the outcome of a commission for the 1900 Birmingham Festival. The idea, he said, had been simmering in his head for eight years. The work he intended for Birmingham was to be on St Augustine, but this was turned down as 'too controversial': he then suggested 'a purely scriptural thing', but nothing came of that. He had, of course, *Gerontius* in mind and Alice Elgar's diary at the time of the 1899 Three Choirs Festival bears the significant remark 'E. walked with Father Bellasis'. He was a priest of the London Oratory and helped Elgar with the cuts that had to be made in the poem, but the composer still hesitated to commit himself. There had been too many disappointments before. He wrote to Novello's, his publishers, 'Will your firm want the work? I want to make this my chief work and to devote myself to it with something like a free mind.' On 5 February 1900 Elgar wrote to A. J. Jaeger—'Nimrod' of the *Enigma Variations*—'I am setting Newman's *Dream of Gerontius*—awfully solemn and mystic.' The vocal score was completed on 6 June—an incredibly short space of time—and the next day Jaeger, who had given invaluable help, had a letter from the composer with the words, 'God bless you, Nimrod, here's the end.' Two months later the orchestral score was finished. Elgar had now fulfilled a wish he had expressed the year before his marriage. 'I hope some day to do a great work, a sort of national thing that my fellow Englishmen might take to themselves and love', and in course of time a large number of them did so. (The rest rejoiced in 'Land of Hope and Glory'!)

At the start of his score Elgar put the initials 'AMDG' ('Ad maiorem gloriam Dei') and at the end a quotation from Ruskin's *Sesame and Lilies*, 'This is the best of me, for the rest, I ate and drank, and slept, loved, and hated, like another: my life was as the vapour, and is not; but this I saw and knew; this, if anything of mine, is worth your memory.' The first six words reveal why *Gerontius* is Elgar's masterpiece. A composer can hardly hope to be visited many times by such a vision.

Elgar, as I have said, was in close touch with Jaeger all through the months he was composing the work, and when the completed score was before him the latter wrote to the composer, 'The more I study the work, the more I marvel. *Gerontius* is miles ahead of anything you have ever done . . . it is the most beautiful and ennobling work since Wagner's *Parsifal*—indeed in a way it *is* another *Parsifal*.'

But Elgar's shrewd friend gave him a warning. 'You must not, cannot expect this work of yours to be appreciated by the ordinary amateur critic after one hearing.' It seems obvious enough, but Jaeger was seeing farther than that.

The first performance took place at Birmingham on 2 October 1900. Elgar was delighted with his three soloists and felt they could not be improved on. Edward Lloyd, the tenor, was in his prime as an artist in 1900 and, as it happened, this event was to be his last important appearance, for he retired this same year. Marie Brema had sung all the great Wagner mezzo-soprano roles at Bayreuth and elsewhere and, as I well remember, was a magnificent Orpheus in Gluck's opera. Plunket Greene had made a reputation as an oratorio and Lieder singer. The great Richter was to conduct. On 24 August Elgar was told that the chorus were delighted with their music and a month later the first rehearsal with them went well. His wife, however, put in her diary at the end of the month, 'Chorus dull and wretched'. Something was going wrong. On 11 June, Swinnerton Heap, a founder of the North Staffordshire Festivals, and a talented conductor who had an innate understanding of Elgar's music, had died of pneumonia, and W. Stockley, in whose orchestra Elgar had once played in earlier years, was called out of retirement to take over the training of the chorus. It became apparent that he was, as a Nonconformist, out of sympathy with the poem, and by the end of August he found the chorus worried with the difficulties of the parts they were now encountering. One of their members wrote some years after the performance, 'One section of the chorus had no idea what the others were doing (or not doing) and being a new work we had not grasped the grand idea of the work as a whole.' It seems that they had been given only single voice parts for reasons of economy.

Elgar came only to the final rehearsal. This, the day before the performance, lasted six hours. The composer stood by Richter trying to explain what he wanted; and not getting this from the chorus told them, 'It's no better than a drawing-room ballad.' Tempers rose, nerves became jagged, and it was a weary, resentful, and apprehensive body of singers who filed on to the platform the next evening. According to one account, 'They dropped in pitch, made ragged entries, and sang with little understanding.' Fuller-Maitland, the newly appointed critic of *The Times*, wrote of the work as 'remarkable and in some ways beautiful'. He was impressed by Elgar's extraordinary instinct for orchestral colour, became weary of 'a succession of strange harmonies arranged in gorgeous clothing' and longed 'for some melodic theme lightly supported'; but he gave high praise to the final sections of both parts, as well as to the Litany in Part 1 and the Prelude to Part 2. He considered Gerontius's dying utterances 'too declamatory for listeners of only moderate cultivation'—a verdict that explains the deadly nature of late nineteenth-century English oratorios. Not a word, you observe, about a poor performance. On the contrary, he wrote, 'the work had been very carefully prepared'.

Jaeger's account in a letter to 'Dorabella' (Mrs Richard Powell) is very different. 'It was *lack* of enthusiasm both in the performers and amongst the critics which riled me at B'ham and afterwards, when I read the critiques. . . . I won't say a word about the performance, but I suffered purgatory!! This disenchantment after my hours of exaltation and refreshment at the pianoforte was too cruel. . . . Old St— the chorus-mess-ter ought to be boiled and served on toast for having had us in purgatory for nigh 2 hours.'

Elgar, for his part, wrote to Jaeger with a bitterness he was to show about his music and the public in later years but never in terms so violent as these. 'I have worked hard for forty years, and at last Providence denies me a decent hearing of my work: so I submit . . . I have allowed my heart to open once—it is now shut against every religious feeling and every soft, gentle impulse for ever.' This seemed to Jaeger 'a weak and wicked "outburst" ', but Elgar's extremely sensitive nature was deeply wounded and he hit out hard. As it happened Providence had not deserted him. A representative group of German musicians was in the audience, headed by Professor Julius Blüths of Düsseldorf Conservatory, and at the end of the performance, Jaeger tells us, 'he grasped my hand (before everyone) and blurted out "A wonderful work; one of the loveliest I know" '. And so it came about that the next performance of *Gerontius*, in a German translation, was given in December 1901, at the Lower Rhine Festival at Düsseldorf. Elgar's wounds began to heal, the fine performance bore out, he said, his own idea of the work. At the repeat performance the next year Richard Strauss gave a luncheon in Elgar's honour and proposed the famous toast, 'I drink to the welfare and success of the first English progressive musician, Meister Elgar.' (The context shows Strauss meant the first in modern times, though I doubt if he had ever heard of Dunstable or Byrd.) The British public stirred in its sleep and asked when they would be given a chance to hear a work that had been called impracticable by some of the critics, and was apparently shelved. When London heard it, in the loving care of Henry Wood, they began to have a glimpse of what Elgar had seen and known and expressed in his masterpiece.

There was certainly some excuse for the audience to be baffled not so much by the music as by the poem at that first performance, and even today one finds people not at all clear about the nature of Gerontius's dream.

Newman dedicated his poem to the memory of a beloved friend, Father John Joseph Gordon—'the *life* of our Oratory at Birmingham' —who died in 1853 at the age of forty-two; but the name 'Gerontius', from a Greek word meaning 'old man', suggests he may have had his own death in mind, for he was then sixty-five. He did not, in fact, die until twenty-five years later.

Elgar formed a clear picture of the old man of the title. 'Look here: I imagined Gerontius to be a man like us, not a priest or a saint, but a sinner, a repentant one of course, but still no end of a worldly man in his life, and now brought to book. Therefore I've not filled his part with church tunes and rubbish, but a good healthy and full-blooded romantic remembered worldliness, so to speak.' It would have been interesting to know how Newman would have regarded that opinion. I recall one of his sermons, 'Neglect of Divine Calls and Warnings', preached at St Mary's, Oxford, and included in the volume *Sermons to Mixed Congregations*, which paints a scarifying picture of just such a worldly sinner, a rich one, who finds himself after death in Hell. 'But you can't mean *me*', he says, emphasizing his respectable position in the world, reciting his charitable deeds—which cost him nothing. It becomes clear as his tortures begin—they are described with sadistic fervour by Newman —that it is indeed he that is meant. There follows a marvellous piece of prose:

> O what a moment for the poor soul when it comes to itself and finds itself suddenly before the Judgement seat of Christ. O what a moment when breathless with the journey and dizzy with the brightness and overcome with the strangeness of what is happening to him and unable to realize where he is, the sinner hears the voice of the accusing spirit, bringing up all the sins of his past life which he has forgotten, or which he has explained away, which he would not allow to be sins, though he suspected they were. Ah poor soul, as it thus fights with that destiny it brought upon itself and those companions it has chosen, the man's name, perhaps, is solemnly chanted forth and his memory decently cherished among his friends on earth.

I daresay the undergraduates were more moved to admire Newman's eloquence than to heed his warnings, for it is hard to discover what the poor man had done to deserve eternal punishment! At any rate Gerontius 'No end of a worldly man . . . a sinner' was a repentant one, which one supposes the other defiantly was not, and for Gerontius the happy issue is never in doubt.

The need to make cuts in the poem, either because the words were intractable for music or, as in the hymn, 'Praise to the Holiest in the height', when there were far too many verses for practical purposes and so on, only matter, as we shall see, when vital explanatory material is omitted and so obscures the exact natures of Gerontius's dream and of his subsequent awakening.

The Prelude is a wonderfully vivid and moving picture of the death of Gerontius. The doctor's work is done, the priest has heard the dying man's confession, assured him of God's pardon, absolved him from his sins, and given him Viaticum—literally provision for a journey and so applied to Holy Communion administered to those in likelihood of immediate death to strengthen them with grace for their journey into eternity. It remains for the priest and the friends round the dying man's bed to recite the 'Recommendation of a departing soul' (the Litanies heard in the first part of the work) and the great prayer beginning 'Proficiscere anima Christiana de hoc mundo' ('Go forth Christian soul from this world'), and at the expiry the beautiful responsory 'Subvenite sancti Dei'. ('Come to his assistance, all ye Saints of God, meet him, all ye Angels of God receiving his soul, offering it in the sight of the Most High. May Christ receive thee, who hath called thee, and may the Angels conduct thee to Abraham's bosom. Eternal rest give to him, O Lord, and let perpetual light shine upon him.') Newman did not quote this responsory.

The themes of the Prelude (all of which except 'sleep' recur in both parts of the work) are expressive of the emotions of Gerontius's last hours. In his conversation with the Angel he says, 'Along my earthly life the thought of death and judgement was to me most terrible', and this is why, even though he is so well prepared for death, the solemn theme of *Judgement* (clarinets, bassoons, and violas in unison with its second, harmonized strain and bringing in other instruments) is followed by a sudden spasm of *Fear* (muted strings) but then at once by *Prayer* (woodwind) which for the moment resolves his fears. We must suppose him to have been conscious up to this point, but now he falls into a fevered *Sleep*. The accompaniment to the muted solo viola melody, at this point, is made out of a version of the *Fear* theme (cello and harp). The viola melody reaches an impassioned climax with the phrases in which Gerontius appeals for mercy. 'Miserere, Judex meus, parce mihi, Domine' (the refrain of 'Sanctus fortis, sanctus Deus'). There succeeds the theme of *Despair*, made more poignant by its scoring at first for cor anglais and solo cello; it is the melody of Gerontius's cry, 'O Jesu, help! Pray for me, Mary.' This melody is raised to a highly emotional pitch in notes of longer length, that bring in the full force of the orchestra. The next theme, 'Go forth upon thy journey, Christian soul', repeated twice, the second time with great orchestral splendour, tells us that the end is near. A stroke on the gong signifies the death of Gerontius, a gentle end, with a sound of harps. The coda briefly recapitulates the themes of *Sleep*, *Fear*, *Despair*, and *Judgement*, and then we hear Gerontius cry 'Jesu, Maria, I am near to death.'

Is he still in the body or not? At the moment of death one is conscious of shock at seeing a loved face become an empty mask. Gerontius is not dreaming his last hours in an empty shell. I mentioned in Chapter 1 the pagan notion, taken over by the early Christians, that the soul hovered near the body for a space before finally quitting it. That is how I picture the dream of Gerontius. No significant lines are omitted in this part of the poem which is headed 'Gerontius'; but in the second section 'Soul of Gerontius', after the inexpressibly beautiful Prelude, true music of felicity, Gerontius recalls his falling asleep and dreaming. All the lines given below are omitted.

> . . . someone softly said
> 'He's gone'; and then a sigh went round the room.
> And then I surely heard a priestly voice
> Cry 'subvenite': and they knelt in prayer.

He cries:

> Ah! whence is this? What is this severance?
> Am I alive or dead? I am not dead,
> But in the body still: for I possess
> A sort of confidence which clings to me
> That each particular organ holds its place
> As heretofore, combining with the rest
> Into one symmetry that wraps me round,
> And makes me man: and surely I could move,
> Did I but will it, every part of me.

But he finds, by trial, that he cannot move or feel or be conscious of any posture, yet towards the end of his long narrative he says, (these words are set) 'Another marvel: someone has me fast within his ample palm', but the omitted following lines explain the inconsistency.

> 'tis not a grasp
> Such as they use on earth, but all around
> Over the surface of my subtle being
> As though I were a sphere, and capable
> To be accosted thus . . .

(Here the libretto continues with 'a uniform and gentle pressure tells me I am not self-moving', etc.)

Clearly the soul of Gerontius now no longer hovers near his body, as he at first thought, but is in outer space.

There is a large cut now from the Angel's solo and the first words of the Soul's awareness of him, but, though this involves the loss of splendid lines in the six stanzas for the Angel, the only ones relevant to this examination come in the Soul's reaction to what he has heard.

> Now know I surely that I am at length
> Out of the body: had I part with earth,
> I never could have drunk those accents in,
> And not have worshipped like a god the voice
> That was so musical!

The Soul's colloquy with the Angel, in the next section, continues from the start to 'What lets me now from going to my Lord!' and the Angel's reply:

> Thou art not let; but with extremest speed
> Art hurrying to the Just and Holy Judge.

What follows is cut:

> For scarcely art thou disembodied yet
> Divide a moment, as men measure time,
> Into its million-million-millionth part,
> Yet even less the interval
> Since thou didst leave the body: and the priest
> Cried 'subvenite', and they fell to prayer;
> Nay, scarcely yet have they begun to pray.

Such lines, and the explanation that follows of the different ways spirits and men measure 'the flow of time', though of interest, would not have been suitable for music, but the allusion to the 'Subvenite' is interesting and the Angel, in an uncut passage, alludes to it again just before the solo of the Angel of the Agony. It is in Section 4, which begins with the Demons, that the most regrettable cut is made. The Soul says:

> I see not those false spirits; shall I see
> My dearest Master, when I reach His throne?

In the rest of his speech, here cut, we learn that the Soul can only hear but not see the Angel. He is bereft of sight, but asks:

... how comes it then
That I have hearing still, and taste, and touch,
Yet not a glimmer of that princely sense
Which binds ideas in one, and makes them live?

The Angel's reply is the essential clue to the true nature of
Gerontius's dream and awakening. One feels Newman is a bit hard-
pressed to explain it.

Nor touch, nor taste, nor hearing hast thou now;
Thou livest in a world of signs and types,
The presentations of most holy truths,
Living and strong, which now encompass thee
A disembodied soul, thou hast, by right,
No converse with aught else beside thyself:
But, lest so stern a solitude should load
And break thy being, in mercy art vouchsafed
Some lower measures of perception,
Which seem to thee, as though through channels brought,
Through ear, or nerves, or palate, which are gone.
And thou art wrapped and swathed around in dreams,
Dreams that are true, yet enigmatical;
For the belongings of thy present state,
Save through such symbols, come not home to thee.

I have italicized the last four lines; they are the heart of the matter.
The Angel makes a nice psychological point in the lines that follow.

Hast thou not heard of those, who, after loss
Of hand or foot, still cried that they had pains
In hand or foot, as though they had it still?
So it is now with thee, who hast not lost
Thy hand or foot, but all which made up man.
So will it be, until the joyous day
Of resurrection, when thou wilt regain
All thou hast lost, new made and glorified.

The missing passages will explain much that may have seemed
'enigmatical'.

Elgar wrote to Jaeger, 'Please remember that none of the action
takes place in the presence of God. I would not have tried *that*, nor
did Newman. The Soul says, 'I go before my God', but *we* don't,
we stand outside. I've thrown over all the machinery for celestial
music, harps, etc.'

Jaeger, ardent Wagnerite, had charged Elgar with 'shirking the
supremest moment' and went on to say 'it wanted a Wagner or a
Richard Strauss to attempt it'. (Strauss's tone poem *Death and Trans-*
figuration had its first performance ten years before Elgar's work and

anything the latter learnt from it cannot have been in the oleographic 'transfiguration' section.) Jaeger, of course, meant to rile Elgar, and did. At his friend's suggestion, the composer added 'a few gloriously great and effulgent chords based on the Judgement theme' to picture the momentary vision of the Almighty.

Jaeger was critical of what he called the Soul's 'whine', the anguished cry, as the solemn chords mentioned above suddenly cease (there is a pause mark for a brief silence). 'Take me away and in the lowest deep there let me be.' It is one of the greatest and most inspired passages in the work. Elgar wrote to Jaeger. 'You must read the poem. I cannot re-write this—I don't think you appreciate the situation—the soul has for an instant seen his God—it is, from that momentary glance, shrivelled, parched, and effete, harmless and finished, and is condemned to purgatory for punishment or purging. . . . I can't see how you can ask for the soul to have a dramatic song here—no, I can't alter that.'

Elgar, for his part, was worried about the long conversation between the Angel and the Soul in Part 2, and wrote to Jaeger, 'Between ourselves this is the only part of the work I fear, or even think twice about. If the words are sufficiently interesting it will do. The words are certainly of great interest, for Gerontius is asking questions that we can imagine ourselves asking in similar circumstances.' Elgar need not have worried, the conversation is excellently composed. The case of the demons is different. Music is incapable of depicting demons. More successful ones are the Furies in Gluck's *Orfeo*, and it is significant that the most effective passage in Elgar's demonic music has a distinct affinity with their choruses in the opera.

Give him his price, Saint tho' he be, From shrewd good sense He'll slave for hire.

Ex. 1

The demons in Anthony Milner's *The Harrowing of Hell* for double choir, tenor and bass soloists, commissioned by the B.B.C. in 1956, are the most convincing of all. The libretto by John Cuddon of this remarkably vivid and dramatic work is based on the account in the apocryphal gospel of Nicholas of Christ's descent into hell between His death and resurrection to redeem the souls of the just from the demons who guard them.

Berlioz, in the Pandemonium section of his *Faust* (Scene XIX) gave his demons nonsense words such as 'Fory my Dinkziorlitz, O meri kariu', etc., which only makes them more ridiculous; Stanford's demons in *Eden* were described by Bernard Shaw as 'brilliant balderdash'; Elgar's music takes a place near the top for what that is worth, in this short list of demonology. When the Soul sings, 'But hark! Upon my sense comes a fierce hubbub which would make me fear, could I be frighted', the music is admirably descriptive, and if Elgar had cut out most of Newman's words for the demons and composed a brief orchestral interlude on these lines with perhaps the Gluck-like chorus woven in, one would feel happier about this section of the work, but it must be admitted that this chorus is far more effective heard and not seen. The eminently respectable members of choral societies cannot possibly be imagined in the role of evil spirits.

To read Newman's poem, in the original, is to come to a fuller realization of Elgar's miraculous identification with those parts of it he set and with his power of inventing memorable themes. The music sounds out of the pages and line after line is wedded so unforgettably to the music that it is impossible to imagine there could be any other setting than this. One example must suffice, Gerontius's great cry for the help of 'Some Angel, Jesu, such as came to Thee, in Thine own agony', with the tremendous impact of the chord under the penultimate word, a chord that is also movingly used again before the solo of the Angel of the Agony and near its end.

Elgar told Jaeger, 'I did not perceive till long after it was in print that (p. 34) "In Thine *own* Agony" and the appalling chords introducing and dismissing the Angel of the Agony were akin, but they are, aren't they?'

Diana McVeagh, Elgar's most perceptive biographer, has pointed out his characteristic habit of slipping one simple chord into a chromatic progression as being at its most effective in the *Death* motive that accompanies the Soul's last word below.

the thought of death and judg——ment was to me most, ter-ri-ble.

Ex. 2

Miss McVeagh does not mention it, and Elgar may not have been conscious of it, but that simple chord, placed where it is, subtly conveys that the Soul has now come to see that the thought of death and judgement are no longer terrible to him and since the same phrase comes before his first utterance, never need have been had he trusted in the mercy of God. There is, it struck me for the first time when writing this chapter, a foreshadowing of the Angel's lovely theme in the Prelude to Part 2, the repeated ascent of the melody to G on first violins, echoed by second violins, with the pattern repeated. This may be a coincidence, but I like to think the Angel was hovering over the sleeping Soul in the Prelude.

Ex. 3

The imaginative scoring of the first of the Angel's heavenly Alleluias, in which the double-basses double the voice part, *pp*, three octaves below, *pppp*, has often been remarked, and remembering Verdi's use of the low register of the flute in *Dies irae* we find Elgar doing the same sort of thing, in two bars only, as the Angel speaks of the 'deep hideous purring' of the damned.

There are five choruses of Angelicals and one of the Angels of the Sacred Stair, in Newman's poem. This entailed severe cutting and even so left Elgar with a problem as to how best to set what was selected.

In June 1900, in a mood of despondency, he wrote to Jaeger, 'I'm so sick of the whole thing. 'Cos why? 'Cos everyone I meet says "I suppose" or "I hope" you are going to keep to the old A. & M. tune!! Blast the British Public—they have no souls, hearts, or minds worth a thought.'

Elgar, when aroused, was generally comprehensive in denunciation! His tune for 'Praise to the Holiest' is far removed from the comfortable eighteenth-century one in the hymn books and he varies and develops it with great skill. The refrain has, so to speak, a built-in climax in its last phrase that can be, and is, reinforced to the utmost limits of vocal and orchestral sound. No one can ever forget the rhythm of the middle section—which begins 'Oh, loving wisdom of our God'—at the words 'that He who smote In man for man the foe, The double agony in man For man should undergo', and particularly the moving passage, with another change of rhythm, 'And in the garden secretly, And on the Cross on high, Should teach His brethren and inspire To suffer and to die.'

As for the Angel's farewell I can only hear the sublimely tender and beautiful words and melody through tears.

Elgar expressly did not want his work to be thought of as a 'Sacred Cantata'. He did most earnestly want it to be thought of as a musical representation of the culminating drama of every human soul.

I only once had the privilege of meeting this great man. Joan Elwes, a soprano who was also an excellent musician, was singing in *The Kingdom* under his direction at the Royal Albert Hall—I think it was one of his last public appearances—and she told me to come round and be introduced to him. Meeting celebrities is, for me, something of an ordeal. On approaching the artist's room, I was not at all reassured at hearing an upraised voice shout 'Get out', and out of the room, like a frightened rabbit, shot a little man—a reporter, I learnt, who had annoyed Elgar. As I entered the room and Joan introduced me his whole expression—which I had seen was severe—changed. He smiled charmingly and said, 'We've met before.' We never had met, but I did not like to contradict him. I believe that my deep love for his music, over so many years, must have been so apparent in my face that it made me look like a known friend. We had a delightful talk, and I went home walking on air.

A few months after his death on 23 February 1934, I was at the bedside of a dying friend. It was very early in the morning and still dark. As the priest began the prayer 'Proficiscere anima Christiana de hoc mundo' Elgar's music came flooding gloriously into my mind. It seemed to fill the room with angels and archangels and, even in my sorrow, I thought how rightly he had said, 'This I saw and knew'.

CHAPTER NINETEEN

HINDEMITH'S *WHEN LILACS LAST IN THE DOOR-YARD BLOOMED*

The music sung at the Requiem Mass for President John F. Kennedy in St John's Cathedral, Washington, on 25 November 1963 included pieces of which he had been especially fond, Schubert's *Ave Maria* and Bizet's *Agnus Dei*. This Mass was celebrated by the Cardinal Archbishop of Boston but, as Mrs Kennedy had wished, without ceremonial. Later Solemn Requiem Masses, with their accompanying ceremonial and fitting music, were celebrated in many countries including, of course, one at London's Westminster Cathedral. All this was as it should be, but I hoped and waited for some more personal expression of sorrow at this tragic loss, which seemed to very many of us the loss of a beloved friend, even if one never seen in the flesh, as well as of a fine and outstanding personality. The work I had in mind was Paul Hindemith's *When lilacs last in the door-yard bloomed*, sub-titled 'A Requiem for those we love'.

Hindemith composed the work in 1945 as the Second World War was ending. In this year, also, Franklin D. Roosevelt had died and Roger Wagner, conductor of a body of singers then known as the Collegiate Chorale, wanted a choral work to commemorate the late President and those who had fallen in the war. Hindemith made the inspired choice of the first and the finest of Walt Whitman's poems collected under the title of *Memories of President Lincoln*, which formed part of a sequel to *Drum-Taps* and was published in 1865. Whitman had been an ardent admirer of Lincoln and his notebooks were crowded with newspaper clippings and observations about the President's assassination on Good Friday, 1865.

I had known of the existence of Hindemith's work for a long time but having failed to take his music, in such orchestral works as *Nobilissima Visione* (a ballet about St Francis), the opera *Mathis der Maler*, and the Rilke *Marien Lieder* (in either version) to my heart because they seemed lacking in true lyrical impulse, I felt no urge to examine his Requiem. But I now got out my Whitman volume and read, with closer attention than ever before, the poet's deeply moving threnody for Lincoln, with Kennedy's death haunting my mind. I recalled hearing Gustav Holst's moving setting of the 'carol' for chorus and orchestra, from Whitman's poem 'Come lovely and soothing death', composed in 1919, with the title *Ode to Death*, and at last I felt impelled to look at Hindemith's work and to hear the recording of it. It soon became clear to me that the poem had called forth a warmer lyricism, a more spiritual feeling than I had found in his work before. His craftsmanship I had always admired, and it here serves him well in tackling the difficulties presented by lines packed with images and symbols and finding an intelligible form for a setting of them.

In Washington, the newspapers, reporting Lincoln's death, had remarked on the profusion of lilacs that banked Lincoln's coffin and Whitman was 'always reminded of the great tragedy of that day by the sight and odour of these blossoms'.

His poem is, so to say, symphonic in structure, and centres round three symbolic themes, 'lilac, star, and bird', all linked in Whitman's mind with the dead President and the American Civil War of 1861. Mr Kay Jaffee, in his informative note on the sleeve of the recording, describes the relevance of the themes.

> The western star, observed after Lincoln's second inauguration and interpreted at first as an omen of good fortune—perhaps even the end of the war—appears in Whitman's elegy as a '*fallen*' star, hidden by 'black murk'; the song of the hermit thrush contained for Whitman combined associations of death (especially in the larger sense of many deaths in war) Nature and 'Death's outlet song of life'; 'the profusion of lilacs'. I have mentioned above the three images recur in leitmotiv fashion throughout the poem, with varied and expanded meanings. A conflict develops between the star and the bird, and at the end of the poem the three symbols unite in Whitmanesque musical imagery 'Lilac and star and bird, twined with the chant of my soul'.

Whitman's poem has sixteen stanzas of varied length out of which Hindemith makes twenty-two movements. Ten of these are allotted to a baritone soloist and the chorus, four are for chorus alone. The mezzo-soprano has four solos and two duets with the baritone and joins him and the chorus in the finales to the two parts of the work. It is scored for an orchestra of normal size, with glockenspiel in the percussion section, and lasts sixty-three minutes. An essential require-ment is a baritone soloist with a big but lyrical voice and impeccable enunciation is demanded of all concerned. A deep C sharp pedal note sounds throughout the fifty-four bars of the orchestral Prelude, over which brass, strings, and woodwind successively play a four-note motif of lamentation which rises, through a series of trills on strings and woodwind, to a high and dissonant point of climax, after which the four-note motif, more fully harmonized and a fifth higher in pitch, returns and gradually takes its original form. It is a powerful picture of a world in mourning. Hindemith sets the first three stanzas of the poem in his first movement, responding most sensitively to the leading images of the words, the lilacs, the drooping star, 'the thought of him I love'.

> When lilacs last in the door-yard bloom'd
> And the great star early droop'd in the western sky in the night,
> I mourn'd, and yet shall mourn with ever-returning spring.

One hears at once how well shaped the music is to the text, the succession of falling intervals that underline the grief, and in the accompanied recitative, a beautiful 'pointing up' of 'lilac', 'star', and 'thought', all with the same motif, the C sharp taking one's mind back to the pedal note in the Prelude. The little motif (for woodwind and glockenspiel) subtly introduced into the orchestral accompaniment is to be associated later with the 'hermit bird'.

Ex. 1

The chorus now sing of the powerful western fallen star 'that first had been an omen of good fortune, but now is hidden in black murk'. As the chorus ends the baritone soloist speaks of the lilac bank growing in the door-yard fronting an old farm-house. The last words, 'A sprig with its flower, I break' are most poignantly set, with a mingling of E minor and C sharp minor tonalities.

Ex. 2

The bird-motif in the woodwind forms the short prelude to an arioso for mezzo-soprano in which the clashing chords and the emphatic rhythm are suggested by the words of the stanza:

> Song of the bleeding throat,
> Death's outlet song of life, for well dear brother I know,
> If thou wast not granted to sing thou would'st surely die.

The third movement is cast in the form of a fairly long chorus followed by a baritone solo. It begins with a march theme on the orchestra, the chorus being at first either unaccompanied or accompanied very sparsely. The clue to the sombre music comes in the last two lines of the stanza.

> Carrying a corpse to where it shall rest in the grave,
> Night and day journeys a coffin.

It is at this point that *pizzicato* strings in unison begin a kind of ghostly funeral march, punctuated here and there by sustained bass notes on the wind; the melodic interest lies in the chorus parts. As the chorus continues, however, the orchestra participate even more fully, but still, as nearly all through this work, the texture is lean, there are no superfluous notes. The chorus ceases at 'with the bells' perpetual clang' and the orchestra closes the section with the march theme *ff*; but there are two more lines of the stanza to come, and these are sung by the baritone in recitative. 'Here, coffin that slowly passes, I give you my sprig of lilac.' Hindemith continues with the seventh stanza set to music in the tempo of the slow march. It is a greeting to 'sane and sacred' death, with a memorable phrase, falling a seventh, at once repeated, and then three times more before the movement ends.

All o ——— ver bou-quets of ros — es, ——— 0 —— death!

Ex. 3

In Stanza 8, for baritone and chorus, the poet muses on the 'Western orb sailing the heavens', and for the first time the shape of the vocal phrases, the few orchestral chords in the bass punctuating a lot of the treble 'running' melodic lines reminded me of somewhat similar writing in Delius's *Sea Drift*.

The thrush's call runs throughout the orchestral accompaniment (woodwind, horns, muted strings) to Stanza 9, a tender arioso for mezzo-soprano, in which come the touching phrases of *Ex.* 4.

Ex. 4

Here, as so often elsewhere in the work, is a Hindemith more sensitive and eloquent than I had ever encountered before. By contrast to this flowing movement Stanza 10, for baritone and chorus, has a square melody of a folksong-like character, beginning with the words 'O how shall I warble myself for the dead one there I loved?' The unaccompanied choral entry and the baritone's completion of the stanza, with a brief and eloquent passage for the orchestra after it, are some of the loveliest pages in the work. The same pattern is followed for Stanza 11 in which the poet asks:

> O what shall I hang on the chamber walls?
> And what shall the pictures be that I hang on the walls,
> To adorn the burial-house of him I love?

The rest of the stanza (for chorus) describes the sights Lincoln loved, growing spring . . . farms and houses . . . the sinking sun . . . and the next movement, Introduction and Fugue (chorus), begins with its remaining five lines, describing other country sights, and then:

> And the city at hand, with dwellings so dense, and stacks of chimneys,
> And all the scenes of life and the workshops, and the workmen
> homeward returning.

This forms the Introduction; the Fugue, which displays all of Hindemith's contrapuntal skill, sets Stanza 12, a wonderful outburst of patriotic emotion, eulogizing Manhattan.

> Lo, body and soul!—this land!
> Mighty Manhattan with spires and the sparkling and hurrying
> tides, and the ships,
> The varied and ample land. . . .

The images crowd in on one another, but the composer has cleverly built a memorable phrase into the start of his fugue subject, one with a marked American flavour and, in addition, he puts a fanfare on the brass to punctuate the spare lines of the orchestral accompaniment at regular intervals. The music goes swiftly and builds up, with repetitions of 'Lo this land' and 'Lo, mighty Manhattan' to a thrilling climax.

In Stanza 13, a beautiful mezzo-soprano solo, the poet speaks again of his trinity of symbols, 'the gray-brown bird . . . the star, the lilac with mastering odour . . .'

Stanza 14, extremely long and packed with images, includes some lines not susceptible to music:

> And the infinite separate houses, how they all went on, each with
> its meals and minutiae of daily usages.

The composer deals with these lines in the only possible way, recitative, but he precedes the lines 'And I knew Death, its thought, and the sacred knowledge of Death' with a chorale for the orchestra marked *Hymn*, 'For those we love', reminding us of the sub-title 'A Requiem for those we love'. The baritone continues in recitative, the orchestra playing phrases of the chorale, *ff*, after each line of the verse, and the relevance of the sub-title is explained by the poet's thought of walking with Death on one side of him and holding the hands of companions on the other.

In the duet that follows for mezzo-soprano and baritone which recapitulates the music of Stanza 13 the gray-brown bird sings the carol of death and 'a verse for him I love'. This is greeted by the poet with rapture and leads to the death carol.

Ex. 5

In the Death Carol (printed in italics in the poem) 'Come lovely and soothing death', the first part is sung by the chorus, with the orchestra, as in the hymn 'for those we love', coming in between the lines for most of its length. The music broadens out into a rapturous section:

Dark mother, always gliding near with soft feet,
Have none chanted for thee a chant of fullest welcome?
Then I chant it for thee, I glory thee above all,
I bring thee a song that when thou must indeed come, come
    unfalteringly.

This splendid rhapsody ends most impressively with the line 'I
float this carol with joy, with joy to thee, O Death!' Stanza 15, a
battle-piece for baritone and chorus, has three orchestral march
sections, the last of which ends with a version of the Last Post on
an army bugle, off stage, sounding through the diminishing tones
of the march. This is effective, but the movement as a whole does
not seem to me on the same high level as the rest.

We come now to Stanza 16 and the last movement of the work.
The key is C sharp minor, the key of the Prelude. With each full
chord for brass in the orchestra a bell tolls. The flute begins a
melody of infinite pathos illustrative, in part, of the words.

Victorious song, death's outlet song, yet varying,
        ever-altering song,
As low and wailing, yet clear the notes,
        rising and falling, flooding the night,
Sadly sinking and fainting, as warning and
        warning, and yet again bursting with joy.

The baritone's part, in lyrical declamation, passes into eloquent
song at the words,

I cease from my song for thee,
From my gaze on thee in the west, fronting the
    west, communing with thee,
O comrade lustrous with silver face in the night.

and again, most beautifully, with cellos doubling the voice melody,

The song, the wondrous chant of the gray-brown bird.

This, with the echo in his soul, 'the lustrous and drooping star . . .
the lilac tall', the poet keeps as 'retrievements out of the night'.

. . . their memory ever I keep, for the dead I loved so well,
For the sweetest, wisest soul of all my days and lands and
    this for his dear sake.

The poignant words are set to music of utter simplicity and of
infinite sadness. The bell tolls again, and so to the end, as the chorus
sing:

Lilac and star and bird twined with the chant of my soul,
There in the fragrant pines, and the cedars dusk and dim.

During these words the mezzo-soprano and baritone soloists sing to the fateful C sharp of the Prelude 'When lilacs last in the door-yard bloom'd'; chorus and soloists transmute the final consonants 'm' and 'd' into a soft humming sound, long sustained over two orchestral chords of C sharp minor.

I was almost as deeply moved, as these sounds ceased, as by the end of Britten's War Requiem, and I cannot think of higher praise than that.

CHAPTER TWENTY

REQUIEMS OF THE FIRST WORLD WAR

Foulds, Elgar, Bliss, Delius

Benjamin Britten's War Requiem, it may surprise all but members of my generation to know, had a predecessor in A World Requiem by J. C. Foulds (1880–1939) composed in 1923 to commemorate those fallen in the First World War. Foulds, a conductor as well as a composer, did good work during the war in providing weekly concerts for the Forces. His other big choral work, described as a concert opera, had a scarcely less grandiose title, *Vision of Dante*. 'A World Requiem' became a semi-national event for some time and drew large audiences to the Albert Hall although it does not seem to have been performed anywhere outside London. The work is laid out for soprano, contralto, tenor and baritone soloists, a small chorus of boys, full chorus, orchestra, piano, and organ. The scoring calls for almost as large a percussion section as Britten uses in the War Requiem. The titles of the twenty-odd movements are in Latin, which seems pretentious, as Latin is used in the text only in *Requiem aeternam*, the first and tenth movements, and is immediately translated into English.

The boys' choir in *Lux Veritatis* (the ninth movement) is placed 'in a distant gallery' and in *Audite* (the fifth movement) fanfares are directed to be played (much as in the Berlioz Requiem) at the north, south, and west ends of the building. In this movement there is a roll-call of the nations and peoples (all except the enemy!), beginning, 'You Greenlander, Kamskatchan, Laplander', etc., and later 'You Australian, New Zealander, Tasmanian', etc. . . .'You Hindu, Buddhist, Parsi, Mahommedan', who are exhorted to live in peace with all men! There follows *Pax*, a movement for the boys' choir, still placed 'in a distant gallery', two harps, sistrum, celesta, and four solo violins. The text, compiled by the composer, is a mixture of Scripture and glosses on Scripture and—as in *Audite*—original material. I can see that this sincerely conceived work, offered as 'a tribute to the memory of the Dead—a message of consolation to the bereaved of all countries', would be bound to make a great impression on the unsophisticated members of the audiences who heard it. The choral writing in the big set pieces and elsewhere shows skill and Foulds has obviously used his experience in writing incidental music for the theatre to good effect. The full score would no doubt show him to be an experienced orchestrator, and he is aware of the harmonic trends of his time, particularly as they appeared in the works of Holst and Vaughan Williams. What is lacking is any sign of a distinctive style, of any genuine melodic gift, of any awareness of banality, or of the fact that well-worn formulas, unless used with imagination, cannot express high aspirations—they merely become clichés.

Different altogether is Elgar's noble setting of three poems from a group called *The Winnowing* by Laurence Binyon, 'The Fourth of August', 'To Women', and 'For the Fallen', and dedicated 'To the memory of our glorious men, with a special thought for the Worcesters'. The work, under the title *The Spirit of England* was performed at the Albert Hall on 24 November 1917 and frequently thereafter on Remembrance Day. But since the last war public sentiment has greatly changed. We know all too much, now, of the devious ways in which wars are started and carried on; patriotic slogans now fall on cynical ears. 'Dulce et decorum est pro patria mori' has a hollow sound.

It is sad indeed that some of Elgar's finest music, especially in 'For the Fallen', has to pay the price of neglect, and the same is true of Arthur Bliss's *Morning Heroes*, a symphony for orator, chorus, and orchestra, composed in 1930 and dedicated 'To the memory of Francis Kennard Bliss, my brother, and all other comrades killed in battle'. Bliss takes his poems from Walt Whitman, Wilfred Owen, Robert Nichols and an eighth-century Chinese poet Li-Tai-Po, and he includes two long extracts from the *Iliad*, the first of which, 'Hector's Farewell to Andromache', is spoken by the orator to orchestral accompaniment—never a happy device. The second extract from the *Iliad* includes a roll-call of the heroes, which is managed by the composer, one need hardly say, with a skill wholly lacking in Foulds's work.

In any circumstances, however, these names, in an age in which the majority of the audience would have no knowledge of the classics, cannot make much of an appeal. The Chinese poem 'Vigil' describes the thoughts that go through the mind of a soldier's wife as she embroiders a white rose on a cushion of silk. She pricks her finger, and the blood falling on the rose turns it red. This delicate, timeless poem has an immediacy lacking in the passages from the *Iliad*.

Bliss imaginatively juxtaposes his lovely setting of 'Vigil' with a very expressive one of Walt Whitman's 'The Bivouac Flame' from *Drum-Taps*, about the sleeping soldiers dreaming of home, and also a setting of Wilfred Owen's 'Spring Offensive', declaimed by the orator with timpani rolls between the lines. One would like to feel that some place could be found, at least, for Elgar's 'For the Fallen' from *The Spirit of England* and of the two movements in Bliss's work. They are too good to be laid for ever on the shelf.

Frederick Delius's Requiem, composed between 1914–16 and his last important choral work, is dedicated 'To the memory of all young artists fallen in the war'. It was first performed in March 1922 at a Philharmonic Concert at the Queen's Hall, and conducted by Albert Coates. On this occasion, and later on by his biographers, it was called by the composer 'A Pagan Requiem', but this designation does not appear in the miniature score published by Boosey and Hawkes in 1965.

There was, if I remember rightly, a general feeling of disappointment with Delius's Requiem at the first performance. Most of us, I suppose, had the *Mass of Life*, composed in 1909, in our minds as a yardstick and perhaps the luke-warm reception was due not so much to the poor quality of some of the music as to the banalities and dogmatism of portions of the libretto. The result anyhow was the virtual shelving of the work until it was revived on 9 November 1965 at a Liverpool Philharmonic Concert under Charles Groves and hailed by the majority of the critics as one of Delius's finest works. The libretto came in for surprisingly little criticism, a great contrast to the way Philip Heseltine (Peter Warlock) slammed it in his biography of the composer.

> With as much dogmatic self-assurance as the most bigoted Christian ever mustered to proclaim the terrors of a material Hell, the anonymous librettist denies the immortality of the soul and survival of human consciousness, as though there were something immoral and offensive in the very possibility.[1]

This is true. The libretto, by the composer, is a strange mixture of quotations or paraphrases from the Old and New Testaments and echoes of Schopenhauer and Nietzsche. The text begins with an altered version of a famous line from Prospero's last speech in *The Tempest*—'Our days here are as one day, for all our days are rounded in a sleep'—not an improvement on the original.

The work is scored for soprano and baritone soloists, double chorus, and a large orchestra, which includes bass oboe and bass clarinet,

---

[1] Delius *by Peter Warlock, with additions, etc., by Hubert Foss (Bodley Head, 1952).*

six horns, three trumpets, three trombones (two tenor and one bass), tuba and a fairly extensive percussion section.

One is struck at once by the austerity of the writing in the short orchestral prelude to the opening chorus, which begins with a theme very much in the mood of the one in the first of Brahms's *Four Serious Songs* to the words 'One thing befalleth the beasts and the sons of men'.

Ex. 1

The baritone soloist replies to the lament of the second chorus, 'Our days here are as one day, for all our days are rounded in a sleep', with 'Why then dissemble we with a tale of falsehoods? We are e'en as day, that's young at morning and old at eventide, departs, and nevermore returns'. The beautiful orchestral detail, gently touched in here and as the chorus repeats the soloist's last words, helps to make the obvious sentiments more acceptable.

So far, then, so good; but now Delius gets up into the pulpit. 'At this regard the weaklings waxéd sore afraid and drugged themselves with dreams and golden visions and built themselves a house of lies to live in.' A storm arose and 'laid it low'—the chorus and the full orchestra are marked *fortissimo* on the last cataclysmic word. Surely this is a version of the parable of the man who built his house on sand? The baritone announces the stern decree, 'Man, thou art mortal and needs must then die', a paraphrase of the words of Ecclesiasticus (14: 17) so unforgettably set by Bach in the great central chorus of the funeral cantata No. 106, *Gottes Zeit ist die allerbeste Zeit*.

After the chorus echo the fateful decree the composer recapitulates the opening chorus, using the whole choral body and the full orchestra. These splendid and dignified pages are followed in the second movement by the crude introduction of a bawling match, mercifully very short, between the Christians shouting 'Alleluia' and the Moslems 'La il Allah' simultaneously. The movement ends with recovered dignity. In the third movement, in which Delius's text has a remote affinity with *The Song of Songs*, the baritone praises a woman who gave her love to all and remained 'chaste and pure as a flower', a remarkable feat. This is, in fact, a picture of that romantic figure the good-hearted harlot. It is a relief to turn to the fourth movement, which moves on a much higher level.

The solo soprano praises the man 'who dies alone and makes no lamentation . . . his soul has ascended to the mountain top'—an ascension, however, that seems to contradict the pessimistic conclusion of what has gone before. With the fifth and last movement the Delius we know and love is on familiar territory. It is a song of 'ever-returning spring' decorated with beautiful orchestral detail and making much use of the motif below, on the orchestra, in various rhythmic forms.

Ex. 2

The two soloists, with the chorus echoing their words, sing rapturously of spring and summer; and, in the orchestral peroration with which the work ends, the cuckoo utters his call, horns and trumpets (outside) sound a fanfare, and the first violins, high up, reiterate the motif above.

Ex. 3

The fine qualities of Delius's Requiem outweigh the moments that are musically poor. Its successful revival is therefore to be welcomed.

CHAPTER TWENTY-ONE

BRITTEN'S WAR REQUIEM

In 1940 Britten composed his *Sinfonia da Requiem*, the score of which bears the inscription 'In memory of my parents'. The three movements take their titles from the Requiem Mass—'Lacrymosa', 'Dies irae', 'Requiem aeternam'. It remains, to date, his only extended work for full orchestra, and after being the subject of patronizing criticism, and of neglect, it is now appreciated at its true worth, as a work of considerable imagination and sensitivity and, to some extent, as we shall see, prophetic of the future.

Eighteen years later the composer compiled an anthology of poems about sleep, setting them for solo tenor, seven obbligato instruments, and strings under the title *Nocturne*. One of the poems in this beautiful work, 'Kind Ghosts', is by Wilfred Owen. It is dated 30 July 1918, but it is not specifically a war poem, though its images of boys, doom, red mouths, blood, are those of the battlefield. I recalled these events when I heard that Britten had been commissioned by the organizers of the Festival to celebrate the consecration of the new St Michael's Cathedral, Coventry by composing a large choral work for performance in the new building, and had decided to intersperse the ancient texts of the Latin *Missa pro defunctis* with nine of Wilfred Owen's bitterly anti-war poems. He had always welcomed a challenge to his creative imagination, spiritual and technical, but this was one of far greater magnitude than any he had met before. I had no doubt that he would overcome all the hazards though how the conjunctions would be made I could not guess.

I was given the privilege of writing the programme note for the first performance on 30 May 1962 and shall never forget the morning when the post brought me a photostat of the vocal score that ended at the *Agnus Dei*—the *Libera me*, a pencil copy made by Imogen Holst, following a week or so later. A sheet with the instrumentation proved to be inaccurate, giving wrong figures for most of the wind instruments and including some instruments—cornets, saxophone, celesta—that were not in the published full score at all. This led me into error in an article written for *The Musical Times*.

A quick first study of the vocal score convinced me that the composer had written a masterpiece. He had solved the problems with inspired simplicity by dividing his forces into three groups: (1) soprano soloist, chorus, and full orchestra for the Latin texts; (2) boys' choir and organ also for the Latin texts; and (3) tenor and baritone soloists and chamber orchestra for the English poems. There were still the transitions to be made from one to another and these, I saw, had been achieved in a most masterly manner.

There are here, then, three contrasted planes of sound and emotion. The Latin texts reveal to us the traditional prayer of the Christian Church for the dead, that they may have light, peace, and rest, and be mercifully regarded at the Last Judgement; there are the prayers of praise of the as yet unborn, the innocent but sentient souls, who also, in the great final movement, add their suffrages for the dead; and—in sharp contrast—the unburdening of the anguished soul of the poet who hated war with his whole soul and was filled with deep compassion for the serving soldier whom his 'very seared conscience' would not let him desert.

Britten told me that he had long cherished the wish to set Owen's war poems but could not see how best to do this. The Coventry commission illuminated his mind and showed the way. Through the huge clear glass window at the west end of the new cathedral can be glimpsed the ruins of the fourteenth-century building, bombed in the war. In that building had been celebrated innumerable Requiem Masses. The new cathedral rising next to it could itself as easily, and more absolutely, become a ruin, and with it a destruction of human life too horrible to contemplate. Britten took heed of the few words of preface Owen wrote for a projected volume of his poems he was preparing shortly before he was killed in action on 4 November 1918, a week before the Armistice, in his twenty-fifth year, while trying to pass his company of the 2nd Manchester Regiment over the Sambre Canal. He wanted to strike at the conscience of England in regard to the continuance of the war.

Britten puts the following words from Owen's preface at the head of the score of the War Requiem: 'My subject is War and the pity of War. The Poetry is in the pity. . . . All a poet can do today is warn.'

Owen concluded—these words are not quoted—'If I thought the letter of this book would last, I might have used proper names: but if the spirit of it survives—survives Prussia—my ambition and those names will have achieved themselves fresher fields than Flanders.' It is vital, for a true appreciation of the War Requiem, to have a clear understanding of Owen's attitude to war and to Christianity.

After abandoning his idea of entering the Anglican Ministry, Owen sought to discover a vocation. In a letter to his mother on this subject on 24 May 1914, he wrote of his love of music being so strong that he felt to declare it might be thought weakness.

This love for music makes one long that he had lived to hear Britten's War Requiem and reminds me of Wilhelm Müller, the poet of Schubert's *Die Schöne Müllerin* and *Winterreise*. He never met the composer and, as far as we know, never knew of the existence of the latter's settings of his poems since he wrote, 'There may be found a sympathetically tuned soul which will discover the melodies in my words and give them back to me.' That, had the poet known it, was what was to happen to Wilfred Owen. The year he died Britten was four years old.

As war poet Owen speaks, Edmund Blunden writes in his Memoir, 'as a soldier, with perfect and certain knowledge of war at grips with the soldier; as a mind, surveying the whole process of wasted spirit, art and blood in all its instant and deeper evils; as a poet, giving his readers picture and tone that whenever they are reconsidered afford a fresh profundity, for they are combinations of profound recognitions. As a man, one of his friends said, the keynote of his character was his intense pity for suffering humanity.'[1]

We reach the heart of his anguish in a letter he wrote from a hospital on the Somme on 2 May 1917:

> Already I have comprehended a light which never will filter into the dogma of any national church; namely, that one of Christ's essential commands was: Passivity at any price! Suffer dishonour and disgrace, but never resort to arms. Be bullied, be outraged, be killed; but do not kill. It may be a chimerical and an ignominious principle, but there it is. It can only be ignored; and I think pulpit professionals are ignoring it very skilfully and successfully indeed. . . . And am I not myself a conscientious objector with a very seared conscience? . . . Christ is literally in 'no man's land'. There men often hear His voice. Greater love hath no man than this, that a man lay down his life for a friend. Is it spoken in English only and French? I do not believe so. Thus you see how pure Christianity will not fit in with pure patriotism.

Pure Christianity was what Owen could not find in any church, but did find in suffering humanity. He wrote to Osbert Sitwell on 4 July 1918 (*Noble Essences*: Macmillan, 1950, p. 106): 'For 14 hours yesterday I was at work—teaching Christ to lift his cross by numbers and how to adjust his crown: and not to imagine he thirst till after

---

[1] *Edmund Blunden's* Memoir *is included in an appendix to* The Collected Poems of Wilfred Owen, *edited, with an introduction and notes, by* C. Day Lewis (Chatto & Windus, 1963).

the last halt. I attended his Supper to see that there were not complaints: and inspected his feet that they should be worthy of the nails. I see to it that he is dumb, and stands at attention before his accusers. With a piece of silver I buy him every day, and with maps I make him familiar with the geography of Golgotha.'

I wish I could remember who it was who said, 'One note on the piano can change the atmosphere of a room.' It is true, and it is one of the unique properties of music. But one note, or one chord, cannot form a musical unit, or idea; that requires two notes, or chords, at least, a beginning and an end. One note may indeed change the atmosphere, arousing expectancy of what will follow.

A two-note motif pervades Britten's War Requiem, and in the extraordinarily imaginative way, spiritual and technical, he uses it, it seems to contain a whole world of mourning.[1] It is formed out of the historic interval of three whole tones, the tritone, known to theorists of the Middle Ages as the *diabolus in musica*, and forbidden in polyphony, either as a chord or as two successive notes; it was, indeed, from the fifteenth up to as late as the nineteenth century, considered a 'dangerous interval', but it has now become common currency. The interval can of course occur on any degree of the chromatic scale. Britten chooses C–F sharp.

The reason for the disturbing sound of this interval is interesting. It lurked in the Lydian mode, which starts on F and continues on the *white* notes only up to F, and because of the possibility of F–B natural occurring in the single melodic line of plainsong, the one permitted accidental is B flat, which changes an augmented fourth into a perfect fourth.

The tritone can sound awkward, unfinished. From this very fact Britten creates one of his most beautiful and unforgettable effects at the end of the *Kyrie*, *Dies irae*, and 'In Paradisum', where the change of one note, F sharp to F natural, opens Heaven.

The Introit *Requiem aeternam* was, as we have seen, a processional piece, sung during the procession of the celebrant, his ministers and attendants, from the sacristy to the altar. Britten, thinking everything in the liturgy anew, brings before us at once, in the orchestral part, a painfully halting procession along the *Via dolorosa*, the highway of war, ever since war began: a procession—I give free play to my imagination—of the dead soldiers of all nations *as they suffered* before death gave them merciful release and, as it were, humanity—their parents, wives, children, friends, watching them, as in some anguished vision, go by. The bells toll, F sharp, then C, and the

---

[1] *The score is dedicated 'in loving memory' to four friends of the composer who lost their lives in the war.*

chorus sing those same notes successively (first F sharp–C then the reverse, C–F sharp) with increasing emotion.

After the cry of 'et lux perpetua luceat eis', in which no light illumines the tragic scene (how different in Verdi!) the four bells clash the mourning intervals as a chord.

Ex. 1

The quietness of the opening measures returns and now Britten makes the first of his wonderful transitions—here from the chorus and full orchestra to the boys' chorus and the organ. The full orchestra rises up to an F major chord, sounded just after by the organ, and then, in quick time, joyfully and, it seems, untroubled, the boys sing the psalm verse 'Te decet hymnus, Deus in Sion' to a fresh and attractive melody beginning with a perfect fourth, C, F. But faintly overshadowing these sounds, high up on the strings, hover C and F sharp. The chromatic shaping of the boys' melody

Ex. 2

to allow of this compels admiration. The boys' voices die away on the intervals C–F sharp; the implication is that these unknown souls will come into a world that is still at war. When writing my note for the first performance I spoke of the boys' choir, always marked 'distant,' as 'a celestial sound' but Britten told me he felt that this was rather 'Walt-Disneyish': and could I introduce the word 'innocent'. I understood what he meant. Innocence and the corruption of innocence have been a major factor in his operas—in *Peter Grimes*, *Lucretia*, *Billy Budd*, *The Turn of the Screw*. It is in this last opera that the poignant words come, 'The ceremony of innocence is drowned'. I therefore changed what I had written into 'an innocent sound from afar' and this he liked.

As the boys' voices die away the tragic procession is resumed. Now comes the first of the beautifully managed transitions to the Owen poems. It is, to my mind, unfortunate that the titles Owen gave his poems are not reproduced in the score, the more so because some of them, as this one, 'Anthem for doomed youth', are so revealing. The mourning motif chord on the bells sounds till the chamber orchestra takes over, with the same chord, most unexpectedly on the harp, and the string basses seem to caricature the halting march theme of the Introit. The words, in this tenor solo, give the clue:

> What passing-bells for these who die as cattle?
> Only the monstrous anger of the guns.
> Only the stuttering rifles' rapid rattle
> Can patter out their hasty orisons.
> No mockeries for them from prayers or bells,
> Nor any voice of mourning save the choirs,—
> The shrill demented choirs of wailing shells;
> And bugles calling for them from sad shires.
> What candles may be held to speed them all?

Britten illustrates vividly the 'rifles' rapid rattle' and the 'wailing shells' in his vocal and orchestral parts.

The poem continues:

> Not in the hands of boys, but in their eyes
> Shall shine the holy glimmers of good-byes.
> The pallor of girls' brows shall be their pall;
> Their flowers the tenderness of silent minds,
> And each slow dusk a drawing-down of blinds.

The melody of the boys' 'Te decet hymnus' sounds on various wind instruments (oboe, clarinet, horn, flute—in a low register—bassoon) throughout most of this section, and also in the voice, which gradually relaxes into the lovely lyrical phrases given to the last line of the poem—the 'Te decet' melody is here put into notes of double length.

Ex. 3

The chamber orchestra (harp and bass strings, as at the start) adds its coda, the bells toll the mourning motif and the chorus, unaccompanied save for the bells tolling between the petitions, sing the *Kyrie*, in very soft sustained chords. The three petitions begin, and the first two end, with the mourning motif, but at the closing 'Kyrie eleison' the music magically resolves on to an utterly peaceful chord of F major.

Ex. 4

Britten's *Dies irae*, as Owen's poems compel, takes place on the battlefield, and this is made abundantly clear by the three bugle calls (on trombone, trumpet, and horn) and a downward scale passage, symbolizing 'Dies irae', with which this tremendous movement begins.

Ex. 5

These simple motifs make clearly recognizable points of reference during the settings of 'Bugles sang', 'On seeing a piece of our artillery brought into action', in *Dies irae*, during 'The parable of the old men and the young', in the Offertory, in *Libera me, Domine*, and in 'Strange meeting' following it.

Whatever horrors war may plunge mankind into in the future they can never be of the kind Owen knew in France. It seems incredible to recall that C. R. W. Nevinson, the distinguished war artist, was obliged, in 1918, by official intervention, to withdraw one of his pictures, ironically called 'The Paths of Glory', from exhibition because of its stark portrayal of dead men caught in barbed wire. D. S. R. Welland, in his book on Wilfred Owen, prints a letter from Paul Nash,[1] an equally realistic and even greater painter:

I have seen the most frightful nightmare of a country more conceived by Dante or Poe than by nature, unspeakable, utterly indescribable. In

---

[1] *This letter, quoted in D. S. R. Welland's* Wilfred Owen (Chatto & Windus, 1960) *is included in the essay by John Rothenstein, in the memorial volume of Paul Nash ed. Margot Fates (Lund Humphries, 1948).*

the fifteen drawings I have made I may give you some vague idea of the horror . . . sunset and sunrise are blasphemous, they are mockeries to man, only the black rain of the bruised and swollen clouds all through the bitter black of night is fit atmosphere in such a land. The rain drives on, the stinking mud becomes more evilly yellow, the shell-holes fill up with green-white water, the roads and tracks are covered in inches of slime, the black dying trees ooze and sweat and the guns never cease. They alone plunge overhead, tearing away the rotting tree stumps, breaking the plank roads, striking down horses and mules, annihilating, maiming, maddening, they plunge into the grave which is this land; one huge grave and cast upon it the poor dead. It is unspeakable, godless, hopeless. I am no longer an artist interested and curious. I am a messenger who will bring back word from the men who are fighting to those who want the war to go on for ever. Feeble, inarticulate will be my message, but it will have a bitter truth and may it burn their lousy souls.

Owen, too, was not a poet 'interested and curious'. 'Above all I am not concerned with Poetry. My subject is War, and the pity of war. The Poetry is in the pity.' He was a changed man as well as a changed poet, passionately involved in the sufferings and endurances of his men, and it is through his eyes and heart and soul that Britten depicts the *Dies irae*.

The composer gives *Dies irae* a trenchant, broken rhythm it had never been subjected to before. This rhythm is maintained in the succeeding three verses of this section ('Quantus tremor'. . .'Tuba mirum'. . .'Mors stupebit') in each of which the last line of the three is repeated to a clinching *legato* phrase.

Ex. 6

The movement has begun very softly, but the bugle call motives on the orchestra between the first and second verses quickly become more strident and urgent until, just before 'Tuba mirum', the whole weight of the brass and percussion are brought into play. On paper the rise and fall of the *Dies irae* scale passages have a deceptive simplicity: in performance they exude terror. Britten does not pause over 'Mors stupebit', feeling perhaps that Verdi had unforgettably set these words. The link to the Owen poem 'Voices' for baritone solo is achieved, as the chorus voices dies away, with a soft roll on the timpani and a sustained bass note on the piano over which, in the same bar, the horn of the chamber orchestra sounds the first of the bugle motives to muted strings accompaniment, and the solo voice takes it up.

> Bugles sang, sadd'ning the evening air;
> And bugles answer'd, sorrowful to hear.
> Bugles sang—Bugles sang.
> Voices of boys were by the river-side.
> Sleep mother'd them; and left the twilight sad.
> The shadow of the morrow weighed on men.
> Bugles sang.
> Voices of old despondency resigned,
> Bowed by the shadow of the morrow, slept.

In turn, flute, clarinet, oboe, with detached notes on the harp outlining their rise and fall, 'sadden the evening air' with the second of the bugle calls, the other two calls on the horn being woven later into the texture. The effectiveness and truth of Britten's cross-references is already made plain. At the words 'The shadow of the morrow weighed on men', the horn, with stressed notes, reflected in the accompanying string chords and the bass drum, heavily descends the scale with the *Dies irae* motif. Those who saw active service in either of the great wars will remember vividly how 'the shadow of the morrow weighed on men'. In training exercises in the First World War, we used to run at stuffed sacks with fixed bayonets, exhorted by loud-voiced sergeants to 'stick it in his guts!' It was very different when the pretence became reality. It was not, I think, the fear of death that made us dread the coming action but the fear of being maimed, or being left wounded and forgotten in No Man's Land. Britten has instinctively put all this into his music.

'Liber scriptus', for soprano solo with chorus, takes us back to the liturgy and a more conventional kind of vocal writing, but with many touches of imaginative orchestration. The timpani beat sternly throughout the chorus part and there are no gracious phrases for 'Salva me, fons pietatis' as in Verdi's Requiem, but a hushed, imploring prayer. After a short pause the chamber orchestra begins a brief introduction to Owen's poem, for solo tenor and baritone, 'The next war', headed with two lines from the last stanza of a poem by Siegfried Sassoon called 'A letter home'. The poet is writing to a friend:

> Yet, through stunning battle storms
> All the while I watch the spark
> Lit to guide me, for I know
> Dreams will triumph, though the dark
> Scowls above me where I go.
> You can hear me; you can mingle
> Radiant folly with my jingle.
> War's a joke for me and you,
> While we know such dreams are true.

Though Owen quotes only the last two lines, they need the context to make the reference intelligible. He gives Sassoon's sentiments a bitter flavour.

> Out there, we've walked quite friendly up to Death;
> Sat down and eaten with him, cool and bland,—
> Pardoned his spilling mess-tins in our hand.
> We've sniffed the green thick odour of his breath,—
>
> Oh, Death was never enemy of ours!
> We laughed at him, we leagued with him, old chum.
> No soldier's paid to kick against his powers.
> We laughed, knowing that better men would come,
> And greater wars; when each proud fighter brags
> He wars on Death—for Life; not men—for flags.

This duet, marked 'fast and gay', delivers the most profound shock, I think, in this disturbing work. The harsh dissonances that mark the first words of some of the lines, the clash of cymbals (struck with a side-drum stick), all the vivid orchestral detail, paint a horrifying picture of the two soldiers to whom Death has come, perforce, to be a friend. The bitter taste is taken away, after a long pause, by chords for four trumpets marked 'sweetly'. They fall gratefully on the ear and lead to the chorus, a meditative singing of 'Recordare, Jesu pie'. Bassoons, and later the rest of the woodwind, double the vocal melody for a space, recalling Verdi's practice; and the accompaniment on the strings is characterized by the constant use of gently clashing seconds.

The two verses 'Recordare, Jesu pie' and 'Qui Mariam absolvisti' are sung only by the women's voices, the two that follow 'Confutatis maledictis' and 'Oro supplex et acclinis' by the men's. In this latter section, in quick tempo, the tenors—their part is marked 'weeping'—respond to the terse phrases of the basses' 'confutatis'.

The music reaches near-hysteria on the part of the tenors, vengeance on the part of the basses. Now comes a fine dramatic stroke, which also forms a masterly link with Owen's poem, 'On seeing a piece of our artillery brought into action'. The orchestra, boiling over, rushes up the scale into thin air, and at this point the timpani (the player using a hard stick) beat out the 'Confutatis maledictis' arpeggio, while, as the baritone begins the poem, woodwind, horns, and strings move upwards in heavily stressed chords.

Be slow — — ly — — lif-ted up, — — — thou long black arm,

Ex. 7

Be slowly lifted up, thou long black arm,
Great gun towering t'ward Heaven, about to curse;
Reach at that arrogance which needs thy harm,
And beat it down before its sins grow worse;
But when thy spell be cast complete and whole,
May God curse thee, and cut thee from our soul!

This is perhaps the most electrifying movement in the work, a masterpiece of concentrated power in a small space. The last word of each line is rammed home with a huge, violently dissonant chord on the orchestra, followed by one or another of the bugle calls. At '(before its sins grow) worse', the trumpet sounds the *Dies irae* downward scale. On the last words 'cut thee from our soul', the voice rises to a climactic high G, and *Dies irae* erupts on chorus and full orchestra. One *sees* that evil black gun slowly rising to kill and maim, the immediacy of the battlefield envelops one. If nothing else of Britten's happened to survive save this fragment, musicians of the future might still say 'This is a work of genius'.

'Lacrimosa', on a larger scale, is no less imaginatively planned. For the first time an Owen poem is incorporated into the Latin text, not put at the end of it. A light accompaniment of strings, and piano, double the chorus part, of which the rhythm is almost the same broken kind as in *Dies irae*. Above the chorus the solo soprano's voice falls and rises in lamentation and, a point of much pathos, with one or another wind instrument doubling the last notes of each of her phrases.

Ex. 8

The movement breaks off at 'parce Deus', and the tenor begins Owen's poem *Futility*. The voice part is marked '*pp* (whispered)'.

> Move him into the sun—
> Gently its touch awoke him once,
> At home, whisp'ring of fields unsown.
> Always it woke him, woke him even in France,
> Until this morning and this snow.
> If anything might rouse him now
> The kind old sun will know.
> > (Chorus: 'Lacrimosa')
> Think how it wakes the seeds—
> Woke, once, the clays of a cold star.
> Are limbs, so dear-achieved, are sides,
> Full-nerved—still warm—too hard to stir?
> > (Chorus: 'Lacrimosa')
> Was it for this the clay grew tall?
> —O what made fatuous sunbeams toil
> To break earth's sleep at all!

This threnody for an unnamed soldier, already itself deeply moving, is made almost intolerably poignant in its inspired setting. The tenor is accompanied by tremolos on the flute, in its lowest register, strings, with touches of quiet cymbal clash, sustained notes here and there on woodwind. It suggests to me the 'whispering of fields unsown' with the gentle sun shining on them and the sleeping boy, but with a deep note of tragedy hovering over the scene. At 'Was it for this the clay grew tall', the tenor's phrase is the one with which the soprano began 'Lacrimosa', a most imaginative touch. Just before he ends 'at all', the chamber orchestra's tremolo has become that of the mourning motif and the bells of the orchestra echo it—a wonderfully devised transition. Then, very softly, unaccompanied, with bells tolling between the lines as in the *Kyrie*, and to the same exquisite music, the chorus sing the concluding lines of the Sequence.

Pie, Jesu Domine, dona eis requiem.
Amen, Amen.

The emotional strain of listening to the whole long movement is great, but the tension is released, at least, at the start of the Offertory as the fresh voices of the distant boys' choir sing, antiphonally, the opening words 'Domine Jesu Christe, Rex gloriae' down to 'ne cadant in obscurum'. Their phrases have a slight affinity to the plainsong of this text. The boys are, as always, accompanied only on the organ, to which is given a 'squashed' chord, the bottom and top notes of which have an important part to play later on in the movement. The tempo, already brisk, becomes more so when the orchestra breaks in and the chorus sing of the coming of Michael the Standard-bearer. The accompaniment here is solely for woodwind and horns.

Britten turns 'Quam olim Abrahae promisisti, et semini ejus' into a loud and jaunty soldiers' song,[1] a tune that rises and falls as they swing along the road, full of optimism about the future promised by the politicians, 'a new heaven and a new earth'.

Ex. 9

The scraps of tune pass from one part to another, all four uniting in its up-and-down phrases as the singing grows more strenuous. The accompaniment is abrupt and fragmented and the whole thing awakens a certain unease in the listener. At the end of the chorus the melody continues, as the woodwind of the chamber orchestra, with strings and timpani support, take it over. So, for a space, do the baritone and tenor soloists for the first lines of the Owen poem, 'The Parable of the Old Men and the Young', which turns out to be the poet's version of the Biblical story of Abraham and Isaac.

> So Abram rose, and clave the wood, and went,
> And took the fire with him, and a knife.
> And as they sojourned both of them together,
> Isaac the first-born spake and said, 'My Father,
> Behold the preparations, fire and iron,
> But where is the lamb for this burnt-offering?'

---

[1] *This tune comes from Britten's Canticle 2, 'Abraham and Isaac', for alto, tenor and piano, the text of which is taken from* The Chester Miracle Play.

The last line of the stanza is sung to an unaccompanied phrase of most touching innocence. The tempo changes to slow and the story moves out of the past into the immediacy of the battlefield as the baritone sings:

> Then Abram bound the youth with belts and straps,
> And builded parapets and trenches there,
> And stretchèd forth the knife to slay his son.

The bassoon, horn (sustained notes) with percussion (gong, bass drum, *pizzicato*, string basses, and later other woodwind), recall motives from the 'Anthem for doomed youth' ('What passing bells for those that die as cattle') and the three bugle motives, to underline the significance of the words. Then, in recitative, tenor and baritone sing:

> When lo! an angel called him out of heav'n
> Saying, lay not thy hand upon the lad,
> Neither do anything to him. Behold,
> A ram, caught in a thicket by its horns;
> Offer the Ram of Pride instead of him.

Britten quotes here again a similar passage from his Canticle, with the harp playing the arpeggios that announce the presence of the angel, and the strings and wind the 'Pride' motif. An interpolation by the horn alone, which includes the first bugle motif, prepares us for the terrible twist Owen gives to the biblical story:

> But the old man would not so, but slew his son,—
> And half the seed of Europe, one by one . . .

To these words of doom the woodwind respond ironically with phrases of the soldiers' song. As the two soloists continually repeat the last line the organ, in march-like time (directed to have no exact connexion with that of the soloists), has a highly dissonant chord of which the separated bass notes are the bottom and top ones of the arpeggiated chord C sharp to D sharp heard at the start of the Offertory—but here with a flattened D. The effect is spine-chilling.

Ex. 10

The boys' choir, as the soloists reiterate with tragic emphasis 'And half the seed of Europe, one by one', now sing the verse of the Offertory.

Hostias et preces tibi Domine, laudis offerimus: tu suscipe pro animabus illis, quarum hodie memoriam facimus: fac eas, Domine, de morte transire ad vitam, quam olim Abrahae promisisti et semini ejus.

We offer unto Thee, O Lord, this sacrifice of prayer and praise: do thou receive it on behalf of the souls of those whose memory we this day recall: make them, O Lord, to pass from death unto life, that life which of old Thou didst promise to Abraham and his seed.

Chorus and orchestra follow this with a repeat of 'Quam olim Abrahae', etc., as heard before but now marked, not loud, but *pp* and *ppp* throughout. The impression given is of a vast stricken battle-field. It made me think of the fourth and last song of Moussorgsky's *Songs and Dances of Death* in which Field-Marshal Death proclaims his victory to the combatants and stamps their battered corpses into the ground. What then has become of God's promise? Unfortunately the Latin words sung by the boys are left without translation in the score and in concert programmes (but not on the record sleeve), so that those who have no Latin may miss the clue to what may seem to them a mockery. It is the words 'to pass from life to death'. *That* is what God promised and it is all, given man's free-will, He could promise. In moments of unbearable tension soldiers would cry out 'Christ, stop this bloody war'. But Christ, who, as Pascal said in unforgettable words, 'will be in agony until the end of the world', suffering with suffering humanity, could not do what God could not do. The whole movement is an outstanding example of Britten's inspired re-thinking of words.

His setting of *Sanctus* is also a most original conception. These words have evoked much beautiful music, but in the context of war they take on a new meaning. This *Sanctus* begins with a clangour of percussion instruments—vibraphone, glockenspiel, antique cymbals (of the kind Debussy used in *L'après-midi d'un faune*), bells—sounding F sharp and continuing so to sound as the soprano sings 'Sanctus' to a brilliant melismatic phrase. The F sharp then falls to C, the mourning motif shadows the hymn of adoration. With 'Pleni sunt coeli et terra gloria tua' we are on earth, a great crowd is gathering to welcome the heroes. This eight-part chorus is built up, with most exciting effect, from the basses' low F sharp to the soprano high G, all declaiming the words freely. 'Hosanna in excelsis' bursts out. Here the full brass are given phrases marked 'glissando'—slides upwards and downwards—and the bass drum loudly booms. It was with such a welcome that the crowd greeted Christ on Palm Sunday, and so it was that the soldiers were greeted in the streets on their way to war. Five days after that vociferous welcome to Christ some among them were calling 'Crucify'. The crowds in the streets were innocent of that, but how much did they really care? Many, of course, did, but there were those who thrived on the war, or who were too unimaginative to realize what it meant to the serving soldier. Siegfried Sassoon satirized them once and for all in his scathing poem 'Blighters'.

> The House is crammed: tier beyond tier they grin
> And cackle at the show, while prancing ranks
> Of harlots shrill the chorus, drunk with din:
> 'We're sure the Kaiser loves our dear old tanks.'
> I'd like to see a tank come down the stalls,
> Lurching to ragtime tunes, or 'Home Sweet Home'
> And there'd be no more jokes in music-halls
> To mock the riddled corpses round Bapaume.

The *Benedictus*, with its hollow procession of consecutive fifths, conveys a note of pain. When Christ said to His disciples 'Let us go up to Jerusalem' He prophesied what lay ahead for Him. But, as always, they did not understand.

What can come after Passion and Death? Owen, alienated from Christianity, could only return a tragic answer in the poem 'The End' for solo baritone that follows. He had written, in this poem, 'Shall God renew the righteous' but substituted 'Shall Life renew these bodies?', indicating that he wished the Deity to be kept out of the poem.

> After the blast of lightning from the East,
> The flourish of loud clouds, the chariot throne:
> After the drums of time have rolled and ceased,
> And by the bronze west long retreat is blown,
> Shall life renew these bodies? Of a truth
> All death will He annul, all tears assuage?—
> Fill the void veins of Life again with youth,
> And wash, with an immortal water, Age?
> When I do ask white Age he saith not so:
> 'My head hangs weighed with snow.'
> And when I hearken to the Earth, she saith:
> 'My fiery heart shrinks, aching. It is death.
> Mine ancient scars shall not be glorified,
> Nor my titanic tears, the sea, be dried.'

Britten sets this fatalistic poem in a declamatory style, passing at the last three lines into *arioso*. He does not fail to illustrate 'the blast of lightning from the East', but softly (flute, clarinet, and timpani, preceded by harp *glissandi* as if from far off) and the drums of Time, and the 'long retreat' (on oboe, clarinet, and bassoon), and he uses the 'retreat' arpeggio to accompany the singer's urgent question in the second half of the poem. Age and the Earth answer the questions put to them in broader phrases, as the strings and oboe begin a curious swaying motif over an *ostinato* bass (double bass, timpani) and this pattern, varied in instrumentation, intervals, and note lengths, continues to the end.

The mourning motif sounds (here as D–G sharp on bassoons and cellos *pizzicato*) at 'my fiery heart shrinks', and then, near the close, (B–E sharp on horn and harp). The music then sinks into the depths of the titanic sea of tears, the ceremony of innocence is drowned— the guilty do not weep.

It is the mourning motif, also, that is built into the chamber and full orchestral parts of the most beautiful *Agnus Dei*. In this movement soloist and chorus share the same accompaniment; and each of the three verses of the tenor soloist is followed by the chorus with each of the three petitions of *Agnus Dei*.

Ex. 11

Owen called his poem *At a Calvary near the Ancre* (once again I regret the absence of his titles in the score).

> One ever hangs where shelled roads part.
> In this war He too lost a limb,
> But His disciples hide apart;
> And now the soldiers bear with Him.
>   (Agnus Dei)
> Near Golgotha strolls many a priest,
> And in their faces there is pride
> That they were flesh-marked by the Beast
> By whom the gentle Christ's denied.
>   (Agnus Dei)
> The scribes on all the people shove
> And bawl allegiance to the state,
> But they who love the greater love
> Lay down their life: they do not hate.
>   (Agnus Dei)

I do not wish to claim that Owen returned to Christianity in this poem but, as a Christian myself, only to say how deeply touched I am by his tender reference to the lonely man on the Cross, who died for all men, and whose image a shell had shattered. How understandable is the poet's anti-clericalism when one remembers that, in the First World War, an army chaplain, safely ensconced at General Headquarters, published a book called *Happy Days in France and Flanders*. But Owen forgot, or perhaps never encountered, the devoted work of many chaplains in the front line. As so often with him, however, compassion succeeds to bitterness and I cannot hear, dry-eyed, these last two lines, 'But they who love the greater love, Lay down their life: they do not hate'. Here is all Owen's hatred of pulpit professionals and politicians, and all his love for the serving soldier. Britten's phrase for the last words by the use of a higher note puts emphasis on 'they (do not hate)'. The last petition of *Agnus Dei*, in the Requiem Mass itself, ends, it will be remembered, with 'Dona eis requiem sempiternam', but Britten has the inspired idea of adding the usual conclusion 'Dona nobis pacem' and giving this—the only time either of the two soloists sings Latin words—to the tenor. His voice goes slowly up the scale over an octave, but in the second half of the phrase ('pacem') the previous C sharp is lowered to C natural and so the progression from C natural to F sharp reveals the mourning motif.

The Absolution *Libera me* is marked 'March' with a gradual *accelerando* up to the highest point of climax in the tremendous movement. Britten told me that it is 'a kind of recapitulation of the whole Mass, with the chorus, up to the climax of *Dies irae* overtaken, as it were, by the steadily accelerating orchestra'. The soprano comes in at 'Tremens factus sum ego' and again at 'quando coeli movendi sunt et terra', and remains with the chorus till the huge final outburst 'Libera me, Domine'. The several voices of the chorus repeat these words in *diminuendo* ending with the tenors, *ppp*. During this section the orchestra has a sustained chord of G minor, very loud at first but dying away on horns and organ. It is then taken over by the chamber orchestra, on the strings, and marked 'cold', as a prelude to Owen's unfinished poem, the last he wrote, 'Strange Meeting'. The portions of this long poem used are set wholly in recitative, with brief sections of arioso. It could have been an anti-climax, but it is, in the outcome, a supremely impressive and moving part of the work. It is amazing what an effect of stillness is given by that cold G minor chord, sustained throughout the first five lines of the poem, and with different harmonies thereafter.

It seemed that out of battle I escaped
Down some profound dull tunnel, long since scooped
Through granites which titanic wars had groined.
Yet also there encumbered sleepers groaned,
Too fast in thought or death to be bestirred.

The dead English soldier moves amongst the dead sleepers:

Then, as I probed them, one sprang up, and stared
With piteous recognition in fixed eyes.
Lifting distressful hands as if to bless.

The English soldier recognizes his German counterpart and Britten, with imaginative realism, gives violins and violas a stabbing *vibrato* chord at 'probed', thereafter often repeated; the symbol of the wounding of enemies who should be, who truly are friends. The mourning motif is built into this chord.

Ex. 12

The English soldier speaks. ' "Strange friend", I said, "here is no cause to mourn" ', and the notes to which the tenor sings 'Strange friend' are C–F sharp, the mourning motif.

The baritone, the German soldier, replies—he continues alone to the end of the poem—'None, save the undone years, the hopelessness', and here the oboe has the 'dona nobis pacem' phrase the tenor sang at the end of *Agnus Dei*, which gives great poignance to the next words: 'Whatever hope is yours, was my life also'—a hope of peace shattered. A little later come these prophetic words:

For by my glee might many men have laughed,
And of my weeping something had been left,
Which must die now. I mean the truth untold,
The pity of war, the pity war distilled.
Now men will go content with what we spoiled.
Or, discontent, boil bloody, and be spilled.
They will be swift, with swiftness of the tigress.
None will break tanks, though nations trek from progress.

An almost sacramental feeling, reproduced in the music, comes into the last lines of the poem.

Then, when much blood had clogged their chariot-wheels
I would go up and wash them from sweet wells.
Even from wells we sunk too deep for war,
Even the sweetest wells that ever were.

The second violins and violas put a lovely aura of sound round the words 'sweet wells'. The 'cold still' chords that have been maintained nearly all through the dialogue now cease, and the German soldier says:

I am the enemy you killed, my friend.
I knew you in this dark; for so you frowned
Yesterday through me as you jabbed and killed.
I parried; but my hands were loath and cold.

(Owen, in one draft of this poem, wrote, in the first line, 'I was a German conscript, and your friend'). The soft stabbing chords are the only sounds that we hear between these lines of the poem. There is a moment of silence. Then as the two soldiers sing, as if in a trance, 'Let us sleep now', to a lulling accompaniment (clarinet, harp, and strings) the boys' voices as always, in the distance and to organ accompaniment, begin the beautiful words of the antiphon, 'In Paradisum'. The attentive ear will recognize this chant-like melody as almost identical, though given a different rhythm, with the soldiers' song 'Quam olim Abrahae'. God's promise, that they should pass from death to life, is here gloriously fulfilled. Angels lead them into Paradise.

In pa-ra – di-sum: de-du-cant te An-ge — li:

Ex. 13

They do not yet understand; they sing continually and almost to the end 'Let us sleep now' and as they sing the chorus and main orchestra, joined by the soprano soloist, gradually build up a radiant welcome, gentle not strenuous in sound, and only reaching one high point of climax. Then the music is halted. Britten will not end on a paradisial note. We are in the world, and it is a tragic world, and so the bells toll and the boys sing, to the chord of the mourning motif 'Requiem aeternam dona eis, Domine': the processional music goes forward, again very quietly, and halts once more. As the bells toll, the boys complete their sentence 'et lux perpetua luceat eis'. On a low note the solo soprano murmurs the last touching words of 'In Paradisum' 'et cum Lazaro quondam paupere aeternam habeas requiem' ('and like Lazarus, the poor man, may you have eternal rest').

The bells toll again, and the chorus very softly sing the final words of the liturgy to the exquisite phrases of the *Kyrie* and *Pie Jesu*, and the mourning motif makes its final resolution onto the utterly peaceful chord of F major. The soldiers sleep at last, the sleep of peace in Christ, by which the early Christians meant the friendship of Christ.

As the long-sustained chord died away—it seemed, into eternity—at the first performance of the War Requiem in Coventry Cathedral, there came that authentic hush that is the finest tribute an audience, deeply moved, can pay to a masterpiece. At length people began to move quietly out of the building, but the young man who had been sitting on my right did not stir. He was looking straight ahead at Graham Sutherland's commanding tapestry of Christ. When, after a slow progress in that large crowd, I reached the door of the cathedral, I looked back and saw that the boy had not moved. He was too young to have known service in the last war, but not too young—and sensitive enough—to receive the profoundly disturbing message of the poet and the musician.

'All a poet can do today is warn. That is why the true Poets must be truthful.'

INDEX

Works discussed in the text which are available on gramophone records at the time of going to press are indicated by an asterisk

Abelard, Peter, 232
*Abraham and Isaac (Britten), 277n, 278
Absalon, fili mi (Josquin), 232
Absolution (*Libera me*):
  Anerio, 47–8
  Britten, 271, 282–5
  Duruflé, 126
  Fauré, 117, 120–1
  Monteverdi, 59
  Pizzetti, 129
  Verdi, 97, 100–1
  Victoria, 51, 52
Acta Mozartiana, 66
Adam, Adolphe, 77
Agnus Dei:
  Berlioz, 95, 108, 113
  Britten, 281, 283
  Brumel, 39
  Cherubini, 80–1, 82, 85
  De la Rue, 41
  Duruflé, 125–6
  Dvořák, 115
  Fauré, 120
  Haydn, M., 64
  Machaut, 26
  Morales, 44
  Mozart, 68, 74
  Palestrina, 44, 45
  Pizzetti, 129
  Verdi, 108
Ahna, Pauline de, 228–30
Aïda (Verdi), 101, 103, 112
Airs or Fantastic Spirits for Three Voices (Weelkes), 215–16
'All glory, laud and honour', 197n
All Souls' Day, 9, 11, 226
Allegri, Gregorio, 166–7
Alleluia, 6, 15, 19, 20, 34
Amalar of Metz, 9
Ambros, A. W., 42–3, 44

An die Musik (Schubert), 225
Anderson, Emily, 65
Anerio, G. F., 46–8, 49
'Anthem for Doomed Youth' (Owen), 269–71, 278
Apparebit repentina dies magna Domini, 16
Aprahamian, Felix, 122–3
Après-midi d'un faune, L' (Debussy), 279
Arcadelt, Jacob, 214–15
Arnold, Denis, 59n
Ars nova, 25, 29
Asola, Giovanni Matteo, 48–9
Assassino nel Cattedrale, L' (Pizzetti), 127
'At a Calvary near the Ancre' (Owen), 281–2
* 'At Sunset' (Strauss), 229–30
Auber, Daniel, 76
Augustine, St, 6, 12, 17, 19, 240
Austin, J., 17
Ave Maria (Arcadelt), 214
*Ave Regina Coelorum (Dufay), 27–8
*Ave verum (Byrd), 136

Bach, Anna Magdalena, 186
Bach, J. S., 30, 44, 56, 59, 62, 69, 71, 78, 156, 172, 174, 177
  * Church Cantatas, 179, 183–201, 227; (No. 8) 193; (No. 20) 190–1; (No. 21) 179; (No. 27) 193; (No. 32) 186; (No. 34) 182; (No. 39) 191; (No. 60) 180, 190–3; (No. 73) 198–200; (No. 75) 191; (No. 82) 200–1; (No. 95) 196–8; (No. 106) 187–90, 263; (No. 140) 200; (No. 156) 198; (No. 159) 156; (No. 161) 193–6
  Mass in B minor, 78

Bach, J. S.—*cont.*
    St Matthew Passion, 156, 177, 200
Bach: the Historical Approach (Terry),
    183–4
Ball, William, 140
Baroque style, 55–6, 58
Barzun, G. Jacques, author of
    Berlioz, 86*n*
basso continuo, 56, 58
Baumstark, Anton, 21
Beecham, Sir Thomas, 69, 72, 222
Beethoven, 59, 75, 76, 115, 225
    Missa Solemnis, 30, 58, 78, 144
    String Quartet in A minor, 37,
        166
    ★ 'Vom Tode', 225
Bellasis, Father, 240
Benedictus:
    Britten, 280
    Cherubini, 80, 101
    De la Rue, 41
    Dvořák, 114
    Haydn, M., 64
    Mozart, 68
    Palestrina, 44
    Verdi, 101
Benedictus Dominus Deus (Canticle of
    Zacharias), 23, 160, 161, 166
Bérard, Christian, 147
Berg, Alban, 193
Berkeley, Lennox, 148–50
Berlioz, Hector, 81–2, 85–95, 107
    Damnation of Faust, 248
    Enfance du Christ, L', 87, 88
    ★ Requiem Mass, 80, 85–95, 101,
        102, 104, 108, 112, 113, 117,
        128, 260
Betulia liberata, La (Mozart), 71
Bienemann, Caspar, 198
Billy Budd (Britten), 269
Binchois, Gilles, 136, 213
Binyon, Laurence, 261
'Bist du bei mir' (Bach), 186–7
'Bivouac Flame, The' (Whitman),
    262
Blake, William, 122
'Blighters' (Sassoon), 280

Bliss, Sir Arthur, 261–2
Blom, Eric, 78
Blume, Professor Friedrich da
    Ponte, 68, 69, 72, 73, 183, 184
Blunden, Edmund, 267
Blüths, Professor Julius, 242
Boito, Arrigo, 96, 97, 99, 102
Boldieu, François, 82
Borromeo, Cardinal, 46
Boulanger, Nadia, 121, 149
Brahms, Johannes, 102, 111
    ★ *Four Serious Songs*, 177, 182,
        227–8, 263
    ★ German Requiem, 110, 175–82
    Three Sacred Choruses, 176
Brahms's Lieder (Friedlander), 182,
    227
Brema, Marie, 241
★ *Brich dem Hungrigen dein Brot*
    (Bach Cantata No. 39), 191
Britten, Benjamin, 72, 149
    ★ Canticles (2–3), 222–5, 277*n*
    ★ War Requiem, 79, 88, 107,
        223, 259, 260, 265–85
Brumel, Antoine, 36–40, 41, 44, 47
Bukofzer, Manfred, 55–6
Bülow, Hans von, 102
★ Burial Service (Croft–Purcell),
    206–9
Burney, Dr Charles, 167
★ 'Busslied' (Beethoven), 225
Byrd, William, 51, 118, 161, 162,
    181, 217–19

Caldara, Antonio, 139–40
Campion, Edmund, 218
Canon of the Mass, 8
Cantatas of J. S. Bach, The (Whit-
    taker), 188
cantus firmus technique, 37, 40, 43,
    47, 51, 52, 58, 124, 135
cantus planus, 33
Capell, Richard, 225
Capriccio (Strauss), 56, 143
Carner, Mosco, 115
'Carol of the Holy Child' (Byrd),
    218–19

Casciolini, Claudio, 57
Charles the Great, Holy Roman Emperor, 9
Cherubini, Luigi:
  Deux Journées, Les, 75, 76
  * Requiem Masses, 75–85, 89, 101, 102, 103, 108; in C minor, 77–82, 84, 86; in D minor, 82–5, 86, 114–15
Chimay, Prince and Princess of, 76–7
Chopin, Frédéric, 151, 193
Christe Eleison:
  Brumel, 38
  Duruflé, 124
  Mozart, 71
  Ockeghem, 33
  Schütz, 173
  Verdi, 103
Christus (Liszt), 154
* *Christus, der ist mein Leben* (Bach Cantata No. 95), 196–8
'Christus factus est' (antiphon), 160–1
Civitate Dei (Augustine), 17
Clarke, Jeremiah, 219–20
Clemenza di Tito, La (Mozart), 66, 69
Coates, Albert, 262
Colet, Dean, 54
Colloredo, Archbishop, 61, 167
'Come lovely and soothing death' (Whitman), 253, 257–8
'Come, sweet death' (Bach), 187
* 'Come, thou lovely hour of death' (Bach Cantata No. 161), 193–6
'Come to me grief for ever' (Byrd), 217
'Come ye sons of Art' (Purcell), 206
'Comme femme desconfortée' (Binchois), 136
Communion (*Lux aeterna*), 22–4
  Brumel, 39
  Cherubini, 80, 81, 85, 108
  De la Rue, 41

Duruflé, 126
Dvořák, 115
Fauré, 120
Haydn, M., 64
Mozart, 74, 108
Verdi, 101, 108–10
Comparative Liturgy (Baumstark), 21
Compère, Loyset, 27
'Confutatis' (*Dies irae* verse):
  Berlioz, 91
  Britten, 274–5
  Cherubini, 79, 84
  Dvořák, 113
  Haydn, M., 62
  Mozart, 72–3
Conolly, Father Joseph, 98
Constantine, Emperor, 6
Cooper, Martin, 146
Così fan tutte (Mozart), 118
Craft, Robert, 220
Credo:
  Dufay, 28–9
  Machaut, 26
Crétin, Guillaume, 213
Croft, William, 206, 208–9
Cuddon, John, 248
Czestochova, 152

Damnation of Faust (Berlioz), 248
Dannreuther, Edward, 140
Danremont, General, 86
David, Laments of, 230–5
Davies, Sir Walford, 209–10
De la Rue, Pierre, 40–1, 44
'De profundis' (Monteverdi), 59, 175
'Death and the Maiden' (Schubert), 70, 225
* *Death and Transfiguration* (Strauss), 229, 247
Debora e Jaele (Pizzetti), 126
Debussy, Claude, 151, 279
Delius, Frederick, 255, 262–4
Dent, E. J., 59
* *Déploration* (Josquin), 30, 213
Deutsch, Professor Otto, 66

Deux Journées, Les (Cherubini), 75, 76

Devil and Kate, The (Dvořák), 112

Dialogue des Carmelites (Poulenc), 147

Dickinson, G. Lowes, 178

Dictionary of Hymnology (Julian), 17

Dido and Aeneas (Purcell), 219

'Die Ehre Gottes aus der Natur' (Beethoven), 225

★ *Die Elenden sollen essen* (Bach Cantata No. 75), 191

Dies irae (Thomas of Celano), 15–19, 24, 30
 Settings by:
 Anerio, 47
 Asola, 48–9
 Berlioz, 90–3
 Britten, 268, 271–7
 Brumel, 36, 38
 Cherubini, 79–80, 83–4
 Dvořák, 112–13
 Fauré, 117–18
 Haydn, M., 62
 Monteverdi, 59
 Morales, 43
 Mozart, 71–3
 Pitoni, 55
 Pizzetti, 128
 Verdi, 101, 103–7

'Do not go gentle into that good night' (Thomas), 220–2

Dr Faustus (Marlowe), 224

Domine Jesu Christe (Offertory), 20–2
 Berlioz, 91, 93–4
 Britten, 277–9
 Casciolini, 57
 Cherubini, 80, 84
 De la Rue, 40
 Duruflé, 124
 Dvořák, 113–14
 Fauré, 118, 119–20
 Haydn, M., 63
 Mozart, 68, 71, 73
 Ockeghem, 35–6
 Palestrina, 44

Verdi, 101, 107

Victoria, 51, 52

★ *Dream of Gerontius, The* (Elgar), 79, 111, 239–51

Drum-Taps (Whitman), 252, 262

Dufay, Guillaume, 25, 26–9, 30, 38, 54

Dukas, Paul, 123

Duparc, Henri, 123

Duruflé, Maurice, 122–6, 128

Dvořák, Antonin, 239–40
 ★ Requiem Mass, 110–16
 ★ *Stabat Mater*, 111, 142–4
 ★ *Te Deum*, 111

Early Christian Prayers (ed. Hamman), 5n

Ecce Homo (Nietzsche), 57

Eden (Stanford), 248

'Ego sum resurrectio et vita' (antiphon), 23

Eichendorff, Joseph von, 229

Einstein, Alfred, 61, 185

Elgar, Sir Edward:
 ★ *Dream of Gerontius*, 79, 111, 239–51
 Spirit of England, 261, 262

Eliot, T. S., 127

Elizabeth I, 216, 218

Elwes, Joan, 251

'End, The' (Owen), 280–1

Enfance du Christ, L' (Berlioz), 87, 88

English Madrigal Composers (Fellowes), 215

★ 'Eternity, thou word of thunder' (Bach Cantatas Nos. 20, 60), 180, 190–3

Eybler, Joseph von, 68, 72

Falstaff (Verdi), 101, 102

Farrar, Dean, 121

Faulte d'argent (Josquin), 53

Fauré, Gabriel, 117–22, 123, 125, 126

Fellowes, Dr Edmund, 206, 215, 218

Ferrand, Humbert, 88

Fidelio (Beethoven), 75
Fifth Book of Madrigals (Arcadelt), 215
First Little Clavier Book (Bach), 186
'For the Fallen' (Binyon–Elgar), 261, 262
Fortunatus, Venantius, 155
Foulds, J. C., 260–1
★ *Four Last Songs* (Strauss), 228–30
★ *Four Sacred Pieces* (Verdi), 97, 101
★ *Four Serious Songs* (Brahms), 177, 182, 227–8, 263
Fra Gherardo (Pizzetti), 126
Francis de Sales, St, 121
Franck, César, 123
Franck, Salomo, 193
French Music (Cooper), 146
Friedlander, Max, 182, 227
Fuller-Maitland, J. A., 241–2
Funeral Hymn (Brahms), 177
'Futility' (Owen), 276–7
Fux, Johann Joseph, 139

Gabrielli, Andrea, 57
Gabrielli, Giovanni, 57, 233
Gassmann, F. L., 69
Gerhardt, Paul, 156
German Requiem:
  ★ Brahms, 176–82
  ★ Schütz, 172–5, 176
Gloria:
  Dufay, 28
  Machaut, 26
Gluck, C. W. von, 75, 248
★ 'God's time is best' (Bach Cantata No. 106), 187–90, 263
Gombert, Nicolas, 53
Gordon, Father John Joseph, 243
Gordon, General, 239
★ *Gottes Zeit ist die allerbeste Zeit* (Bach Cantata No. 106), 187–90, 263
Gounod, Charles François, 110, 146
★ 'Gracious God, when wilt thou call me' (Bach Cantata No. 8), 193
Gradual, 12, 13–14

Asola, 48
Cherubini, 78–9, 82–3
Dvořák, 112
Morales, 43
Ockeghem, 30, 34
Victoria, 52
Gray, Cecil, 30, 166
Greek View of Life, The (Dickinson), 178
Green, Julian, 122, 186
Greene, Harry Plunket, 241
Gregorian Melodies, The (Wagner), 15
Gregory, St, 9, 14
Gregory XIII, Pope, 50
Groves, Charles, 262

Habeneck, F. A., 86–7
Hadrian I, Pope, 9
Haec dies, quam fecit Dominus, 14
Hallé, Sir Charles, 87
Hamburger, Michael, 178
Hampton, John, 54
Handel, Georg F., 69, 71, 231–2
Hardy, Thomas, 99
Harrison, Dr F., 53–4
Harrowing of Hell, The (Milner), 248
Hassler, Hans Leo, 156, 194
Haydn, Joseph, 60, 61, 69, 76, 80
Haydn, Michael, 60–4, 68, 70, 71, 77, 79
Heap, Swinnerton, 241
Heine, Heinrich, 140
Heinrich, Prince, Lord of Plassen, 171–2, 174
★ *Herr, wie du willt, so schick's mit mir* (Bach Cantata No. 73), 198–200
Herzlich thut mich verlangen (Hassler), 156
Heseltine, Philip (Peter Warlock), 262
Hiller, Ferdinand, 82
Hindemith, Paul, 252–9
History of the Church, A (Hughes), 3
History of Music (Gray), 30, 166

Hölderlin, J. C. F., 178
Holst, Gustav, 253
Holst, Imogen, 265
How to Become a Music Critic
(Shaw), 111*n*
Hughes, Father Philip, 3
Hussey, Dyneley, 103
Hymns of the Roman Liturgy
(Conolly), 98
Hyperion's Song of Destiny (Hölderlin), 178

I Promessi Sposi (Manzoni), 100
★ 'I stand with one foot in the grave' (Bach Cantata No. 156), 198
★ *Ich habe genug* (Bach Cantata No. 82), 200–1
★ *Ich hatte viel Bekümmerniss* (Bach Cantata No. 21), 179
★ *Ich steh' mit einem Fuss im Grabe* (Bach Cantata No. 156), 198
'If thou but suffer God to guide thee' (Neumark), 179
'Il bianco e dolce cigno' (Arcadelt), 214
Il combattimento di Tancredi e Clorinda (Monteverdi), 58
Iliad, 261
★ 'Im Abendroth' (Strauss), 229–30
★ *In Memoriam Dylan Thomas* (Stravinsky), 221–2
★ 'In Paradisum deducant te Angeli' (antiphon), 24, 97, 118, 126, 129, 268, 284
'In the midst of life' (Purcell), 207, 208, 209
Ingegneri, Marc Antonio, 164
'Ingemisco' (*Dies irae* verse), 106
Innocent VIII, Pope, 121
Intermezzo (Strauss), 229
Introit, 12–13
  Berlioz, 88–90, 95
  Britten, 268–70
  Brumel, 37–8
  Cherubini, 77–8, 82
  De la Rue, 40

Dufay, 28–9
Duruflé, 123–4
Dvořák, 112
Haydn, M., 61
  Mozart, 68, 69–71, 74
  Ockeghem, 31–3
  Palestrina, 47
  Pizzetti, 127
  Verdi, 102–3
★ 'It is enough' (Bach Cantata No. 82), 200–1

Jacobi, J. G., 225
Jacopone da Todi, 133, 154
Jaeger, A. J., 240–1, 242, 247–8, 249
Jaffee, Kay, 253
'Je ne mange point porc', 31
Jennens, Charles, 231
Jeremiah, Lamentations of, 160, 231
Jerome, St, 6
Jeronimo de Florencia, Padre, 51
Joseph and his Brethren (Méhul), 76
Joseph II, Holy Roman Emperor, 10, 64
Josquin Des Prés, 53, 173, 232
  ★ *Déploration*, 30, 213–14
  Miserere mei, Deus, 167
  ★ *Planxit David*, 231
  ★ *Stabat Mater*, 135–6, 137
Julian, John, 17
Jungmann, Joseph A., 8–9, 108
'Juste judex ultionis' (*Dies irae* verse):
  Cherubini, 79
  Haydn, M., 62
Justin Martyr, St, 7

Kalbeck, Max, 175
Kennedy, John F., 252, 253
Kerner, Dr Dieter, 66
Kerner, Julius, 226
'Kind Ghosts' (Owen), 265
Knoll, Christoph, 194
Köchel, Ludwig, 61
★ *Komm', du süsse Todesstunde* (Bach Cantata No. 161), 193–6, 201

Komm, süsser Tod (Bach), 187
Krênek, Ernst, 33
Kyrie, 8, 13, 19, 26
  Berlioz, 90
  Brumel, 38
  Cherubini, 77–8, 83
  De la Rue, 40
  Duruflé, 124
  Dvořák, 112
  Haydn, M., 61
  Machaut, 26
  Mozart, 68, 69–70, 71, 74
  Ockeghem, 32
  Palestrina, 44–5
  Pizzetti, 127
  Schütz, 173
  Verdi, 101, 103
  Victoria, 52

'Lacrimosa' (*Dies irae* verse):
  Berlioz, 92–3
  Britten, 275–6
  Cherubini, 79, 84
  Dvořák, 113
  Haydn, M., 62
  Mozart, 68, 73
  Pizzetti, 128
  Verdi, 101, 106
Laetabundus, 133
Lamentations, 160, 161, 231
  * Palestrina, 161–3
  * Tallis, 163
  Victoria, 164–6
Laments of David, 230–5
Lämmerhirt, Tobias, 188
Lassus, Orlando de, 31, 51, 53, 161,
  181
'Last Judgment' (Michelangelo),
  105
* *Lauda Sion Salvatorem*, 19, 133
Lavigna, Vincenzo, 102
Legrenzi, Giovanni, 139
Lehmann, Lotte, 228
Leopold I, Holy Roman Emperor,
  167
Leopold II, Holy Roman Emperor,
  66

Leopold of Anhalt-Cöthen, Prince,
  184
Lesueur, Jean François, 86
'Letter home, A' (Sassoon), 274
Li–Tai–Po, 261
'Liber scriptus' (*Dies irae* verse):
  Anerio, 47
  Berlioz, 91
  Britten, 273
  Brumel, 38
  Cherubini, 79
  Dvořák, 113
  Pizzetti, 128
  Verdi, 101
Libera me (Absolution), 15, 23–4
  Anerio, 47–8
  Britten, 271, 282–5
  Duruflé, 126
  Fauré, 117, 120–1
  Monteverdi, 59
  Pizzetti, 129
  Verdi, 97, 100–1
  Victoria, 51, 52
Libertine, The (Shadwell), 206
Licinius, Emperor, 6
* *Liebster Gott, wann werd' ich
    sterben?* (Bach Cantata No. 8),
    193
* *Liebster Jesu, mein Verlangen* (Bach
    Cantata No. 32), 186n
Lincoln, Abraham, 252, 253, 256
Liszt, Franz, 135, 154–8
'Litanei auf das Fest aller Seelen'
  (Schubert), 225–6
Litanies à la Vierge Noire (Poulenc),
  146
Liturgy Constitution (Paul VI), 6, 20
Lloyd, Edward, 241
* 'Lord, as thou wilt so deal with
    me' (Bach Cantata No. 73),
    198–200
Luther, Martin, 171, 197
Lux aeterna (Communion), 22–3
  Brumel, 39
  Cherubini, 80, 81, 85, 108
  De la Rue, 41
  Duruflé, 126

Lux aeterna—cont.
  Dvořák, 115
  Fauré, 120
  Haydn, 64
  Mozart, 74, 108
  Verdi, 101, 108–10
Lydgate, John, 209
Lydia (Fauré), 119

Machaut, Guillaume de, 25–6
McVeagh, Diana, 249
Madrigali guerrieri et amorosi (Monteverdi), 58
Maffei, Contessa, 99, 100
Magic Flute, The (Mozart), 67, 68, 69
Malcolm, George, 46, 160
'Man that is born of a woman' (Purcell), 206, 208
Manning, Cardinal, 121
Manzoni, Alessandro, 96, 97, 99, 101, 108
'Marcellus Mass' (Palestrina), 46, 47
Maria, Dowager Empress, 49–50, 51
Marien Lieder (Hindemith), 252
Marlowe, Christopher, 224
Martin, George, 96, 100
Martinengo, G. C., 57
Martini, Padre, 69
Mary II, Queen, 206, 207
Masonic Funeral Music (Mozart), 69, 71
Mass of Life (Delius), 262
Mass of the Roman Rite, The (Jungmann), 8n, 108
Massenet, Jules, 148, 229, 230
Mathis der Maler (Hindemith), 252
May, Florence, 176
'Media vita in morte sumus' (Notker), 193, 207
Mediaeval Latin Lyrics (Waddell), 232n
Medici, Alessandro dei, 215
Méhul, Etienne, 76, 86
Memories of President Lincoln (Whitman), 252
Men and Music (Carner), 115

Mendel, Arthur, 171
Mendelssohn, 161
Messiah (Handel), 69
Metastasio, 71
Mewton-Wood, Noel, 222
Michelangelo, 16, 42, 105
Milanese Mass, 11, 14
Milner, Anthony, 248
Miserere mei, Deus (Psalm 50), 160, 161
  Allegri, 166–7
  Josquin des Prés, 167
  Victoria, 164, 166
Missa Solemnis (Beethoven), 30, 58, 78, 144
Molinet, Jean, 213
★ 'Montes Gelboe' (antiphon), 230
Monteverdi, Claudio, 56, 174, 233, 234
  Requiem Mass, 58–9, 175
  ★ *Sonata sopra Sancta Maria*, 58, 93
  ★ *Vespers*, 57, 59, 93
Morales, Cristóbal, 42–4, 49, 51
Morley, Thomas, 206, 215–16
Morning Heroes (Bliss), 261–2
Mors et Vita (Gounod), 110
'Mors stupebit' (*Dies irae* verse):
  Berlioz, 91
  Britten, 272, 273
  Cherubini, 79, 83
  Dvořák, 113
  Haydn, M., 62
  Mozart, 72
  Pizzetti, 128
  Verdi, 104, 105
Morton, H. V., 4
Moussorgsky, Modeste, 279
Mozart, Wolfgang, 102, 141, 167
  Betulia liberata, La, 71
  Magic Flute, 67, 68, 69
  Masonic Funeral Music, 69, 71
  ★ Requiem Mass, 61, 64–74, 76, 77, 79, 86, 88, 102, 103, 108, 118
Mozart, Constanze, 61, 67, 68
Müller, Wilhelm, 267

Murder in the Cathedral (Eliot), 127
Music in the Baroque Era (Bukofzer), 55–6
Music in Mediaeval Britain (Harrison), 53–4
Music on Henry Purcell's Death (Clarke), 219–20
musica mensurabilis, 33
musica reservata, 55, 56
★ *Musikalisches Exequien* (Schütz), 171–5, 176
★ 'My spirit was in heaviness' (Bach Cantata No. 21), 179

Napoleon, 76
Nash, Paul, 271–2
'Nature's praise of God' (Beethoven), 225
Neumark, George, 179
Nevinson, C. R. W., 271
Newman, Cardinal, 9, 81, 239, 243, 244, 249, 250
Newman, Ernest, 195
'Next war, The' (Owen), 273–4
Nichols, Robert, 261
Niemetschek, Franz, 66, 67
Nietzsche, Friedrich, 57
Nissen, Georg, 67
Nobilissima Visione (Hindemith), 252
Noble Essences (Sitwell), 267
Nocturne (Britten), 265
Noel, Henry, 216
'Noel, adieu thou Court's delight' (Weelkes), 216, 218
Notker Balbulus, 193, 207
Novello, Vincent, 65, 68

★ 'O Christ, my all in living' (Bach Cantata No. 95), 196–8
★ 'O Death, how bitter art thou' (Brahms), 227–8
★ *O Ewigkeit, du Donnerwort* (Bach Cantatas Nos. 20, 60), 180, 190–3
O Haupt voll Blut und Wunden (Gerhardt), 156

★ 'O light everlasting' (Bach Cantata No. 34), 182
★ 'O teach me, Lord, my days to number' (Bach Cantata No. 27), 193
★ 'O Tod, wie bitter bist du' (Brahms), 227–8
Obrecht, Jacob, 53
Ockeghem, Johannes, 27, 29, 30–36, 37, 40, 213–14
Ode to Death (Holst), 253
Odo, St, 9
★ *O ewiges Feuer* (Bach Cantata No. 34), 182
Offertory (*Domine Jesu*), 20–22
  Berlioz, 91, 93–4
  Britten, 277–9
  Casciolini, 57
  Cherubini, 80, 84
  De la Rue, 40
  Duruflé, 124
  Dvořák, 113–14
  Fauré, 118, 119–20
  Haydn, M., 63
  Mozart, 68, 71, 73
  Ockeghem, 35–6
  Palestrina, 44
  Verdi, 101, 107
  Victoria, 51, 52
★ *Officium Defunctorum* (Victoria), 50
Officium Hebdomedae Sanctae (Victoria), 164–6
Omnium bonorum plena (Dufay), 27
'On seeing a piece of our artillery brought into action' (Owen), 275
Ophüls, Dr, 227
Orfeo (Gluck), 248
Origen, 121
Osborne, George A., 87
Otello (Verdi), 101, 107
Owen, Wilfred, 261, 262, 265, 266–8, 269, 271, 272–8, 280, 281–4
Oxyrhynchus hymn to Holy Trinity, 7
'Pagan Requiem, A' (Delius), 262–4

Paisiello, Giovanni, 76
Palestrina, 48, 51, 57, 58, 77, 102,
    108, 119, 139, 145, 164, 181
  * Lamentations, 161–3, 166
  * 'Marcellus Mass', 46, 47
    Requiem Mass, 44–6, 52
  * Stabat Mater, 136–7, 152
'Parable of the Old Men and the
    Young' (Owen), 277–9
Pascal, Blaise, 279
'Paths of Glory, The' (Nevinson),
    271
Paul, St, 4, 182
Paul III, Pope, 42
Paul V, Pope, 57
Paul VI, Pope, 6, 20
Pelléas et Mélisande (Fauré), 118
Penelope (Fauré), 118
'Penitence' (Beethoven), 225
Pergolesi, Giovanni Battista, 137–
    8, 139, 143
Pericles, 177–8
Peter, St, 4
Peter Grimes (Britten), 269
Petti, Anthony G., 46n
Philip of Castille, 31
Philip of Neri, St, 49
Philip II of Spain, 49, 50
Pico della Mirandola, Giovanni, 121
'Pie Jesu Domine' (Dies irae verse),
    20
  Berlioz, 92, 93
  Cherubini, 80, 84
  Duruflé, 125
  Dvořák, 113, 114–15
  Fauré, 120
  Haydn, M., 62
  Morales, 43
  Pizzetti, 128
  Verdi, 106
Pirro, André, 183, 195
Pitoni, Giuseppe, 55
Pius IV, Pope, 11, 46
Pius V, Pope, 11
Pius VIII, Pope, 167
Pius XII, Pope, 159
Pizzetti, Ildebrando, 126–9

* Plainsong Requiem Mass, 11–24
  Agnus Dei, 22
  Alleluia, 15, 19, 20
  Communion, 22–4
  Gradual, 12, 13–14
  Introit, 12–13
  Kyrie, 13, 19
  Offertory, 20–2
  Sanctus, 22
  Sequence, 11, 15–20
  Tract, 12, 15, 20
Planxit David (Josquin), 231
Plath, Wolfgang, 68
Ponte, Lorenzo da, 65, 66, 70
Porpora, Nicolo, 60
Poulenc, Francis, 146–8, 149
Powell, Mrs Richard, 242
Prayer Book of Queen Elizabeth
    (1559), 205
Puccini, Giacomo, 112
Puchberg, Michael, 66
Pujol, Dom David, 51
Purcell, Henry, 206–9, 217, 219–20

Quattro Pezzi Sacri, 97–9, 101
'Qui Mariam absolvisti' (Dies irae
    verse):
  Britten, 274
  Cherubini, 79
  Pizzetti, 128
  Verdi, 106
'Quid sum miser' (Dies irae verse):
  Berlioz, 91
  Dvořák, 113
  Pizzetti, 128
  Verdi, 105

Radaut, Else, 67
'Recordare' (Dies irae verse):
  Anerio, 47
  Berlioz, 91, 92
  Britten, 274
  Brumel, 38
  Cherubini, 79
  Dvořák, 113
  Mozart, 69, 72
Reese, Gustave, 53, 136, 214

Reinhalter, Dr Karl, 176–7, 182
Renaissance style, 55–6
Requiem (Walford Davies), 209–10
Requiem aeternam (Introit), 12–13
  Berlioz, 89
  Britten, 268–70
  Dufay, 28
  Ockeghem, 31–3
  Pizzetti, 127
  Verdi, 102–3
  Victoria, 52
Requiem Masses:
  * Anerio, 46–8
  Asola, 48–9
  * Berlioz, 80, 85–95, 104, 108,
    111, 112, 113, 117, 128
  Brumel, 36–9, 41, 44
  Casciolini, 57
  * Cherubini, 75–86, 88, 103,
    108, 114–15
  * De la Rue, 40–1, 44
  Dufay, 25, 27, 28–9, 54
  * Duruflé, 122–6, 128
  * Dvořák, 110–16, 142
  * Fauré, 117–22, 123, 125
  * Haydn, M., 60–4, 77, 79
  Lassus, 31, 53
  Monteverdi, 58–9
  Morales, 42–4, 51
  * Mozart, 60, 65, 66–74, 77, 79,
    86, 88, 103, 108, 118
  * Ockeghem, 29–36, 40, 213
  Palestrina, 44–5, 52
  Pitoni, 55
  Pizzetti, 126–9
  Plainsong Requiem Mass, 11–24
  Richafort, 53
  Scarlatti, 59
  * Verdi, 88, 90, 91, 97–110, 111,
    115, 117, 120, 273
  * Victoria, 49–54
Responsories (*Tenebrae*):
  Ingegneri, 164
  Victoria, 164–6
'Rex tremendae' (*Dies irae* verse):
  Berlioz, 91, 92
  Cherubini, 79, 84

Dvořák, 113
Mozart, 72
Pizzetti, 128
Verdi, 105–6
Richafort, Jean, 53
Richter, Hans, 241
Ricordi, Giulio, 100
Rist, Johann, 190, 191
Roma Sotterranea Cristiana, La
  (Rossi), 4
Roosevelt, Franklin D., 252
Rossi, G. B. de, 4
Rossini, Giachino, 99, 101, 109,
  140–2, 143
'Royal banners forward go, The',
  155
Ruffo, Vincento, 46
Ruskin, John, 240

Sacred Latin Poetry (Trench), 16
St Matthew Passion (Bach), 156, 177,
  200
Salieri, Antonio, 66
Sanctus, 22
  Berlioz, 95
  Britten, 279–80
  Brumel, 39
  Cherubini, 80, 84, 101
  De la Rue, 40, 41
  Dufay, 28
  Duruflé, 125
  Dvořák, 114
  Fauré, 118, 120, 125
  Haydn, M., 63
  Machaut, 26
  Mozart, 68
  Palestrina, 44
  Pizzetti, 129
  Verdi, 101, 107–8
Sarti, Giuseppe, 77
Sassoon, Siegfried, 274, 280
* *Saul* (Handel), 231–2
Scarlatti, Alessandro, 59, 138–9, 143
Schemelli, Georg Christian, 187
'Schlechtes Wetter' (Strauss), 229
Schöne Müllerin, Die (Schubert),
  267

Schrattenbach, Archbishop Sigismund von, 60
Schrems, Joseph, 46n
Schubert, Franz, 70, 92, 143, 225–6, 267
Schumann, Robert, 176
Schütz, Heinrich:
　* *Musikalisches Exequien*, 171–5
　Symphoniae Sacrae, 232–4
Schweitzer, Albert, 183, 201
Sea Drift (Delius), 255
Sebastian, St, 4, 6
Second Little Clavier Book (Bach), 186
Sequence, 11–12, 15–20, 30. See also *Dies Irae*
Sermons to Mixed Congregations (Newman), 243
Sesame and Lilies (Ruskin), 240
Shadwell, Thomas, 206
Shaw, Bernard, 110–11, 248
Short History of Music, A (Einstein), 185
Sidney, Sir Philip, 217
Silverstolpe, F. S., 73
Simeon, Song of, 175
* *Sinfonia da Requiem* (Britten), 265
Sitwell, Dame Edith, 222–3
Sitwell, Sir Osbert, 267
* 'Sleepers wake' (Bach Cantata No. 140), 200
Smetana, Bedrich, 111
Sonata sopra Sancta Maria (Monteverdi), 58, 93
Song of Songs, 263
Songs and Dances of Death (Moussorgsky), 279
Songs of Sadness and Piety (Byrd), 217–18
Spanish Cathedral Music in the Golden Age (Stevenson), 49
Spirit of England, The (Elgar), 261, 262
Spontini, Gasparo, 79
'Spring Offensive' (Owen), 262
Stabat Mater, 19, 133–53
　Berkeley, 148–50
　Caldara, 139–40

* Dvořák, 111, 142–4
Gounod, 146
* Josquin, 135–6, 137
Liszt, 154, 156, 157
* Palestrina, 136–7, 152
* Pergolesi, 137–8, 143
* Rossini, 110, 140–2
* Poulenc, 146–8
Scarlatti, 138–9, 143
* Szymanowski, 150–3
Verdi, 144–6
Stabat Mater speciosa (*Jacopone*), 154
Stanford, Charles V., 248
Stepchildren of Music (Blom), 78
Stevens, Denis, 28
Stevenson, Robert, 49, 51, 52
stile concertato, 233
'Still falls the rain' (Sitwell), 222–4
Stockley, W., 241
'Strange Meeting' (Owen), 282–4
Strauss, Richard, 151, 242, 247
　Capriccio, 56, 143
　* *Four Last Songs*, 228–30
Stravinsky, Igor, 149, 151, 220–2
Strepponi, Giuseppina, 96
Strozzi, Giulio, 58–9
style antico, 56
style moderno, 56
Süssmayer, Franz, 68–9, 72, 74
'Sweet white swan, The' (Arcadelt), 214
Swieten, Baron von, 66
Symphoniae Sacrae (Schütz), 232–3
Szymanowski, Karol, 150–3

Tallis, Thomas, 30, 161, 163, 218
Taverner, John, 31
Te Deum:
　* Berlioz, 87
　* Dvořák, 111
　* Verdi, 97–9, 145
Tempest, The (Shakespeare), 262
Tenebrae, 159–67
　Byrd, 161, 162
　Palestrina, 161, 162–3, 166
　* Tallis, 161, 163
　* Victoria, 160, 161, 164–6

Terry, Richard, 166
Terry, Sanford, 183–4
Teschner, G. M., 197
'This is the day which the Lord hath made', 14
Thomas Aquinas, St, 9
Thomas of Celano, 15
Thomas, Dylan, 220–2
'Thou knowest, Lord' (Purcell), 206–7, 209
★ Three Sacred Choruses (Brahms), 176
Thucydides, 177–8
'To Death' (Beethoven), 225
★ 'To rest, to rest' (Wolf), 226
★ Tod und Verklärung (Strauss), 229, 247
Tomkins, Thomas, 232, 234–5
Tournemire, Charles, 123
Tract, 12, 15, 20
    Asola, 48
    De la Rue, 40–1
    Ockeghem, 30, 34–5
Traveller in Rome, A (Morton), 4
Traviata, La (Verdi), 104
Treatise on Orchestration (Berlioz), 93
Trench, Archbishop Chevenix, 16
Trent, Council of: (1562) 46, 84; (1563), 11, 19, 46
'Tuba mirum' (Dies irae verse):
    Anerio, 47
    Berlioz, 91, 92
    Britten, 272
    Brumel, 38
    Cherubini, 79
    Dvořák, 112–13
    Haydn, M., 62
    Mozart, 69, 71–2
    Pizzetti, 128
    Verdi, 91, 104
Tudway, Thomas, 206
Turandot (Puccini), 112
Turn of the Screw, The (Britten), 269
Turner, Bruno, 31, 34

★ Veni sancte Spiritus, 19, 133

Verdi, Giuseppe:
    Aïda, 101, 103, 112
    Four Sacred Pieces, 97–9, 101
    ★ Requiem Mass, 72, 79, 88, 90, 91, 96–110, 111, 115, 117, 120, 250, 273, 274
    ★ Stabat Mater, 144–6
    ★ Te Deum, 97–9, 145
Vesperae Solennes de Confessore (Mozart), 70
Vespers (Monteverdi), 57, 58, 59, 93
Vestale, La (Spontini), 79
'Vexilla regis prodeunt' (Venantius), 155, 156
★ Via Crucis (Liszt), 135, 154–8
Victimae Paschali laudes, 19, 133
Victoria, Tomás Luis de:
    ★ Requiem Masses, 49–53
    ★ Responsories, 59, 111, 160, 161, 164–6
'Vigil' (Li-Tai-Po), 261
Vincentino, Don Nicola, 46
Vision of Dante (Foulds), 260
Visitation of the Sick, Order of, 205
Vitellozi, Cardinal, 46
Vitry, Philip de, 25
'Voices' (Owen), 273
★ 'Vom Tode' (Beethoven), 225
'Vox ultima crucis' (Lydgate), 209

Wachet auf (Bach Cantata No. 140), 200
Waddell, Helen, 232
Wagner, Richard, 102
Wagner, Roger, 252
Wagner, Professor, 15
Walpole, Henry, 218
Walsegg, Count Franz von, 61
★ War Requiem (Britten), 79, 88, 107, 223, 259, 260, 265–85
Warlock, Peter, 262
Weelkes, Thomas, 215–17, 218
Welland, D. S. R., 271
Wer nur den lieben Gott lässt walten (Neumark), 179–80
★ Wer weiss, wie nahe mir mein Ende (Bach Cantata No. 27), 193

'Western Wynde' (Taverner), 31
★ 'When David heard that Absalom was slain' (Tomkins), 234–5
★ *When lilacs last in the door-yard bloomed* (Hindemith), 252–9
Whitman, Walt, 252–3, 261, 262
Whittaker, W. G., 188
'Why do I use my paper, ink, and pen?' (Byrd), 218
Willaert, Adrian, 57
Winnowing, The (Binyon), 261

★ *Winterreise* (Schubert), 267
Wittgenstein, Princess, 156
Wolf, Hugo, 225, 226–7, 229
Wood, Sir Henry, 222, 242
World Requiem, A (Foulds), 260–1

'Ye sacred Muses' (Byrd), 218

Zacharias, Canticle of, 23, 160, 161, 166
★ 'Zur Ruh, zur Ruh' (Wolf), 226